The Independence of the Judiciary in Bangladesh

M. Ehteshamul Bari

The Independence of the Judiciary in Bangladesh

Exploring the Gap Between Theory and Practice

M. Ehteshamul Bari
Thomas More Law School
Australian Catholic University
Melbourne, VIC, Australia

ISBN 978-981-16-6221-8   ISBN 978-981-16-6222-5   (eBook)
https://doi.org/10.1007/978-981-16-6222-5

© The Editor(s) (if applicable) and The Author(s), under exclusive license to Springer Nature Singapore
Pte Ltd. 2022
This work is subject to copyright. All rights are solely and exclusively licensed by the Publisher, whether
the whole or part of the material is concerned, specifically the rights of translation, reprinting, reuse of
illustrations, recitation, broadcasting, reproduction on microfilms or in any other physical way, and
transmission or information storage and retrieval, electronic adaptation, computer software, or by similar
or dissimilar methodology now known or hereafter developed.
The use of general descriptive names, registered names, trademarks, service marks, etc. in this publication
does not imply, even in the absence of a specific statement, that such names are exempt from the relevant
protective laws and regulations and therefore free for general use.
The publisher, the authors, and the editors are safe to assume that the advice and information in this book
are believed to be true and accurate at the date of publication. Neither the publisher nor the authors or the
editors give a warranty, expressed or implied, with respect to the material contained herein or for any
errors or omissions that may have been made. The publisher remains neutral with regard to jurisdictional
claims in published maps and institutional affiliations.

This Springer imprint is published by the registered company Springer Nature Singapore Pte Ltd.
The registered company address is: 152 Beach Road, #21-01/04 Gateway East, Singapore 189721,
Singapore

Dedicated to my beloved parents,
Mrs. Umme Salma Atiya Bari and late
Professor M. Ershadul Bari, to whom I owe
everything.

Preface

When the South Asian nation of Bangladesh achieved its independence almost 50 years ago on 16 December 1971 following a 9-month long brutal war with Pakistan, the founding fathers aspired to establish a democratic society in which the judiciary will operate independently to ensure the observance of the rule of law and the enforcement of the fundamental rights of individuals. Accordingly, the ideal of safeguarding the independence of the judiciary has found a prominent place in the Constitution of Bangladesh, 1972. However, the key elements for realising such an ideal, such as a transparent method of appointment of judges, have not adequately been guaranteed by the Constitution. Consequently, succeeding generations of executives have sought to undermine the independence of the judiciary. Thus, there exists a gap between the theory and practice concerning the independence of the judiciary in Bangladesh. The book, therefore, endeavours, in the first place, to fill a significant gap in the existing literature regarding the weaknesses of the constitutional provisions concerning the appointment of the Chief Justice of Bangladesh and other judges of the Supreme Court. Second, this book will evaluate from comparative constitutional and normative perspectives the effectiveness of the method of removal of judges involving a body of judicial character, namely the Supreme Judicial Council, as had been incorporated in the Constitution of Bangladesh through the Proclamations (Tenth Amendment) Order, 1977 and later validated by the Constitution (Fifth Amendment) Act, 1979. It will be made manifestly evident that the recent attempts to dispense with this transparent method of removal of the judges have been preferred to bring the superior judiciary under the control of an all-power executive.

Since no systematic and structured research has so far been carried out critically examining the above issues, this book will enhance knowledge by not only identifying the flaws, deficiencies, and lacunae of the constitutional provisions concerning the method of appointment of the judges of the Supreme Court but also examining the measures undertaken by the current government of the Bangladesh Awami League to dispense with the transparent method of removal of the judges involving the Supreme Judicial Council. Consequently, based on these findings, recommendations will be put forward to rectify these defects from comparative constitutional law and normative perspectives. The outcome of this proposed book will not only establish the best means for excluding the possibility of appointment of judges of the Supreme Court on extraneous considerations but also for guaranteeing their security of tenure, thereby safeguarding the independence of the superior judiciary of Bangladesh.

Melbourne, Australia   M. Ehteshamul Bari

Acknowledgements

I could not have completed the writing of this book without the kind and generous support of a number of individuals. First, I am deeply grateful to my dearest mother, Mrs Umme Salma Atiya Bari, for her limitless love and unconditional support. She has been my protector, my rock, and my strength.

I owe a profound debt of gratitude to my beloved father, late Professor M Ershadul Bari, who was the foremost authority on Bangladeshi Constitutional Law. He was not only my father but also my greatest teacher. His teachings and lessons have shaped both personal and professional aspects of my life.

I would like to thank my sister, Safia Naz, for her support whenever asked. I am also thankful to my wife, Samia Islam, for her love and support. Since I completed the task of writing this book after the birth of our first baby, Samaira Bari, my wife's patience during this process has been of immense comfort and help. I hope one day my beautiful daughter, Samaira, will read this book with great interest!

Finally, I would like to thank my mentor, Professor David Weisbrot AM (Former President of the Australian Law Reforms Commission) for his invaluable guidance and support.

About This Book

When the South Asian nation of Bangladesh achieved its independence on 16 December 1971 following a 9-month long brutal war with Pakistan, the founding fathers aspired to establish a democratic society in which the judiciary will operate independently to ensure the observance of the rule of law and the enforcement of fundamental rights. However, notwithstanding such an aspiration, the Constitution of Bangladesh, 1972, does not prescribe a transparent method for appointing the judges of the superior judiciary – the Supreme Court of Bangladesh – which would enable judges to decide cases according to the oath of their office. Rather it entrusts the executive with the power to appoint the judges, thereby paving the way for intrusion of political or personal favouritism in the appointment process. Furthermore, although the Constitution, as amended by the Proclamations (Tenth Amendment) Order, 1977 and later validated by the Constitution (Fifth Amendment) Act, 1979, guaranteed security of tenure by stipulating a transparent procedure for the removal of judges of the Supreme Court, the current government of Bangladesh Awami League (BAL) has taken several measures to dispense with this transparent procedure.

This book makes it manifestly evident that the absence of a transparent method of appointment of judges of the Supreme Court has often resulted in the appointment of judges not on merit, but through political or personal patronage. Furthermore, the measures taken by the BAL regime to replace the transparent method of removal of the judges of the Supreme Court have substantially impaired the independence of the judges to decide cases independently of the wishes of the appointing authority. Consequently, in light of these findings, this book puts forward recommendations from comparative constitutional law and normative perspectives for the insertion of detailed norms in the Constitution of Bangladesh so as to establish the best means for excluding patronage appointments to the bench and for guaranteeing the security of tenure of the judges, thereby safeguarding the independence of the superior judiciary to decide cases without fear or favour.

This book will be of particular interest and use to scholars and students of comparative constitutional law and Asian Law. Given the law reform analysis undertaken in this work, policymakers represent another primary target for this book.

Although the recommendations put forward in the proposed title will be of particular benefit to the policymakers in Bangladesh, they will nevertheless be also relevant for the policymakers of those nations – the constitutions of which do not contain adequate guarantees for securing the independence of the judiciary.

Contents

1 Introduction 1
  1.1 Introduction 1
  1.2 The Standards Concerning the Independence of the Judiciary
       and Their Recognition in Domestic Constitutions 4
  1.3 The Constitution of Bangladesh and the Guarantee
       of Judicial Independence 6
      1.3.1 The Constitution of Bangladesh and the Method
           of Appointment of Judges of the SC 11
      1.3.2 The Constitution of Bangladesh and the Method
           of Removal of Judges of the SC 13
  1.4 Objectives of the Book 14
  1.5 Structure of the Book 15
  References 17

**2 The Principle of Judicial Independence and Its Recognition
in the Constitution of Bangladesh, 1972** 19
  2.1 Introduction 19
  2.2 The Importance of an Independent and Impartial
       Judiciary in a Democratic State 20
  2.3 Traditional and New Conceptual Dimensions
       (Four Meanings) of Judicial Independence 26
      2.3.1 Four Meanings of Judicial Independence 26
  2.4 The Importance of the Method of Appointment and the Security
       of Tenure of the Judges as Constituent Elements of Judicial
       Independence 32
      2.4.1 The Importance of a Transparent Method
           of Appointment of the Judges 32
      2.4.2 The Importance of a Transparent Method
           of Removal of Judges 44

xiii

| 2.5 | Case Study: The Independence of the Judiciary in Pakistan | 47 |

2.5 Case Study: The Independence of the Judiciary in Pakistan 47
2.6 The Principle of Judicial Independence as Enshrined
in the Constitution of Bangladesh, 1972 50
References... 54

**3 The Method of Appointment of the Judges of the Supreme
Court Under the Constitution of Bangladesh, 1972.** 57
3.1 Introduction 57
3.2 The Appointment of the Chief Justice of Bangladesh 58
3.3 The Provisions of the Constitution of Bangladesh, 1972,
Concerning the Appointment of Judges of the AD
of the SC of Bangladesh 65
3.4 The Constitutional Provisions Concerning the Appointment
of the Judges of the HCD of the SC....................... 67
3.5 Dispensation of the Constitutional Requirement
of "Consultation with Chief Justice" in the Appointment
of Judges of the SC 70
    3.5.1 Deletion of the Constitutional Requirement
       of Consultation with the Chief Justice
       by the Constitution (Fourth Amendment) Act, 1975 71
    3.5.2 Restoration of the Constitutional Requirement
       of Consultation with the Chief Justice and Deletion
       of this Requirement Again by the First Martial
       Law Regime (1975–1979) 73
    3.5.3 The Method of Appointment of Judges Under
       the Second Martial Law Regime (1982–1986) 74
    3.5.4 Breach of the Convention of Consulting
       the Chief Justice in 1994 in Appointing
       the Judges of the SC.............................. 76
    3.5.5 Judicial Interpretation of the Requirement
       of "Consultation with the Chief Justice"
       in Bangladesh.................................... 78
3.6 Restoration of the Requirement of "Consultation
with the Chief Justice" in the Constitution of Bangladesh
in July 2011 83
3.7 The Establishment of the Supreme Judicial Commission
in Bangladesh to Recommend Candidates for Appointment
as Judges to the SC 84
    3.7.1 Composition of the Supreme Judicial Commission....... 85
    3.7.2 Selection Process 87
    3.7.3 Functions and Selection Criteria 88
    3.7.4 Selection Meeting of the Commission................. 88
    3.7.5 Consideration of Report by the President 89
3.8 Validity of the Supreme Judicial Commission Ordinance........ 90
References... 92

Contents

4 The Intrusion of Extraneous Considerations in the Appointment of the Chief Justice and the Other Judges of the Supreme Court of Bangladesh 95

4.1 Introduction 95

4.2 Contravention of the Convention of Seniority in Appointing the Chief Justice of Bangladesh 96

 4.2.1 Supersession during the Regime of the BNP-Jamaat Alliance (2001–2006) 96

 4.2.2 Supersession during the Non-Party "Care-Taker" Government (2007–2008) 98

 4.2.3 Supersession during the Present BAL Government (2009- to Date). 99

4.3 The Violation of the Convention of Seniority in Appointing the Judges of the AD 108

 4.3.1 Contravention of the Principle of Seniority in Appointing Judges of the AD during Martial Law and Autocratic Regimes 108

 4.3.2 Breach of the Violation of the Principle of Seniority in Appointing the Judges of the AD following the Return to Parliamentary Democracy 110

4.4 The Appointment of the Judges of the HCD 123

References. 126

5 The Guarantee of Security of Tenure of the Judges of the Supreme Court under the Constitution of Bangladesh, 1972 129

5.1 Introduction 129

5.2 The Original Provisions of the Constitution of Bangladesh, 1972, Concerning the Retirement Age and the Method of Removal of the Judges of the Superior Courts 129

5.3 The Changes Introduced to the Security of Tenure of the Judges of the SC of Bangladesh by the Constitution (Fourth Amendment) Act, 1975 130

5.4 The Changes Introduced to the Security of Tenure of the Judges by the Martial Law Regime of 1975 131

5.5 The Changes Introduced to the Security of Tenure of the Judges by the Martial Law Regime of HM Ershad (1982–1986). 133

5.6 The Changes Introduced to the Retirement Age of the Judges by the BNP Government (2001–2006) 134

References. 135

xvi

6 The Functioning of the Supreme Judicial Council, the Changes Introduced to the Method of Removal of Judges of the Supreme Court of Bangladesh in 2014 and the Subsequent Scathing Attack on the Judiciary 137

6.1 Introduction 137

6.2 The Functioning of the Supreme Judicial Council 138

6.3 The Omission of the Constitutional Provisions Concerning the SJC by the Constitution (Sixteenth Amendment) Act, 2014 142

6.4 The SC's Invalidation of the Sixteenth Amendment and the Consequent Attack on the Chief Justice 144

6.5 The Impact of Justice Sinha's Resignation on the Independence of the Judiciary 148

References.. 154

7 Conclusion 157

7.1 Introduction 157

7.2 The Constituent Elements of Judicial Independence............ 157

7.2.1 The Importance of a Transparent Method of Appointment 158

7.2.2 The Importance of Security of Tenure................. 161

7.3 The Constitution of Bangladesh and the Principle of Judicial Independence 163

7.4 Does the Constitution of Bangladesh Guarantee a Transparent Method of Appointment of Judges of the Superior Judiciary? 163

7.4.1 The Appointment of the Chief Justice 164

7.4.2 The Appointment of the Judges of the AD.............. 165

7.4.3 The Appointment of the Judges of the HCD 166

7.4.4 The Fate of the Supreme Judicial Council, 2008......... 166

7.5 Does the Constitution Adequately Safeguard the Security of Tenure of the Judges of the SC? 167

7.6 Recommendations: Incorporation of Effective Safeguards in the Constitution of Bangladesh, 1972 for Guaranteeing the Independence of the Judiciary 168

References.. 172

Table of Cases 173

Bibliography 175

About the Author

M. Ehteshamul Bari, PhD (Macquarie, Sydney), is a Senior Lecturer in Law and the Higher Degree Research Coordinator in the Thomas More Law School at the Australian Catholic University (ACU), Melbourne, Australia. He previously served as the Acting Deputy Dean of Law at ACU. Dr Bari's primary research expertise lies in the areas of constitutional law, human rights law, Asian law, and public international law. Apart from this monograph, he is also the author of two other monographs, namely, *States of Emergency and the Law: The Experience of Bangladesh* (London and New York: Routledge, 2017) and *The Use of Preventive Detention Laws in Malaysia: A Case for Reform* (Singapore: Springer, 2020). He has also published numerous research articles in reputed peer-reviewed journals, including the *Oxford University Commonwealth Law Journal*, *Wisconsin International Law Journal*, *George Washington International Law Review*, *Emory International Law Review*, *Cardozo International & Comparative Law Review*, *Transnational Law and Contemporary Problems*, *Michigan State International Law Review*, *Suffolk Transnational Law Review*, and *San Diego International Law Journal*. Dr Bari has received prestigious research awards in recognition of his scholarship.

Chapter 1
Introduction

1.1 Introduction

It is a common feature of modern democracies to distribute power among the three organs of the government, namely, executive, legislature and judiciary. The idea underlying such division of power, according to French Jurist, Baron de Montesquieu—the architect of the modern formulation of the doctrine of separation of powers—is to prevent the concentration of too much power in any particular arm of government[1] and thereby limit the possibility of abuse of power. As Montesquieu remarked:

> To prevent ... abuse [of power], it is necessary from the nature of things that one power should be a check on another ... When legislative power is united with executive power in a single person or in a single body of the magistracy, there is no liberty ... Nor is there liberty if the power of judging is not separated from legislative power and from executive power. If it were joined to legislative power, the life and liberty of the subject would be exposed to arbitrary control; for the judge would then be the legislator. If it were joined to executive power, the judge might behave with violence and oppression. Thus would be an end of everything if the same person or the same body, whether of the nobles or of the people, were to exercise these three powers: that of enacting laws, that of executing public resolutions, and that of judging the crimes or the disputes of individuals.[2]

Although Montesquieu's conception of separation of powers has certainly influenced the framers of the constitutions of the democratic countries of the world, it has not strictly been implemented, particularly in countries with a Westminster system. For the separation of powers between the executive and the legislature in this form of government does not in practice exist. As the ministers, who head the ministries, are simultaneously members of the executive and the legislature, thereby mandating significant overlap between the functions of these two arms of

---

[1] Gustaf (1980), p. 95.
[2] Montesquieu (1989), p. 157.

© The Author(s), under exclusive license to Springer Nature Singapore Pte Ltd. 2022
M. E. Bari, *The Independence of the Judiciary in Bangladesh*,
https://doi.org/10.1007/978-981-16-6222-5_1

government. It can be argued that such an overlap is necessary for avoiding the sort of political deadlocks that have in recent times become the characteristic feature of the American system of government, which goes further than any other in applying Montesquieu's pure doctrine of separation of powers. In the USA, the absence of any overlap between the functions of the executive, i.e., the President and his cabinet, and the legislature, i.e., the Congress, has resulted in these branches engaging in an unhealthy competition of trying to exert supremacy over one other. For instance, in October 2013 political infighting between the Republican Party controlled House of Representatives on the one hand, and President Barack Obama and Democratic Party-led Senate on the other, resulted in a budget impasse, which in turn forced the federal government to enter a shutdown for a period of 16 days.[3] A similar budget impasse also occurred in December 2018, which resulted in a shutdown of the federal government for 35 days—the longest in the history of the USA.[4]

The doctrine of separation of powers may now be said to have received its main application in democratic countries with parliamentary form of government by securing the independence of the courts from the control of the political branches of the government, namely, the executive and the legislature. Such independence is an indispensable feature of any democratic society proclaiming the rule of law. As it enables the courts to interpret and apply the law independently and impartially,[5] thereby ensuring the supremacy of law over the arbitrary exercise of power by either the executive or legislature and guaranteeing the equal protection of law to all people without exception. The judiciary's ability to decide cases impartially in accordance with the dictates of law guarantees that the "lamp of justice" does not go "out in darkness"[6] and public confidence in the administration of justice also remains unshaken and unaffected. The importance of an independent judiciary can be gathered from the observations of Henry Sidgwick, who as early as in 1897, remarked that "in determining a nation's rank in political civilization, no test is more decisive than the degree in which justice as defined by the law is actually realised in its judicial administration; both as between one private citizen and another, and as between citizens and members of the Government."[7]

Inextricably linked with the independence of the judges to interpret and apply the law in an impartial manner are the procedures concerning their appointment and security of tenure. For a transparent method of appointment of judges, which obviates the possibility of intrusion of extraneous considerations into the process, enables judges to decide cases without feeling beholden to the appointing authority

---

[3]Appleton and Stracqualursi (2014), https://abcnews.go.com/Politics/heres-happened-time-government-shut/story?id=26997023

[4]Aljazeera (2019), https://www.aljazeera.com/news/2019/1/25/us-govt-shutdown-how-long-who-is-affected-why-did-it-begin

[5]Phillips and Jackson (1997), p. 15.

[6]Bryce (1921), p. 384.

[7]Sidgwick (1897), p. 481.

1.1 Introduction

while the guarantee of security of tenure permits them to make decisions without the apprehension of suffering personally as a result of such decision-making.

When the South Asian nation of Bangladesh achieved its independence on 16 December 1971 following a 9-month long brutal war with Pakistan, the founding fathers aspired to establish a democratic society in which the judiciary will operate independently to ensure the observance of the rule of law and the enforcement of fundamental rights. However, notwithstanding such an aspiration, the Constitution of Bangladesh, 1972, does not prescribe a transparent method for appointing the judges of the superior judiciary—the Supreme Court of Bangladesh—which would enable judges to decide cases according to the oath of their office. Rather it entrusts the executive with the power to appoint the judges, thereby paving the way for intrusion of political or personal favouritism in the appointment process. Furthermore, although the Constitution, as amended by the Proclamations (Tenth Amendment) Order, 1977 and later validated by the Constitution (Fifth Amendment) Act, 1979, guaranteed security of tenure by stipulating a transparent procedure for the removal of judges of the Supreme Court, the current government of Bangladesh Awami League (BAL) has taken several measures to dispense with this transparent procedure. This book will make it manifestly evident that the absence of a transparent method of appointment of judges of the Supreme Court has often resulted in the appointment of judges not on merit, but through political or personal patronage. Furthermore, the measures taken by the BAL regime to replace the transparent method of removal of the judges of the Supreme Court have substantially impaired the independence of the judges to decide cases independently of the wishes of the appointing authority. Consequently, in light of these findings, this book will put forward recommendations from comparative constitutional law and normative perspectives for the insertion of detailed norms in the Constitution of Bangladesh so as to establish the best means for excluding patronage appointments to the bench and for guaranteeing the security of tenure of the judges, thereby safeguarding the independence of the superior judiciary to decide cases without fear or favour.

In this chapter, first, the standards concerning the independence of the judiciary and their recognition in domestic constitutions will briefly be discussed. Second, an attempt will be made to briefly examine the guarantee of judicial independence as enshrined in the Constitution of Bangladesh, 1972. Third, the objectives of the book will be discussed. Finally, an outline of the chapters which will make up this book will be provided.

1.2 The Standards Concerning the Independence of the Judiciary and Their Recognition in Domestic Constitutions

It should be stressed here that in order to assist the comity of nations to put in place effective guarantees for enabling judges to decide cases independently and impartially, various international non-governmental organizations since the 1950s have developed standards, such as the International Bar Association's Minimum Standards, 1982, the Montreal Universal Declaration on the Independence of Justice, 1983 and the Beijing Statement of the Principles of the Independence of the Judiciary, 1995, for thickening the concept of judicial independence. These standards contend that in order to safeguard the independence of the judiciary it is imperative to safeguard not only the independence of the individual judges but also the independence of the judiciary as a whole.[8] The individual independence, which was recognized by the Congress of the International Commission of Jurists held in New Delhi in January 1959, consists of two elements, namely, substantive and personal independence. The substantive independence of the judges refers to the independence of the judges to decide cases brought before them in accordance with their oath of office without submitting to any kind of internal or external pressures. On the other hand, personal independence implies the competence of the judges to adjudicate cases without the apprehension of suffering personally for such adjudication. In this context, the observations of the International Bar Association's Minimum Standards of Judicial Independence, 1982, are instructive. The Standards note that personal independence of the judges is guaranteed when "the terms and conditions of judicial service are adequately secured so as to ensure that individual judges are not subject to executive control".[9] Arguably, the personal independence of the judges can only be safeguarded by stipulating a transparent method of appointment and guaranteeing their security of tenure. For, in the first place, a transparent method of appointment would ensure that judges are appointed on merit and not on the basis any extraneous considerations, thereby ensuring that judges do not feel obliged to the appointing authority. Second, the guarantee of security of tenure enables judges to decide cases, particularly where the executive is a party, without fear or favour.

However, it can be argued that the expansion of the concept of judicial independence by including in it the additional elements of collective and internal independence in the 1980s, has been the most significant contribution of the international standards concerning judicial independence. For, it has been argued that independence of the individual judges—composed of both substantive and personal independence—would be virtually ineffective without the internal and collective independence of the judiciary. In this context, it is pertinent to note that collective

---

[8] Green (1985), p. 135.
[9] International Bar Association (1982), art. 1(b).

1.2 The Standards Concerning the Independence of the Judiciary and Their...

independence has been construed to mean the institutional, administrative and financial independence of the judiciary as a whole *vis-a-vis* the executive and legislative branches of the government. The Beijing Statement of Principles of the Independence of the Judiciary in the LAWASIA Region, 1995 contends that such independence is safeguarded when the judiciary itself is entrusted with the task of administering the affairs of the court.[10] The importance of safeguarding the collective independence of the judiciary for enabling the individual judges to perform their judicial functions can be gathered from the following observations of the Canadian Supreme Court in *Valente v R*[11]:

> an individual judge may enjoy the essential conditions of judicial independence but if the court or tribunal over which he or she presides is not independent of the other branches of government, in what is essential to its function, he or she cannot be said to be an independent tribunal.[12]

While internal independence means the independence of a judge to decide individual cases free from any kind of pressure or interference from his judicial superiors and colleagues.[13] This element of judicial independence has most prominently been recognised in the Montreal Universal Declaration on the Independence of Justice, 1983, which provides that "[i]n the decision-making process, judges shall be independent vis-a-vis their judicial colleagues and superiors. Any hierarchical organisation of the judiciary and any difference in grade or rank shall in no way interfere with the right of the judge to pronounce his judgment freely".[14]

Thus, it is evident from the brief discussion above that the concept of independence of the judiciary has currently four meanings or facets:

I. substantive independence;
II. personal independence;
III. collective independence; and
IV. internal independence.

However, notwithstanding the recognition of the above facets of judicial independence, this book will make it evident that it is more common for the constitutions of modern democracies to guarantee the individual independence, namely substantive and personal independence of the judges. To this end, it will be shown that some constitutions have gone further than others in seeking to safeguard such independence of the judges by guaranteeing a transparent method of appointment for obviating the possibility of intrusion of extraneous consideration into the process of appointing the judges of the superior courts. For instance, in the United Kingdom (UK), the Constitutional Reform Act was passed in 2005 to provide for the establishment of a Judicial Appointments Commission (JAC), which is headed

---

[10] Law Association for Asia and the Pacific (LAWASIA) (1995), art. 36.

[11] *Valente v R* [1985] 2 SCR 673.

[12] Ibid., [15].

[13] Shetreet (1985), p. 399.

[14] Montreal Declaration (1983), art. 2.03.

by a lay person and does not allow for representation of either the executive or the legislature, to perform the task of recommending the appointment of judges "solely on merit".[15] Thus, the objective underlying the enactment of the JAC is to deprive the political branches of the government the opportunity to adversely influence the selection process of the judges.

Furthermore, some constitutions seek to guarantee the security of tenure of the judges by incorporating a difficult process of removing judges from office. In this context, reference can be made to the constitutional arrangement in Pakistan. The Constitution of Pakistan, 1973, entrusts a permanent disciplinary body of judicial character with the responsibility of conducting an inquiry into allegations of incapacity or misconduct brought against a judge of the superior judiciary and of, subsequently, recommending the removal of the concerned judge if it found merit in the allegation.[16] It is noteworthy that in order to enable the disciplinary body to perform its functions in an independent manner, the Constitution of Pakistan deprives the executive branch the opportunity to choose the membership of the body by stipulating that the latter would be composed solely of the senior-most judges of the superior judiciary.[17]

This book will argue that the guarantee of substantive and personal independence in modern constitutions has enabled judges of superior courts to decide cases free from the influences of the political branches, thereby upholding the independence of the judiciary.

1.3 The Constitution of Bangladesh and the Guarantee of Judicial Independence

Prior to emerging as an independent state on 16 December 1971, Bangladesh was in a union with Pakistan for 24 years as its eastern province. During the continuance of this union, the Punjab-dominated central government in West Pakistan not only centralised power but also routinely subjected Bangladeshis—then the inhabitants of East Pakistan—to discrimination "in every sphere of governmental and public activity."[18] As Paul Dreyfust noted: "Over the years, West Pakistan behaved like a poorly raised, egotistical guest, devouring the best dishes and leaving nothing but scraps and leftovers for East Pakistan."[19]

Alarmed at the prospect of their province being reduced to a "mere colony" of West Pakistan, Bangladeshis pinned their "last hope of being part of a participatory

---

[15] Constitutional Reform Act, 2005 (UK) s. 63(2).

[16] Constitution of Pakistan, 1973 (Pakistan) Art. 209(1) read together with arts 209(5, 6).

[17] Constitution of Pakistan, 1973 (Pakistan) Art. 209(2).

[18] See Bari (2017), p. 7.

[19] Boissoneault (2016), https://www.smithsonianmag.com/history/genocide-us-cant-remember-bangladesh-cant-forget-180961490/

1.3 The Constitution of Bangladesh and the Guarantee of Judicial Independence

democracy" on a favourable outcome for the Awami League of East Pakistan in the first general election in Pakistan's history.[20] As the Awami League contested the election, which was held on 7 December 1970, on the promise of safeguarding greater provincial autonomy for East Pakistan. Although the Awami League won the right to form a government by winning 167 of the 300 parliamentary seats in the election, the Pakistani military junta refused to honour the mandate given to the party by the people. Instead, the Martial Law regime of General Yahya Khan "postponed the convening of the National Assembly, *sine die*" on 1 March 1971.[21] This latest arbitrary move of the military junta triggered the first "massive civil disobedience movement" in East Pakistan.[22] However, Yahya termed the movement an "armed rebellion" and ordered, on 25 March 1971, the military to carry out the genocidal "Operation Searchlight" to put down the movement.[23] This in turn persuaded East Pakistan to declare its independence from Pakistan on 26 March 1971.[24]

Bangladesh's "Proclamation of Independence", which was issued on 10 April 1971, contained "provisional arrangements" for the governance of the People's Republic of Bangladesh. Although the Proclamation declared that in order to give effect to the mandate granted to the Awami League in the general election held in December 1970, the party's elected representatives had "duly constituted" themselves "into a Constituent Assembly", it did not vest the legislative power of the Republic in the Assembly. Rather it proclaimed that the President would "exercise all the Executive and Legislative powers of the Republic" till "such time as a Constitution" was framed for the newly independent nation.[25] It should be stressed here that investing the President, instead of the Constituent Assembly, with legislative power contravened the doctrine of separation of powers. Furthermore, it marked a clear departure from the previous example set by the British in the Subcontinent under the Indian Independence Act, 1947. For the Act of 1947 firmly established the Constituent Assemblies of Pakistan and India as the central legislatures for both the nations until such time as the enactment of their respective constitutions.[26] It is also pertinent to note here that the Proclamation of Independence, which is considered the first interim Constitution of Bangladesh, was not only silent as to the exercise of judicial powers but also did not provide for the creation of a superior court for Bangladesh.

Within a month of securing independence, on 11 January 1972, the Provisional Constitution of Bangladesh Order, 1972 was issued in pursuance of the Proclamation of Independence. Instead of a Supreme Court, the Provisional Constitution provided for the establishment of a High Court as the highest court of law of the newly

---

[20] See above n 18, p. 7; Proclamation of Independence, 1971 (Bangladesh) para 2.

[21] Dunbar (1972), p. 452.

[22] See above n 18, p. 7.

[23] Ibid.

[24] Ibid.

[25] Proclamation of Independence, 1971 (Bangladesh).

[26] Indian Independence Act, 1947 (UK) s. 8(1).

8   1 Introduction

independent nation. The Provisional Constitution merely provided that the High Court would consist of "a Chief Justice and so many other Judges as may be appointed from time to time".[27] It was silent both as to the authority who would appoint such judges of the High Court and to the terms and conditions on which such judges were to hold office. This lacuna, however, was removed by the High Court of Bangladesh Order (President's Order No. 5 of 1972), which was issued only six days after the issuance of the Provisional Constitution of Bangladesh Order on 17 January 1972. This Order provided that the President from time to time would appoint the Chief Justice and other Judges of the High Court "who... [would] hold office on such terms and conditions as the President may determine".[28] Thus the President was not only given the power to appoint the Chief Justice and other Judges of the High Court, but he was also given the authority to determine the terms and conditions of their service. This left the door too wide open for the President to assess the suitability of candidates for judgeship in terms of their political allegiance and ideological outlook. These fears were, indeed, realised when the President did not reappoint Chief Justice of the erstwhile "Dacca" High Court[29] and another four senior judges[30] to the newly established High Court of Bangladesh, without assigning any reason whatsoever. These instances of non-appointment contravened the international norms developed in this regard, thus: "Where a court is abolished or restructured, all existing members of the court must be reappointed to its replacement or appointment to another judicial office of equivalent status and tenure."[31] It seems that the President did not consider these five judges as persons who shared his philosophy or ideology and, as such, dropped them unceremoniously ignoring their competence, integrity, seniority and experience.

However, although the President was given the unilateral authority to choose the composition of the High Court, the Court was nevertheless given "all such original, appellate, special, revisional, review, procedural and all other power as were exercisable in respect of the ... territories [of Bangladesh] by the High Court at 'Dacca' under any law in force before the 26th day of March, 1971". Within seven months of the issuance of the High Court of Bangladesh Order, the government of the day felt the necessity to establish an Appellate Division of the High Court to deal with all "appeals and petitions, which immediately before the commencement of the Provisional Constitution of Bangladesh Order, 1972, were pending before the erstwhile Supreme Court of Pakistan arising out of matters within the territories of Bangladesh".[32] Accordingly the High Court of Bangladesh (Amendment) Order (President Order No. 91 of 1972) was issued on 2 August 1972, which provided that

---

[27] Provisional Constitution of Bangladesh Order, 1972, art. 9.

[28] High Court of Bangladesh Order, 1972, art. 3.

[29] Justice B. A. Siddiqui was the Chief Justice of erstwhile Dhaka High Court.

[30] The other four judges who were dropped are Maksumul Hakim, Abdul Hakim, Nurul Islam and T. H. Khan.

[31] Beijing Statement of Principles of the Independence of the Judiciary in the LAWASIA Region, art. 29.

[32] High Court of Bangladesh (Amendment) Order, 1972, art. 4.

1.3 The Constitution of Bangladesh and the Guarantee of Judicial Independence

"[t]here shall be an Appellate Division of High Court of Bangladesh which shall consist of the Chief Justice and two other Judges to be appointed by the President after consultation with the Chief Justice".[33] Thus the power of the President, who could not reasonably be expected to know the members of the Bar so as to properly assess their fitness for appointment to the bench, to appoint the judges of the Appellate Division of the High Court was sought to be qualified by the requirement of mandatory consultation with the Chief Justice, who was in the best possible position to provide expert advice about the legal acumen and expertise of the prospective candidates for judgeship. The High Court of Bangladesh with its Appellate Division remained in force until the establishment of the Supreme Court of Bangladesh under the Constitution of Bangladesh.

It is pertinent to mention here that the founding fathers of Bangladesh completed the task of enacting the Constitution within a year of the nation securing its independence. Thus, the Constitution of Bangladesh was given effect from 16 December 1972 to commemorate the First Anniversary of the Victory Day of Bangladesh.[34] It should be further stressed here that the founding fathers in a deliberate attempt to give effect to the aspiration of the people to be part of a democratic society, pledged in the preamble of the Constitution that:

> it shall be a fundamental aim of the State to realise through the democratic process a socialist society, free from exploitation—a society in which the rule of law, fundamental human rights and freedom, equality and justice … will be secured for all citizens.[35]

Since an independent judiciary is an essential feature of any democratic society seeking to uphold the rule of law and the fundamental liberties of individuals, it is imperative to secure its position in the constitution,[36] which is considered the supreme law of a nation. In particular, the constitution should vest the judicial power of a nation in the judiciary. Although the Constitution of Bangladesh vests the "executive power of the Republic" in the Prime Minister[37] and confers the "legislative powers of the Republic" on the Parliament,[38] it does not explicitly invest judiciary with the judicial power of the Republic. Thus, the framers of the Constitution embraced the spirit of separation of powers only in respect of the executive and legislature, but they preferred to remain silent with regard to vesting judicial power in the judiciary. This marked a clear departure from the constitutional practice of other states.[39]

---

[33] Ibid.

[34] See above n 18, at 7.

[35] Constitution of Bangladesh, 1972 (Bangladesh) Preamble.

[36] Singh (2000), p. 249.

[37] Constitution of Bangladesh, 1972 (Bangladesh) art. 55(2).

[38] Constitution of Bangladesh, 1972 (Bangladesh) art. 65(1).

[39] For instance, the Commonwealth of Australia Constitution Act, 1900 (Aus.) s. 71 stipulates that "the judicial power of the Commonwealth shall be vested in a Federal Supreme Court, to be called the High Court of Australia, and in such other federal courts as the Parliament creates, and in such

10 1 Introduction

However, notwithstanding the constitutional silence regarding the vesting of judicial power in the judiciary, it should be stressed here that the highest court of law in Bangladesh, namely, the Supreme Court,[40] exercises the judicial power of the Republic in pursuance of the Constitution itself. In this context, Justice Mustafa Kamal applying the rule of construction, which was enunciated by Lord Diplock in *Hinds and others v. The Queen*[41] to hold that the "absence of express words [in the Constitution] does not prevent" the judicial power of the state being exercised by the judiciary "if it is intended that previously existing courts shall continue to function",[42] forcefully observed in *Mujibur Rahman v. Bangladesh*[43] that:

> Our Constitution expressly provides in paragraph 6 of the Fourth Schedule the continuity of the incumbent Chief Justice and the Judges of the erstwhile High Court of Bangladesh in the new dispensation and the transfer of legal proceedings from the previous Courts to... the Supreme Court... Our Constitution, therefore, expressly intended that the previously existing superior Courts shall continue to function, albeit in a new dispensation... Although the Constitution itself omitted to confer judicial power on the Supreme Court... by any express provision, there can be no doubt whatsoever that the Supreme Court ... [is] the repository of judicial power of the State, because ...[it has] been previously existing and the Constitution allows ...[it] to function, although in a new form.[44]

It should be further stressed here that although the framers of the Constitution of Bangladesh did not expressly vest the judicial power of the Republic in the judiciary, they sought to make the principle of independence of judiciary a cornerstone in the scheme of the Constitution. To this end, reference can be made, for instance, to the provisions contained in Articles 22 and 94(4) of the Constitution. First, Article 22 of the Constitution stipulates that the "State shall ensure the separation of the judiciary from the executive organs of the State". Second, Article 94(4) provides that: "Subject to the provisions of this Constitution the Chief Justice and the other Judges shall be independent in the exercise of their judicial functions." Thus, the Constitution not only recognises the necessity to safeguard the independence of the judiciary as a whole, but, critically, also to maintain the individual independence of the judges. It can be argued that these constitutional provisions for protecting the independence of the judiciary, particularly from the executive, are aimed at realising the fundamental aim of the state, as is evidenced from the third preamble paragraph of the Constitution, of establishing "a society in which the rule of law, fundamental human rights and freedom, equality and justice ... will be secured for all citizens."[45] For it is only an independent judiciary which can promote the rule of law and protect the fundamental human rights of individuals.

---

other courts as it invests with federal jurisdiction". In the same vein, Article 92 of the German Basic Law, 1949, invests the judicial power in the judges.

[40] Commonwealth of Australia Constitution Act, 1900 (Aus.) art. 94(1).

[41] *Hind and others v The Queen (1976) 1 All ER 353.*

[42] Quoted in *Mujibur Rahman v Bangladesh* 44 DLR (AD) 1992 111 [22] (J. Mostofa Kamal).

[43] *Mujibur Rahman v Bangladesh* 44 DLR (AD) (1992) 111.

[44] Ibid., [22] (J. Mostofa Kamal).

[45] Constitution of Bangladesh, 1972 (Bangladesh) Preamble.

1.3 The Constitution of Bangladesh and the Guarantee of Judicial Independence 11

It should be stressed here that in addition to the above provisions, the Supreme Court of Bangladesh in the seminal case of *Anwar Hossain Chowdhury and Others v. Bangladesh,*[46] has recognized the principle of the independence of the judiciary as one of the basic features or structures of the Constitution,[47] i.e., one of the structural pillars on which the constitutional edifice is built upon and which if altered will cause the entire edifice to crumble. Thus, the principle of judicial independence, as guaranteed by the Constitution of Bangladesh, has been placed beyond the powers of the transient majority in the Parliament to wipe out by the "amendatory process".[48]

An attempt will now be made to briefly examine the manner in which the Constitution of Bangladesh seeks to give effect to the ideal of safeguarding the independence of the judiciary.

1.3.1 The Constitution of Bangladesh and the Method of Appointment of Judges of the SC

Before discussing the method of appointing the judges of superior courts of Bangladesh as stipulated by the 1972 Constitution of Bangladesh, it is necessary to briefly examine the provisions concerning the structure and function of the Supreme Court (SC)—the highest court of the land—which are contained in Part V, Chapter I of the Constitution.

The Constitution stipulates that the SC shall be composed of two divisions, namely the Appellate Division (AD) and the High Court Division (HCD).[49] It has conferred original and appellate jurisdictions and powers on the HCD,[50] while the AD has been invested with the authority "to hear and determine appeals from judgments, decrees, orders or sentences" of the HCD.[51]

The Constitution of Bangladesh contains provisions relating to the appointment of three types of judges, namely, the Chief Justice, judges of the AD and additional as well as regular Judges of the HCD of the SC.

First, with regard to the appointment of the Chief Justice, who is the head of the Bangladeshi judiciary, the Constitution has provided the President with the unfettered power to make such an appointment. This discretion ignores the benefit of shared responsibility: responsibility, for instance, shared between the President and a selection committee consisting of majority members from the superior judiciary, in order to prevent a politically motivated appointment to suit the designs the government of the day. In this context, reference can be to the constitutional

---

[46] *Anwar Hossain Chowdhury and Others v Bangladesh* (1989) 18 CLC (AD).

[47] Ibid., [347].

[48] Ibid., [416].

[49] Constitution of Bangladesh, 1972 (Bangladesh) Preamble.

[50] Constitution of Bangladesh, 1972 (Bangladesh) art. 101.

[51] Constitution of Bangladesh, 1972 (Bangladesh) art. 103.

arrangements in Armenia, Poland, Saudi Arabia, Spain, Namibia, Nepal and Nigeria. For the constitutions of these nations stipulate that the head of the judiciary should be appointed by the head of the state either on the proposal or recommendation of, or in consultation with, an independent selection body of judicial character to obviate the possibility of questionable appointments to the highest judicial office of the land.[52] It should, however, be stressed that in order to ensure that extraneous considerations did not play a part in the pivotal appointment of the Chief Justice of Bangladesh, a convention of appointing the senior-most judge of the AD as the Chief Justice had been developed.

Second, in appointing the judges of both the Divisions of SC, the President is required by the Constitution to act on the advice of the Prime Minister, after consulting the Chief Justice.[53] Furthermore, a convention of appointing the senior-most judges of the HCD as the judges of the AD had been developed to preserve the integrity and impartiality of the appointment process. However, this book will make it evident that both these conventions with regard to the appointment of the Chief Justice of the nation and of the judges of the AD have been transgressed at regular intervals by succeeding generations of executives, particularly by the current government of the Bangladesh Awami League, for politicising the superior judiciary of the nation, thereby undermining its credibility in the eyes of the litigants as an impartial arbitrator of disputes.

Finally, although there exists a constitutional obligation to consult the Chief Justice when appointing the regular judges of the HCD, there is an absence of such an obligation when appointing the additional judges of the HCD for a period of two years under Article 98 of the Constitution. This book will make it evident that successive governments in Bangladesh have taken advantage of the lacuna in Article 98 to pack the HCD with judges who share their political philosophy with the hope that these judges would support their action, omission and legislation if and when challenged.

---

[52] See Constitution of the Republic of Armenia, 1995 (Arm.) art. 95, s. 3. (providing that the President of the Court of Appeals shall be appointed on the proposal of the Judicial Council); Constitution of the Republic of Poland, 1997 (Pol.) art. 144, s. 3(1) ("The First President of the Supreme Court shall be appointed by the President of the Republic from amongst candidates proposed by the General Assembly of the Judges of the Supreme Court"); See Basic Law of the Government, 1992 (Saudi Arabia) art. 52 (stipulating that the appointment of judges, including the Chief Justice, by Royal Decree upon a proposal from the Higher Council of Justice); See *Constitución Española, Boletín Official del Estado*, 1978 (Spain) n. 123(2) (providing that the President of the Supreme Court shall be appointed by the King at the proposal of the General Council of the judicial branch); See Constitution of the Republic of Namibia, 1990 (Namibia) art. 82(1) (stating that the appointment of the Judge-President of the High Court shall be "made by the President on recommendation of the Judicial Service Commission."); See Nēpālakō Sanvidhāna [Constitution of Nepal] 2015, art. 129(2) (providing that the President shall appoint the Chief Justice of Nepal on the recommendation of the Constitutional Council); Constitution of Nigeria, 1999 (Nigeria) art. 231(1) ("The appointment of a person to the office of Chief Justice of Nigeria shall be made by the President on the recommendation of the National Judicial Council subject to confirmation of such appointment by the Senate.)

[53] Constitution of Bangladesh, 1972 (Bangladesh) article 95(1).

1.3.2 The Constitution of Bangladesh and the Method of Removal of Judges of the SC

The Constitution of Bangladesh originally provided that a judge of the SC could only be removed from office "by an order of the President passed pursuant to a resolution of Parliament supported by a majority of not less than two-thirds of the total number of members of Parliament, on the ground of proved misbehavior or incapacity".[54] However, the Constitution (Fourth Amendment) Act, which was enacted by the Parliament during the regime of Sheikh Mujibur Rahman, on 25 January 1975 changed the method of removal of the judges of the SC. It inserted a new provision in the Constitution which stated: "A judge may be removed from his office by the President on the ground of misbehavior or incapacity."[55] Thus, the President was given the unfettered power to remove the judges of the SC at his pleasure.

Since security of tenure of the judges, which enables them to administer justice without fear or favour, is a constituent element of the individual independence of the judges, it was the extra-constitutional Martial Law regime of General Ziaur Rahman which, on 22 April 1979, changed the method of removing the judges of the SC through a Proclamation Order, which was later validated by the Constitution (Fifth Amendment) Act, 1979. This removal procedure stipulated that a judge of the SC could only be removed from office by the President on the recommendation of the Supreme Judicial Council (SJC), which was to be composed of the Chief Justice and the two next senior judges. However, the current regime of Bangladesh Awami League (BAL) dispensed with this method of removal of judges of the SC by persuading the Parliament to pass the Constitutional (Sixteenth Amendment) Act on 17 September 2014. This new amendment vested the power to remove judges of the SC in the Parliament, thereby bringing the SC under the control of the executive and curtailing in the process its independence. For unlike the parliaments of democratic nations, the present Parliament of Bangladesh, which is the product of an election that was rigged in favour of the incumbent BAL,[56] is not only devoid of any real opposition but is also subservient to the executive.

Accordingly, in August 2017, the AD led by Chief Justice SK Sinha in *Bangladesh v. Advocate Asaduzzaman Siddiqui (the Sixteenth Amendment Case)*[57] unanimously upheld the decision of the HCD invalidating the Sixteenth Amendment, thereby restoring the constitutional provisions concerning the SJC. However, this ruling ultimately led to Justice Sinha being unceremoniously forced out of his high office, which is an unprecedented event in the judicial history of the nation (See Sect. 6.4). Following Justice Sinha's ouster from office, the BAL regime has cast considerable

---

[54] Constitution of Bangladesh, 1972 (Bangladesh) art. 96(2).

[55] Constitution (Fourth Amendment) Act, 1975 (Bangladesh) s. 15.

[56] Bari and Dey (2019), pp. 621–622.

[57] *Bangladesh v Advocate Asaduzzaman Siddiqui (the Sixteenth Amendment Case)* (2017) Civil Appeal No. 06 of 2017 (AD).

doubt on the restoration of the constitutional provisions concerning the SJC apparently due to the pendency of a review petition before the AD seeking the reversal of the decision in the *Sixteenth Amendment Case* (See Sect. 6.5). Furthermore, the current Chief Justice, who was also a part of the AD which invalidated the Sixteenth Amendment, instead of seeking to speedily dispose of the review petition, has proceeded to take disciplinary action against judges of the SC accused of misconduct or incapacity in consultation with the executive branch of government. This book will demonstrate that these adverse measures have substantially impaired the independence of the judges to decide cases, particularly where the executive is a party, without the apprehension of suffering personally.

1.4   Objectives of the Book

It is evident from the discussion in Sect. 1.3 that although the ideal of safeguarding the independence of the judiciary has found a prominent place in the Constitution of Bangladesh, the key elements for realising such an ideal have not adequately been guaranteed by the Constitution. Consequently, succeeding generations of executives have sought to undermine the independence of the judiciary. Thus, there exists a gap between the theory and practice concerning the independence of judiciary in Bangladesh. The book, therefore, endeavours, in the first place, to fill a significant gap in the existing literature regarding the weaknesses of the constitutional provisions concerning the appointment of the Chief Justice of Bangladesh and other judges of the SC. In order to address these deficiencies, this book will, in part, rely on comparative constitutional analysis. In particular, this analysis will draw on the process of appointing the judges of the superior courts as stipulated under the constitutional arrangement of India, and on the transparent methods of appointment introduced in the UK through the enactment of the Constitutional Reform Act of 2005 and in Pakistan through the enactment of the Constitution (Eighteenth Amendment) Act, 2010. The comparative experiences of these jurisdictions will provide insight into the mechanisms necessary for obviating the possibility of intrusion of extraneous considerations into the process of selecting the judges of the superior courts. Second, this book will evaluate from comparative constitutional and normative perspectives the effectiveness of the method of removal of judges involving the SJC, as had been incorporated in the Constitution of Bangladesh through the Proclamations (Tenth Amendment) Order, 1977 and later validated by the Constitution (Fifth Amendment) Act, 1979. It will be made manifestly evident that the recent attempts to dispense with this transparent method of removal have been preferred to bring the superior judiciary under the control of an all-power executive.

Since no systematic and structured research has so far been carried out critically examining the above issues, this research will enhance knowledge by not only identifying the flaws, deficiencies and lacunae of the constitutional provisions concerning the method of appointment of the judges of the SC but also examining the measures undertaken by the current BAL regime to dispense with the transparent method of removal of the judges involving the SJC. Consequently, based on these findings, recommendations will be put forward to rectify these defects from comparative constitutional law and normative perspectives. The outcome of this book will not only establish the best means for excluding the possibility of appointment of judges of the SC on extraneous considerations but also for guaranteeing their security of tenure, thereby safeguarding the independence of the superior judiciary of Bangladesh.

1.5 Structure of the Book

Following this introductory chapter, the structure of this book is divided into six chapters.

In Chap. 2, titled "The Principle of Judicial Independence and its Recognition in the Constitution of Bangladesh, 1972", light will first be shed on: a) the importance of an independent judiciary in a democratic state; b) the traditional and modern meanings of judicial independence; and c) the importance of a transparent method of appointment of judges and the security of tenure of judges, as constituent elements of judicial independence. Subsequently, the principle of judicial independence as enshrined in the Constitution of Bangladesh will be outlined.

Chapter 3, titled "The Method of Appointment of the Judges of the Supreme Court under the Constitution of Bangladesh, 1972," will deal with the provisions concerning the appointment of judges of the SC with special reference to the leading decisions of the court in this regard. In particular, it will be shown that in order to ensure that extraneous considerations do not play any part in the pivotal process of appointing the Chief Justice of the country, a convention of appointing the senior most judge of the AD—the higher division of the SC—as the Chief Justice was developed. In the same vein, a convention of appointing the senior-most judges of the HCD, which is the lower division of the SC, as the judges of the AD was established. The method prescribed by the Constitution for appointing the regular as well as the additional judges of the HCD will also be discussed. Finally, light will be shed on the short-lived Supreme Judicial Commission, which was established in March 2008 to recommend the best candidates to the executive for appointment as judges of the HCD and the AD.

After gaining insight into the constitutional process of appointing the Chief Justice of Bangladesh and the other judges of both the Divisions of the SC, Chap. 4, titled "The Intrusion of Extraneous Considerations in the Appointment of the Chief Justice and the Other Judges of the Supreme Court of Bangladesh", will, in the first place, shed light on the transgression of both the conventions of appointing the senior-most judge of the AD as the Chief Justice and of appointing the senior-most judges of the HCD as the judges of the AD. Second, it will be shown that the absence of a constitutional obligation to consult the Chief Justice in appointing additional judges to the HCD has resulted in governments packing the bench with loyalists. Finally, the manner in which the journey of the Supreme Judicial Commission, which was established in 2008 through the promulgation of an Ordinance, to recommend the best candidates to the President for appointment as the judges of the HCD and the AD, was calculatedly brought to an end by the current Government of BAL in February 2009, will be discussed. The objective of these analyses is to demonstrate that the weaknesses of the constitutional provisions concerning the appointment of the judges have enabled the politicization of the superior judiciary of the nation, thereby eroding public confidence in its credibility.

Chapter 5, titled "The Guarantee of Security of Tenure of the Judges of the Supreme Court under the Constitution of Bangladesh, 1972", will critically examine the two crucial elements connected with the security of tenure, namely, retirement age and the method of removal of judges of the superior courts, as originally stipulated by the 1972 Constitution of Bangladesh and the various amendments introduced to these components over the years. The objective of this examination is to demonstrate that the method of removal of judges involving the SJC, as introduced by the Martial Law regime of General Zia, was more conducive to maintaining the independence of the judiciary.

Chapter 6, titled "The Functioning of the Supreme Judicial Council, the Changes Introduced to the Method of Removal of Judges of the Supreme Court of Bangladesh in 2014 and the Subsequent Scathing Attack on the Judiciary", will, in the first place, critically evaluate the functioning of the SJC for safeguarding the independence of the judiciary. Subsequently, it will be made manifestly evident that the deletion of the constitutional provisions concerning this transparent procedure of removal of the judges through the Constitution (Sixteenth Amendment) Act, 2014 and the subsequent measures, e.g. forcing the Chief Justice of the country to not only resign from office but also to leave the country for declaring the Sixteenth Amendment unconstitutional, have been preferred for exerting the supremacy of the BAL government over the judiciary. Furthermore, light will be shed on the fact that these adverse measures have substantially impaired the ability of the judges of the SC to administer justice without the fear of adverse consequences.

Finally, the concluding chapter, Chap. 7, in light of the findings detailed in Chaps. 3, 4, 5 and 6, will put forward recommendations for ensuring that the superior judiciary in Bangladesh can more properly assume its status as "an impenetrable bulwark against"[58] arbitrary exercise of power by the political branches of the government, thereby upholding the rule of law and the human rights of individuals.

---

[58] Carlton Jr. (2002), pp. 835–836.

References

Aljazeera. (2019). *US gov't shutdown: How long? Who is affected? Why did it begin?*. Available at https://www.aljazeera.com/news/2019/1/25/us-govt-shutdown-how-long-who-is-affected-why-did-it-begin

Appleton, K., & Stracqualursi, V. (2014). *Here's what happened the last time the government shut down*. Available at https://abcnews.go.com/Politics/heres-happened-time-government-shut/story?id=26997023

Bari, M. E. (2017). *States of emergency and the law: The experience of Bangladesh* (p. 7). Routledge.

Bari, M. E., & Dey, P. (2019). The enactment of digital security laws in Bangladesh: No place for dissent. *George Washington International Law Review, 51*(4), 621–622.

Boissoneault, L. (2016). *The genocide the U.S. can't remember, but Bangladesh can't forget*. Available at https://www.smithsonianmag.com/history/genocide-us-cant-remember-bangladesh-cant-forget-180961490/

Bryce, J. (1921). *Modern democracies* (Vol. II, p. 384). The Macmillan Company.

Carlton, A. P., Jr. (2002). Preserving judicial independence – An exegesis. *Fordham Urban Law Journal, 29*, 835–836.

Dunbar, D. (1972). Pakistan: The failure of political negotiations. *Asian Survey, 12*(5), 452.

Green, G. (1985). The rationale and some aspects of judicial independence. *Australian Law Journal, 59*, 135.

Gustaf, P. (1980). The independence of the judiciary. In *Report of the symposium on the independence of judges and lawyers* (p. 95).

International Bar Association. (1982). *Minimum standards of judicial independence* (art. 1(b)).

Law Association for Asia and the Pacific (LAWASIA). (1995). *The Beijing statement of the principles of the independence of the judiciary in the LAWASIA region* (art. 36).

Montesquieu. (1989). *The spirit of the laws* (p. 157). Cambridge University Press.

Montreal Declaration. (1983). *Universal declaration on the independence of justice* (art. 2.03).

Phillips, O. H., & Jackson, P. (1997). *Constitutional and administrative law* (p. 15). Sweet & Maxwell Ltd.

Shetreet, S. (1985). The emerging transnational jurisprudence on judicial independence: The IBA standards and Montreal declaration. In S. Shetreet & J. Deschenes (Eds.), *Judicial independence: The contemporary debate* (p. 399)). Martinus Nijhoff Publishers.

Sidgwick, H. (1897). *The elements of politics* (p. 481). Macmillan and Co..

Singh, M. P. (2000). Securing the independence of the judiciary – The Indian experience. *Indian International and Comparative Law Review, 10*(2), 249.

Chapter 2
The Principle of Judicial Independence and Its Recognition in the Constitution of Bangladesh, 1972

2.1 Introduction

The judiciary is that organ of the government, which according to Alexander Hamilton, has "no influence over either the sword or the purse; no direction either of the strength or of the wealth of the society; and can take no active resolution whatever. It may truly be said to have neither force nor will, but merely judgment."[1] In countries with a written constitution—the supreme law which cannot be changed like any other law—the judges perform the pivotal task of acting as the guardians of the constitution, which involve delivering judgments declaring statutes contravening the tenets of the constitution null and void, and thereby maintaining the rule of law. As Alexander Hamilton observed:

> No legislative act… contrary to the constitution, can be valid. To deny this would be to affirm that the deputy is greater than his principal… It [constitution] therefore belongs to them [the judges] to ascertain its meaning as well as the meaning of any particular act proceeding from the legislative body… the constitution ought to be preferred to the statute, the intention of the people to the intention of their agents.[2]

In the same vein, James Bryce says:

> When questions arise as to the limits of the powers of the Executive or of the Legislature, or- in a Federation- as to the limits of the respective powers of the Central or National and those of the State Government, it is by a Court of Law that the true meaning of the Constitution, as the fundamental and supreme law, ought to be determined, because it is the rightful and authorised interpreter of what the people intended to declare when they were enacting a fundamental instrument.[3]

---

[1] Hamilton (1948), pp. 396–397.

[2] Ibid.

[3] Bryce (1921), pp. 384–385.

© The Author(s), under exclusive license to Springer Nature Singapore Pte Ltd. 2022
M. E. Bari, *The Independence of the Judiciary in Bangladesh*,
https://doi.org/10.1007/978-981-16-6222-5_2

It should be stressed here that the judiciary can only stand up for the rule of law in a democratic nation. For in an authoritarian state, the judiciary is expected to adopt a highly deferential attitude when called upon to scrutinise governmental actions and decisions.[4] In this context, Harold Laski aptly noted that "[i]f the executive could shape judicial decision in accordance with its own desires, it would be the unlimited master of the State".[5] Thus, the role of the judiciary as the guardian of the rule of law necessitates that it should completely be separated from the two other organs of the government, namely the executive and the legislature. As the UN Special Rapporteur on the Independence of Judges and Lawyers, who in his Report of 2004, noted:

> The rule of law and separation of powers not only constitute the pillars of the system of democracy but also open the way to an administration of justice that provides guarantees of independence, impartiality and transparency. These guarantees are ... universal in scope.[6]

It is against the above background that this chapter will, first, outline the importance of an independent judiciary in a democratic state. Second, it will explore the traditional and modern meanings of judicial independence. Third, the importance of a transparent method of appointment of judges and the security of tenure of judges as constituent elements of judicial independence will be emphasised. Fourth, in an effort to demonstrate the effectiveness of these core elements in safeguarding judicial independence, this chapter will shed light on the manner in which the superior judiciary of Pakistan has been operating independently of the political branches, particularly the executive. Finally, the principle of judicial independence as enshrined in the Constitution of Bangladesh will be outlined.

2.2 The Importance of an Independent and Impartial Judiciary in a Democratic State

A fundamental feature of any democratic society is the maintenance of the rule and the enforcement of the fundamental rights of individuals. To this end, it is common for democratic constitutions around the word to contain *ex ante* norms for constraining the scope of the powers of the political branches of the government so as to obviate the possibility of substitution of the rule of law with rule of man and to prevent the imposition of long-lasting limitations on the rights of individuals. Consequently, it is incumbent on the judges to intervene to ensure that no executive action or law passed by the parliament contravenes these norms, thereby preserving public confidence in the administration of justice. As Justice Saleem Akhter

---

[4] For example, in the Nazi era in Germany, there was no independent judiciary as the judges were expected to follow the wishes and orders of the Fuehrer. In the Third Reich (the Federation), judges were under a duty to consider "the will of the Fuehrer" as being supreme.

[5] Laski (2015), p. 542.

[6] UN Special Rapporteur on the Independence of Judges and Lawyers (2004, 28].

2.2 The Importance of an Independent and Impartial Judiciary in a Democratic State 21

observed in the case of *Sharaf Faridi v the Federation of Islamic Republic of Pakistan:*[7]

> In a set-up where the Constitution is based on trichotomy of powers, the judiciary enjoys a unique and supreme position within the framework of the Constitution as it creates balance amongst the various organs of the State and also checks the excessive and arbitrary exercise of power by the Executive or the Legislature ... The jurisdiction and the parameters for exercise of powers by all three organs have been mentioned in definite terms in the Constitution. No organ is permitted to encroach upon the authority of the other and the Judiciary by its power to interpret the Constitution keeps the Legislature and the Executive within the spheres and bounds of the Constitution.[8]

However, in order for the judges to perform such functions, it is imperative that their independence to dispense justice is adequately secured. In this context, the independence of the judges "connotes not only a state of mind but also a status or relationship to others ... particularly to the executive branch of government".[9] The importance of an independent judiciary can be gathered from the fact that as back as in 1776, the American revolutionaries listed the absence of judicial independence in the Declaration of Independence as one of the causes of their Revolution, thus:

> The history of the present King of Great Britain is a history of repeated injuries and usurpations, all having in direct object the establishment of an absolute Tyranny over these States ... He has made judges dependent upon his will alone, for the tenure of their offices and the amount of their salaries.

An attempt will now be made to explore how an independent judiciary in a democratic society can: (i) uphold the rule of law, (ii) defend constitutional guarantees of fundamental rights, and (iii) ensure the administration of fair justice so as to maintain and enhance public confidence.

(i) **Maintaining the Rule of Law**

An independent judiciary is the essential, indeed indispensable, component of a free and democratic society[10] and the hallmark of a modern democracy is the observance of the rule of law. An enlightened, independent and courageous judiciary is, therefore, a fundamental requisite for the very existence of any society that respects the rule of law as a subservient judiciary cannot be relied upon to accomplish the task of maintaining the rule of law and as such, absolutism is likely to have free rein.[11] It is an independent judiciary which remains "alert to see that any coercive action is justified in law"[12] and consequently, is not afraid of making unpopular decisions against powerful interests. As James Bryce pertinently aptly noted:

---

[7] *Sharaf Faridi v the Federation of Islamic Republic of Pakistan* PLD 1989 Karachi 404.

[8] Ibid., p. 444.

[9] The Supreme Court of Canada in *Walter Valente v Her Majesty the Queen,* (1985) 2 RCS 673.

[10] Larkin (1997), p. 7.

[11] Bari (1993), p. 10.

[12] Lord Atkin in his memorable war-time dissent in *Liversidge v Anderson,* [1942] AC 206, 244.

[in] all countries cases, sometimes civil, but more frequently criminal, arise which involve political issues and excite party feeling. It is then that the courage and uprightness of the judges become supremely valuable to the nation commanding respect for the exposition of the law which they have to deliver.[13]

Thus, an independent judiciary by upholding the supremacy of law over the arbitrary exercise of power, guaranteeing equal protection of law to all people without exception, and ensuring that judgments are based upon legal and factual merits, facilitates the flourishing of a true democracy based on the rule of law. As James Madison said: "Independent tribunals of justice will consider themselves .... an impenetrable bulwark against every assumption of power in the Legislature or Executive."[14]

(ii) Upholding the Fundamental Rights

A constitutional guarantee of human rights would be rendered meaningless unless the judiciary possesses the requisite independence to interpret and enforce those rights. As James Madison, who, on 8 June 1789, proposed the incorporation of a Bill of Rights in the US Constitution, stressed:

Independent tribunals of justice will consider themselves in a peculiar manner the guardians of those (constitutionally protected) rights. They will be naturally led to resist every encroachment upon rights expressly stipulated in that Constitution by the declaration of rights.[15]

In the same vein, one of the conclusions of the International Conference of Jurists, held in Bangkok in 1965, emphasised the importance of judicial independence for the enforcement of fundamental rights: "The ultimate protection of the individual in a society governed by the Rule of Law depends upon the existence of an enlightened, independent and courageous judiciary and upon adequate provision for the speedy and effective administration of justice."

Hence, the peoples of the world affirmed, *inter alia*, in 1945 in the Charter of the United Nations, their determination to establish conditions under which justice can be maintained to achieve international cooperation in promoting and encouraging respect for human rights and fundamental freedoms without any discrimination. Since the adoption of the Universal Declaration of Human Rights (UDHR) in December 1948, the international community has made considerable progress towards the incorporation, promotion, and development of transnational jurisprudence of substantive human rights along with the principle of judicial independence. These guarantees have been embodied in a number of global and regional conventions on human rights. Effective mechanisms for the enforcement of human rights in the national, regional and international systems of justices are a fundamental requisite as without such mechanisms human rights will remain unfulfilled injunctions in the constitutions or in the regional and international conventions. Thus, the

---

[13] See above n 3, p. 384.

[14] Agresto (1984), p. 25.

[15] Ibid., p. 25.

2.2 The Importance of an Independent and Impartial Judiciary in a Democratic State 23

UDHR—the adoption of which marked the beginning of the real journey towards safeguarding human rights globally[16]—provides that: "Everyone has the right to an effective remedy by the competent national tribunals for acts violating the fundamental rights granted to him by Constitution or by law."[17] It further enshrines the principle of the independence of judiciary by providing that "[e]veryone is entitled in full equality to a fair and public hearing by an independent and impartial tribunal, in the determination of his rights and obligations and of any criminal charge against him".[18] Similarly, the European Convention for the Protection of Human Rights and Fundamental Freedoms, 1950 provides that '[i]n the determination of his civil rights and obligations or of any criminal charge against him, everyone is entitled to a fair and public hearing within a reasonable time by an independent and impartial tribunal established by law".[19] Later in 1966, the community of states adopted the International Covenant on Civil and Political Rights, which is considered the most important universal instrument on human rights, guaranteeing therein that all person shall be equal before the courts, and that "in the determination of any criminal charge or of rights and obligations in a suit at law, everyone shall be entitled, without undue delay, to a fair and public hearing by a competent, independent and impartial tribunal established by law".[20]

The American Convention on Human Rights, 1969, also invests every person with "the right to a hearing, with due guarantees and within a reasonable time, by a competent, independent and impartial tribunal .... in the substantiation of any accusation of a criminal nature made against him, or for the determination of his rights and obligations of a civil or any other nature".[21] The latest regional convention on human rights, the African Charter on Human and Peoples' Rights, 1981, in a similar manner states that "[e]very individual shall have the right to have his cause heard. This comprises: a) the right to an appeal to competent national organs against the acts of violating his fundamental rights as recognised and guaranteed by conventions [and] laws .... d) the right to be tried within a reasonable time by an impartial court or tribunal."[22]

The incorporation of the principle of judicial independence into the global and regional human rights law jurisprudence demonstrates the realisation of the international community that the independence of courts is essential for effectively upholding the constitutional guarantees of human rights. Various international organisations, such as the International Commission of Jurists, the International Bar Association

---

[16] Baderin & Ssenyonjo (2016), p. 3.

[17] Universal Declaration of Human Rights (1948), art. 8.

[18] Ibid., art. 10.

[19] European Convention for the Protection of Human Rights and Fundamental Freedoms (1950), art 6(1).

[20] International Covenant on Civil and Political Rights (1966), art. 14(1).

[21] American Convention on Human Rights (1969), art. 8(1).

[22] African Charter on Human and Peoples' Rights (1981), art. 7.

24 2 The Principle of Judicial Independence and Its Recognition in the Constitution...

and the Law Association of Asia and the Western Pacific (LAWASIA),[23] have similarly emphasised that the constitutional guarantees concerning fundamental rights can only be upheld and protected through a competent, independent and impartial judiciary. The establishment of the Office of the United Nations Special Rapporteur on the Independence of Judges and Lawyers in 1994 was another manifestation of the international community's realisation of the need to safeguard human rights by an independent judiciary.

(iii) Dispensation of Fair Justice to Maintain Public Confidence

Warren Burger, who served as the Chief Justice of the US Supreme Court from 1969 to 1986, aptly noted in an address to American Bar that "[i]deas, ideals and great conception are vital to a system of justice, but it must have more than that—there must be delivery and execution. Concepts of justice must have hands and feet or they remain sterile abstractions."[24] Without a free and independent judiciary, ready to adjudicate between individuals and between the state and individuals in an impartial manner, justice would, indeed, be a meaningless word. As James Bryce noted:

> [t]here is no better test of the excellence of a government than the efficiency of its judicial system, for nothing more nearly touches the welfare and security of the average citizen than his sense that he can rely on the certain and prompt administration of justice .... if the Law be dishonestly administered, the salt has lost its savour; if it be weakly or fitfully enforced, the guarantees or order fail, for it is more by the certainty than by the severity of punishment that offences are repressed. If the lamp of justice goes out in darkness, how great is that darkness![25]

The perception of the aggrieved parties that the judicial power is exercised independently and impartially is imperative to ensure the maintenance of public confidence in the administration of justice. Justice Pathak of the Indian Supreme Court portrayed this dimension eloquently in *S. P. Gupta v. Union of India:*[26]

> Public confidence in the administration of justice is imperative to its effectiveness, because ultimately the ready acceptance of a judicial verdict alone gives relevance to the judicial

---

[23] International Commission of Jurists' Standards on Judicial Independence adopted in Athens (Greece) in 1955, in New Delhi in 1959, in Lagos (Nigeria) in 1961, in Rio de Janeiro (Brazil) in 1962, in Bangkok (Thailand) in 1965, and in Caracas (Venezuela) in 1989; International Bar Association's Minimum Standards of Judicial Independence (adopted in New Delhi), 1982; the Montreal Universal Declaration on the Independence of Justice, adopted in Montreal by the First World Conference on the Independence of Justice, 1983; the United Nations Basic Principles on the Independence of the Judiciary, 1985; the Law Association of Asia and the Western Pacific's (LAWASIA) Tokyo Principles on the Independence of the Judiciary in the LAWASIA Region, 1982; the Beijing Statement on the Principles of the Independence of Justice, 1995; the Harare Declaration of the Commonwealth; the Bangalore Principles of Judicial Conduct; and the Latimer House Guidelines and the Suva (Fiji) Statement on the Principles of Judicial Independence and Access to Justice, 2004.

[24] Burger (1972), http://www.hcourt.gov.au/speeches/kirbyj/kirbyj_20mar05.html.

[25] See above n 3, p. 384.

[26] *S. P. Gupta v Union of India* (1981) Supp SCC 87; AIR 1982 SC 149.

2.2 The Importance of an Independent and Impartial Judiciary in a Democratic State

system. While the administration of justice draws its legal sanction from the Constitution, its credibility rests in the faith of the people. Indispensable to that faith is the independence of the judiciary. An independent and impartial judiciary supplies the reason for the judicial institution, it also gives character and content to the constitutional milieu.[27]

Thus, an independent judiciary promotes public confidence by ensuring to litigants that their claims would be determined fairly. Without such confidence, the effective functioning of the judiciary is a well-nigh impossibility.[28] As James Bryce pertinently noted:

[n]othing does more for the welfare of the private citizen, and nothing more conduces to the smooth working of free government than a general confidence in the pure and efficient administration of justice between the individual and the State as well as between man and man.[29]

In the same vein, Justice William O Douglas, who served as a Justice of the US Supreme Court, observed that:

The strength of the judiciary is in the command it has over the hearts and minds of men. That respect and prestige are the product of innumerable judgments and decrees, a mosaic built from the multitude of cases decided. Respect and prestige do not grow suddenly; they are the products of time and experience. But they flourish when judges are independent and courageous.[30]

Since judicial misconduct has the dreadful impact of undermining public confidence in the administration of justice, it is imperative for a "judge... [to] exhibit and promote high standards of judicial conduct in order to reinforce public confidence in the judiciary which is fundamental to the maintenance of judicial independence".[31] The significance of public perception in the judiciary is well reflected in the oft quoted maxim: "Justice must not only be done, but must also be seen to be done." It implies that "[a] judge shall not knowingly, while a proceeding is before, or could come before, the judge, make any comment that might reasonably be expected to affect the outcome of such proceeding or impair the manifest fairness of the process. Nor shall the judge make any comment in public or otherwise that might affect the fair trial of any person or issue".[32] This point has further been elaborated by the Bangalore Principles of Judicial Conduct, 2002, in the following manner:

A judge shall not allow the judge's family, social or other relationships improperly to influence the judge's judicial conduct and judgment as a judge[33]... A judge shall not use or lend the prestige of the judicial office to advance the private interests of the judge, a member of the judge's family or of anyone else, nor shall a judge convey or permit others to convey the

---

[27] Ibid., p. 705.

[28] Frankfurter (1957), p. 796.

[29] See above n 3, p. 389.

[30] Douglas (1956), p. 345.

[31] UN Transparency Joint Initiative (2002), art. 1.6.

[32] Ibid., art. 2.4.

[33] Ibid., art. 4.8.

impression that anyone is in a special position improperly to influence the judge in the performance of judicial duties.[34]

It should be kept in mind that judicial independence is something which must never be taken for granted, and like freedom, exacts the price of eternal vigilance.[35] In the long run, the manner in which judges perform their duties can build up public opinion for the courts. The public, particularly the lawyers and all sections of civil society, will support the judiciary if the latter is seen as an effective and impartial forum for the dispensation of justice.[36]

2.3 Traditional and New Conceptual Dimensions (Four Meanings) of Judicial Independence

The concept of independence of the judiciary implies that the judges should be able to decide cases free from the interference of the political branches, especially the executive, and without the apprehension of suffering personally as a consequence of such decision-making. The Congress of the International Commission of Jurists held in New Delhi in January 1959 accepted this approach when it observed that judicial independence "implies freedom from interference by the Executive or Legislative with the exercise of the judicial function".[37] Sir Harry Gibbs, the former Chief Justice of Australia, also referred to the traditional meaning of judicial independence when he remarked: "no judge should have anything to hope or fear in respect of anything which he or she may have done properly in the course of performing judicial functions. So neither the parliament nor the executive, nor anyone else, should be able to bring pressure of any kind to bear upon a judge in the performance of judicial duties."[38]

2.3.1 Four Meanings of Judicial Independence

Since the 1950s, international and regional organisations, as discussed earlier in Sect. 1.2, have developed norms concerning judicial independence. Although these norms are non-binding, they have strengthened and broadened the concept of judicial independence. The concept is now said to include the following four facets:

(a) substantive independence;

---

[34] Ibid., art. 4.9.

[35] See above n 11, p. 10.

[36] Ibid., p. 11.

[37] International Congress of Jurists (1959), art. 1.

[38] Quoted in Sturgess & Chubb (1988), p. 149.

2.3 Traditional and New Conceptual Dimensions (Four Meanings) of Judicial... 27

(b) personal independence;
(c) collective independence; and
(d) internal independence.

It should be pointed out that among these four facets, only substantive and personal independence are universally recognised by law and legal scholars. These two elements of judicial independence comprise the independence of an individual judge. The guarantee of individual independence of the judges has the salutary effect of imposing both negative and positive duties on the state apparatus. The negative duty involves ensuring that judges are free from undue pressures, improper influences or threats from any quarter, thereby enabling them to perform their functions without the fear of suffering any adverse consequences.[39] While the positive duty involves guaranteeing the freedom of the judges to decide cases in accordance with their own understanding of law and fact.[40]

On the other hand, the elements of collective independence and internal independence constitute the independence of the judiciary as a whole and were developed in the 1980s. They were recognised first by the International Bar Association's Minimum Standards of Judicial Independence adopted in New Delhi in October 1982, and were subsequently recognised by the Montreal Universal Declaration on the Independence of Justice, 1983, the Beijing Statement of Principles of the Independence of the Judiciary in the LAWASIA Region, 1995 and the Bangalore Principles of Judicial Conduct, 2002. The inclusion of collective independence and internal independence in the expression "independence of judiciary" as its component parts is considered an important milestone in recent legal history. For scholars argue that institutional independence of the judiciary further serves to shield the individual judges from undue influence.[41]

An attempt will now be made to shed light on the manner in which the international and regional norms have sought to expand these facets of judicial independence and the extent to which they have been recognised in various constitutions of the world.

(a) *Substantive Independence*

Substantive independence, which is also described as "functional or decisional independence",[42] means the independence of judges to decide cases in accordance with their oath of office without submitting to any kind of pressure, whether internal or external, but only to their own sense of justice and the dictates of law.[43] In this context, Erkki Juhani Taipale, a European Jurist, notes that judges in "administering justice can only be subordinate to the law, and that only the law can influence the contents of the decisions made by [them] …. No other state authority, not even the

---

[39] Karlan (1999), p. 536, 558.

[40] Ibid.

[41] Green (1985), p. 135.

[42] Josan & Shah (2002), p. 175; Dakolias & Thachuk (2000), p. 361.

[43] Dakolias & Thachuk (2000), p. 361.

28 2 The Principle of Judicial Independence and Its Recognition in the Constitution...

highest, is allowed to influence the decisions made by the judicial organ".[44] Thus a substantively independent judge is one who "dispenses justice according to law without regard to the policies and inclinations of the government of the day".[45]

The international norms concerning judicial independence have recognized substantive independence in similar terms. For instance, the International Bar Association's Minimum Standards of Judicial Independence, 1982, define the concept to mean that "in the discharge of his judicial function, a judge is subject to nothing but the law and the commands of his conscience".[46] The concept has been further elaborated in the 1983 Universal Declaration on the Independence of Justice, thus:

> Judges individually shall be free, and it shall be their duty, to decide matters before them impartially, in accordance with their assessment of the facts and their understanding of the law without any restrictions, influences, inducements, pressures, threats or interferences, direct or indirect, from any quarter or for any reason.[47]

This elaboration was echoed in the 1985 UN Basic Principles on the Independence of the Judiciary in the follower manner: "The Judiciary shall decide matters before them impartially, on the basis of facts and in accordance with the law, without any restrictions, improper influence, inducements, pressures, threats or interferences, direct or indirect, from any quarter or for any reason."[48] Finally, the Beijing Statement of Principles of the Independence of the Judiciary in the LAWASIA Region, 1995, also followed the 1983 Universal Declaration on the Independence of the Judiciary: "The judiciary shall decide matters before it in accordance with its impartial assessment of the facts and its understanding of the law without improper influences, direct or indirect, from any source."[49]

It should, however, be stressed here that even prior to the development of the above international norms, the notion of substantive independence, which is considered as the kernel of judicial independence, had received due recognition in the constitutions of some of the countries of the world. For instance, the Constitution of Japan, which was adopted in 1946, provides that "[all Judges shall be independent in the exercise of their conscience and shall be bound only by this Constitution and the laws".[50] A year later in 1947, when South Korea—Japan's maritime neighbour—enacted its Constitution, the principle of substantive independence was articulated in similar terms. The Constitution of the Republic of Korea, 1947, recognizes the concept by stipulating that "[judges shall rule independently according to their conscience and in conformity with the Constitution and law".[51]

---

[44] Taipale (1980), p. 118.

[45] Stephen (1985), p. 531.

[46] International Bar Association (1982), art. 1(c).

[47] Universal Declaration on the Independence of Justice (1983), art. 2.02.

[48] UN Basic Principles on the Independence of the Judiciary (1985), art. 2.

[49] Law Association for Asia and the Pacific (LAWASIA) (1995), art. 3(a).

[50] Constitution of Japan, 1946 (Japan) art. 76(3).

[51] Constitution of the Republic of Korea, 1981 (South Korea), art. 103.

Thus, it is evident from the above discussion that substantive independence means the independence of individual judges to carry out the task of judicial decision-making on the basis of their assessment of the facts and understanding of law in accordance with their oath of office without any kind of inducement, pressure or threat from any quarter and without taking into account the policies of the government of the day. Such a frame of mind can be demonstrated only by those judges, to use the words of Justice Bhagwati of the Indian Supreme Court, who are of "stern stuff and tough fibre, unbending before power" and can "uphold the core principle of the rule of law which says 'Be you ever so high, the law is above you.'"[52]

(b) *Personal Independence*

Personal independence has been defined by the 1982 International Bar Association's Minimum Standards of Judicial Independence as meaning "that the terms and conditions of judicial service are adequately secured so as to ensure that individual judges are not subject to executive control".[53] Thus, it implies that the individual judges shall be independent of the political branches of the government, especially the executive, in respect of the terms of judicial service, including transfer, remuneration, pension and the security of tenure, for instance, until a mandatory retiring age.[54] Consequently, it can be argued that personal independence corresponds to the traditional and central meaning of the independence of the judiciary, i.e. "that judges... [should] not [be] dependent on Government in any way which might influence them in coming to decisions in individual cases".[55]

(c) *Collective Independence*

Collective independence means the institutional, administrative and financial independence of the judiciary as a whole from the political branches of the government, namely the executive and the legislature. In particular, it virtually aims at the abolition of the dominant role that the executive plays in the administrative and financial matters of the judiciary. Thus, collective independence demands greater effective judicial participation in the administration of the courts, including control over administrative personnel, maintenance of court buildings, preparation and formulation of its budget and allocation of resources.[56] For interference in the management of the judiciary by the executive, has adverse impact on individual judges in performing their judicial functions. The collective independence of the judiciary is considered an important means to protect and buttress the freedom of an individual judge in his decision-making from executive interference by way of administrative control. In this context, it is necessary to shed light on the manner in which the

---

[52] *S. P. Gupta and others v President of Union of India*, AIR 1982 SC 149 at p. 672.

[53] See above n 46, art. 1(b).

[54] Dawson (1954), p. 486.

[55] Griffith (1977), p. 29.

[56] See above n 43, pp. 361–62.

concept of collective independence has been recognised by various international declarations.

The Commonwealth Law Ministers claimed in their meeting held in Kuala Lumpur, Malaysia in 1996 that "[t]he protections enjoyed by judges, including financial independence… are an important defence against improper interference and free the judiciary to discharge the particular responsibilities given to it within national constitutional frameworks".[57] The Montreal Universal Declaration on the Independence of Justice, 1983, has given emphasis on this important conceptual aspect of the judicial independence by stating that:

> It shall be a priority of the highest order, for the state to provide adequate resource to allow for the due administration of justice, including physical facilities appropriate for the maintenance of judicial independence, dignity and efficiency, judicial and administrative personnel, and operating budgets.[58]

In the same vein, the Beijing Statement of Principles of the Independence of the Judiciary in the LAWASIA Region, 1995, stresses that '[t]he principal responsibility for court administration, including appointment, supervision and disciplinary control of administrative personnel and support staff must vest in the Judiciary, or in a body in which the Judiciary is represented and has an effective role.'[59]

In this context, it is noteworthy that in 1993, the Courts Administration Act was passed in the Australian state of South Australia providing for the establishment of the State Courts Administration Council, which is independent of the control of the executive, consisting of the Chief Justice of the Supreme Court, the Chief Judge of the District Court, the Chief Magistrate of the Magistrates Court and associate members appointed by each of these three office bearers.[60] The Council is entrusted with the responsibility of "providing or arranging for the provision of, the administrative facilities and services for participating courts that are necessary to enable those courts and their staff properly to carry out their judicial and administrative functions".[61] This can serve as an important model for other democratic countries to follow in order to safeguard the collective independence of the judiciary.

(d) **Internal Independence**

Internal Independence of the judiciary means the independence of a judge from any kind of order, indication or pressure from his judicial superiors and colleagues in coming to decisions in individual cases.[62] This means that the threat to judicial independence may not only stem from external sources but also from internal sources, such as fellow and senior judges. Thus, a judge should not only be independent from the interference of the executive and legislative branches of the govern-

---

[57] Meeting of Commonwealth Law Ministers, Memoranda (1996), p. ix.

[58] Montreal Declaration (1983), art. 2.41.

[59] See above n 49, art. 36.

[60] Courts Administration Act, 1993 (SA) s. 7.

[61] Courts Administration Act, 1993 (SA) s. 10.

[62] See above n 43, p. 362.

2.3 Traditional and New Conceptual Dimensions (Four Meanings) of Judicial...

ment but also from his judicial colleagues and superiors, in deciding a case. Although the International Bar Association's Minimum Standards and UN Basic Principles on the Independence of the Judiciary recognise the concept of internal judicial independence, the notion has received more elaboration and prominence in the text of the Montreal Universal Declaration on the Independence of Justice, 1983. For the International Bar Association's Minimum Standards of Judicial Independence merely states that "[i]n the decision-making process, a judge must be independent vis-a-vis his judicial colleagues and superiors".[63] In the same vein, the UN Basic Principles on the Independence of the Judiciary, 1985 simply states that "[t]here shall not be any inappropriate or unwarranted interference with the judicial process."[64]

Whereas the Montreal Universal Declaration on the Independence of Justice provides that "[i]n the decision-making process, judges shall be independent vis-a-vis their judicial colleagues and superiors. Any hierarchical organisation of the judiciary and any difference in grade or rank shall in no way interfere with the right of the judge to pronounce his judgment freely".[65] In the same vein, the Beijing Statement of the Principles of the Independence of the Judiciary in the LAWASIA Region, 1995, provides: 'In the decision-making process, any hierarchical organisation of the Judiciary and any difference in grade or rank shall in no way interfere with the duty of the judge exercising jurisdiction individually or judges acting collectively to pronounce judgment.'[66]

Thus, it is evident from the above discussion that only the International Bar Association's Minimum Standards recognise the four different concepts of judicial independence, namely, substantive, personal, collective and internal. Although the Montreal Universal Declaration on the Independence of Justice contains express provisions concerning substantive and internal independence of the judges, it does not provide for personal independence of the judges and only contains implied reference to the collective independence of the judiciary. On the other hand, the UN Basic Principles of the Independence of the Judiciary only expressly recognise the substantive independence of the judges and contain merely implied reference to the internal independence of the judges. Finally, although the Beijing Statement of the Principles of the Independence of the Judiciary in the LAWASIA Region, 1995 embodies explicit provisions concerning substantive, internal, and collective independence of the judges, it does not contain any reference whatsoever to their personal independence. Thus, it is clear that all these international norms have a uniform approach to only one aspect of the judicial independence, namely the substantive independence of the judges.

---

[63] See above n 46, art. 46.

[64] See above n 48, art. 4.

[65] See above n 58, art. 2.03.

[66] See above n 49, art. 6.

2.4 The Importance of the Method of Appointment and the Security of Tenure of the Judges as Constituent Elements of Judicial Independence

The judiciary is considered a fair arbiter which dispenses justice between man and man, between individuals and the state and which ultimately stands between the people and the government as a bulwark against the arbitrary exercise of power. In order for the judiciary to carry out these functions, its interpretation of the law must not be bound by the will of the executive. In other words, in order for the judges to call the executive to account by protecting the life as well as the liberty of the governed, it is imperative that the judges are insulated from political pressure. Any attempt to insulate judges from such pressure, however, necessitates securing their individual independence, namely substantive and personal independence. For such independence, as pointed out earlier in Sect. 2.3, enables judges to decide cases in accordance with their oath of office without the apprehension of suffering personally for such decision-making. An attempt will now be made to demonstrate that the individual independence of the judges can be guaranteed by ensuring that the method of their appointment is transparent and that they enjoy security of tenure.

2.4.1 The Importance of a Transparent Method of Appointment of the Judges

Although the question of judges performing their functions independently comes after their appointment, the method of their appointment is one of the crucial and dominant factors to ensure their individual independence—the independence which greatly depends upon the independent character, integrity, equanimity, legal knowledge and keen intellect of the persons who would hold the office of judges. For the appointment of a judge on account of political or personal favouritism in disregard of essential qualities, such as qualifications, merit, competency, integrity and earlier performance as an advocate or judicial officer, may produce "spineless puppets" incapable of dispensing justice independent of the wishes of the government of the day.[67] It can hardly be expected that after a judge appointed on the consideration of political allegiance, "takes oath, there is a sudden transformation and he forgets his past connections and turns a new leaf of life".[68] As Enid Campbell and HP Lee notes:

> Judicial independence can ... be subverted by the appointment of persons who do not possess an outstanding level of professional ability, intellectual capacity and experience and integrity, and who cannot shake off a sense of gratitude to the appointing authority. It is ...

---

[67] Roosevelt (1937), http://www.presidency.ucsb.edu/ws/?pid.15381

[68] Bari (2014), p. 15.

2.4 The Importance of the Method of Appointment and the Security of Tenure... 33

in the interests of the ... people [not] to have their judicial tribunals reduced to timorous institutions.[69]

Litigants come to courts of law to have their disputes adjudicated with the expectation that judges are impartial, independent and of integrity—which according to Francis Bacon means the "portion and proper virtue"[70] of the judges. Therefore, "in appointing judges, a government owes a duty to the people ... to ensure appointees of the highest calibre".[71] Lord Halisham, who as Lord Chancellor was responsible for selecting candidates for appointment to the bench in England and Wales, underscored this necessity when he remarked:

> My first and fundamental policy is to appoint solely on merit the best potential candidate ready and willing to accept the post. No considerations of party politics, sex, religion, or race must enter into my calculations and they do not. Personality, integrity, professional ability, experience, standing and capacity are the only criteria, coupled of course with the requirement that the candidate must be physically capable of carrying out the duties of the post, and not disqualified by any personal unsuitability. My overriding consideration is always the public interest in maintaining the quality of the Bench and confidence in its competence and independence.[72]

It is, therefore, evident that the appointment of the right kind of judges having the requisite qualities of professional skill, ability and integrity will go a long way in ensuring the interpretation and enforcement of the law without fear or favour. Accordingly, some of the national constitutions stipulate the qualities that an individual should possess in order to be considered for appointment as a judge of the superior courts. For instance, the Constitution of the Islamic Federal Republic of the Comoros, 1978, provided that the members of the Supreme Court shall be chosen on the basis of their competence, their integrity and their knowledge of law.[73]

Furthermore, the international standards as contained in the Universal Declaration on the Independence of Justice, 1983 and the Beijing Statement of Principles of the Independence of the Judiciary in the LAWASIA Region, 1995, as amended in Manila on 28 August 1997, also provide for certain criteria for the selection of judges. The Universal Declaration provides that candidates for appointment to the bench should be individuals of integrity, ability and "well-trained in the law".[74] In the same vein, the Beijing Statement calls for "judges [to] be chosen on the basis of proven competence, integrity and independence".[75]

In light of the above discussion, it can be argued that in order to select the best candidates for appointment to the bench, a suitable and appropriate method of

---

[69] Campbell and Lee (2001), p. 95.

[70] Bacon (1612).

[71] Ibid.

[72] Quoted in Gibbs (1987), p. 142

[73] Constitution of the Islamic Federal Republic of the Comoros, 1978 (Comoros) art. 32. However, this provision has been dispensed with in the 2001. Constitution of Comoros (available with automatic translation at http: //www.wipo.int/wipolex/en/text. jsp? file_id.208361).

[74] See above n 47, art. 2.11

[75] See above n 49, art. 11

34   2 The Principle of Judicial Independence and Its Recognition in the Constitution...

appointment is necessary. This argument gains further credence by reference to the Latimer House Guidelines on Parliamentary and Judicial Independence, 1998, which stress that an elaborate "appointment process [is necessary].... to guarantee the quality and independence of mind of those selected for appointment at all lives of the judiciary.'[76] However, the manner in which judicial appointments are made in nations around the world may broadly be grouped into the following three categories:

a Appointment by the head of the state (as in Sri Lanka, South Korea, Israel, Nigeria, and Republic of Chile);[77]
b Election by the legislature (as in Switzerland);[78]
c Appointment by a judicial service commission (such as the Superior Council of the Judiciary in Italy and the National Judicial Council in Croatia).[79]

It should be noted that notwithstanding the different methods of appointing judges of the superior courts prevalent in various nations, appointment by the head of the state is the most commonly followed method, particularly in most of the common law nations. However, there remains within these nations significant diversity regarding the entities that either need to be consulted or on whose recommendation or confirmation, the executive is required to make such appointments. It is needless to say that any process for appointing judges which retains a dominant role for the executive would inevitably pave the way for intrusion of extraneous considerations in the selection of judges, thereby undermining the credibility of the judges as fair arbitrators in the eyes of the litigants. But commenting on the system of vesting the authority in the hands of the executive to appoint judges of the superior courts, Justice Bhagwati of the Indian Supreme Court in *SP Gupta v. Union of India*[80] observed:

> This is, of course, not an ideal system of appointment of judges, but the reason why the power of appointment of judges is left to the Executive appears to be that the Executive is responsible to the Legislature and through the Legislature, it is accountable to the people, who are consumers of justice, ... [for making] any wrong or improper appointment.[81]

It is, however, submitted that in a parliamentary democracy, which is prevalent in many countries, such as Australia, India and Malaysia, the Prime Minister commands a majority in Parliament and, as such, it can hardly be expected that a vote of censure will be passed against him disapproving his "wrong or improper

---

[76] The Commonwealth Latimer House Guidelines (1998), pp. 28–29.

[77] Constitution of Sri Lanka, 1978 (Sri Lanka) art 107; Constitution of Republic of South Korea, 1948 art. 104(2); Basic Law – Judicature, art. 4(a). The Judicial Committee of Israel, which is chaired by the Minister of Justice, is comprised of nine members: three judges of the Supreme Court, two lawyers, two members of Parliament, and two cabinet ministers; Constitution of Federal Republic of Nigeria, 1999 (Nigeria) ch. VII, pt. 1(A)(231).

[78] Lienhard (2008), 2.

[79] Constitution of Italy, 1948 (Italy) Title IV, art. 105; Constitution of Croatia, 1990 (Croatia) art. 123.

[80] *SP Gupta v. Union of India* 1981 Supp SCC 87.

[81] Ibid., p. 230.

2.4 The Importance of the Method of Appointment and the Security of Tenure... 35

appointment" of judges to the superior courts. Even the Speaker of the Parliament, who is usually elected to office on the ticket of the ruling party, may not allow putting down a question in the Parliament regarding controversial appointments to the bench.

Accordingly, in order to insulate judges from the influence of the political branches of the government, particularly the executive, the international norms concerning judicial independence developed since the 1980s, forcefully recommend the appointment of judges of superior courts either by, on the recommendation of, proposal/advice of, or after consultation with, an appropriately constituted and representative judicial body.[82] Consequently, there is a growing tendency among modern constitutions, such as the Constitutions of Guyana, Algeria, Croatia, Namibia, Fiji, Nepal, Saudi Arabia, South Africa, Rwanda, Poland, Albania, Nigeria and Iraq—adopted in the 1980s and shortly thereafter—to invest an independent nominating body with the power of selecting and recommending best candidates to the head of the state for judicial appointment.[83] More recently in 2005, fundamental changes were introduced to the British constitutional process of appointing judges in an effort to make the process more transparent and merit-based. The British Parliament in 2005 passed the Constitutional Reform Act (CRA) providing for the establishment of selection commissions to select and recommend candidates for appointment as judges in the UK, thereby precluding the unilateral authority of the Lord Chancellor—a government minister—to make such selections and recommendations. First, the CRA establishes a Judicial Appointments Commission (JAC) to select and recommend the appointment of the majority of the judges in the UK, including those of the High Court.[84] The JAC is headed by a lay person and is additionally composed of 14 members—all of whom are selected through open competition among the judiciary, the legal profession, non-legally qualified judicial officer holders and the public.[85] Second, the Act contains provisions for convening special selection commissions for recommending the appointment of judges to senior posi-

---

[82] See International Commission of Jurists (1961), art. 3; Principles and Conclusions on the Independence of the Judiciary in the LAWASIA Region (1982), art. 10(d); International Bar Association (1982), art. 3(a); Universal Declaration on the Independence of Justice (1983), art. 2.14(b); UN Basic Principles on the Independence of the Judiciary (1985), art. 10; Beijing Statement of Principles on the Independence of the Judiciary in LAWASIA Region (1995), art. 14; Latimer House Guidelines for Parliamentary Supremacy and Judicial Independence in the Commonwealth (1998), art. II(1).

[83] Constitution of the Co-operative Republic of Guyana, 1980 (Guyana) art. 128; Constitution of Algeria, 1989 (Algeria) art. 155; Constitution of the Republic of Croatia, 1990 (Croatia) art. 82(1); Constitution of Namibia, 1990 (Namibia) art. 132(2); Constitution of the Sovereign Democratic Republic of Fiji, 1990 (Fiji) art 87(1); Constitution of Nepal, 1990 (Nepal) art. 52; Constitution of the Kingdom of Saudi Arabia, 1992 (Saudi Arabia) art. 174(3); Constitution of South Africa, 1996 (South Africa) art. 147 and 149; Constitution of the Federation of Rwanda, 2003 (Rwanda) art 179; Constitution of Poland, 1997 (Poland) art. 136(4); Constitution of Albania, 1998 (Albania) art. 44(E), Constitution of the Republic of Iraq, 2005 (Iraq) art. 104(1); Constitution of the Republic of Trinidad and Tobago, 1976 (Trinidad and Tobago) art. 231(1) and 231(2).

[84] Constitutional Reform Act, 2005, s 61(1) read together with schedule 12.

[85] Ibid.

tions. For instance, the Act stipulates that an appointments commission will be convened for recommending candidates to the executive for appointment as Justices of the Supreme Court—the highest court of appeal in the UK. The CRA, as amended by the Crime and Courts Act, 2013, also provides for the membership of such a special commission. It states that the commission will be chaired by the President of the Supreme Court and will additionally be composed of four members—one senior judge nominated by the President of the Court and one each from the Judicial Appointments Commission for England and Wales, the Judicial Appointments Board in Scotland and the Judicial Appointments Commission in Northern Ireland.[86]

It is noteworthy that the CRA does not provide representation to the political branches of the government either in the permanent or the ad hoc appointments commission, thereby depriving them of the opportunity to unduly influence the process of selecting the judges. Furthermore, both types of commissions are obligated to select and recommend candidates "solely on merit".[87] Another striking feature of both the permanent and ad hoc appointments commissions is that they are more than mere "recommending" bodies.[88] Although the executive branch retains the authority to appoint the judges, the CRA significantly constrains its exercise of discretion in this regard. First, while the appointing authority has been given the discretion to reject the recommendations put forward by the commissions or to request their reconsideration, such actions must be accompanied by reasons. Second, the appointing authority has no other option but to select a candidate after three separate recommendations have been put forward by the commissions.[89]

Thus, the objective underlying the establishment of the appointments commissions is to ensure transparency in the process of appointing judges in the UK by reducing the role of the executive in the process to "almost a purely formal one".[90] In this context, it is pertinent to note the remarks made by the first Chairman of the Judicial Appointments Commission of the UK, in her first speech in November 2006: "For the first time in its 1,000-year history, the Judiciary is fully and officially independent of the government. This has been described as the most significant change since *Magna Carta* in 1215."[91] Gordon Brown—the then British Prime Minister—after the enactment of the CRA went even further by advocating the dispensation of the executive's last vestiges of power to make judicial appointments, when he remarked on 3 July 2007 that:

> For centuries, they [the Executive] have exercised authority in the name of the monarchy without the people and their elected representatives being consulted. So I now propose that in 12 important areas of our national life, the Prime Minister and the Executive should

---

[86] Constitutional Reform Act, 2005, s. 25.

[87] Constitutional Reform Act, 2005, s. 63(2)

[88] Sackville (2006), p. 130.

[89] The Supreme Court (Judicial Appointments) Regulations 2013 (UK), reg 20; The Judicial Appointments Regulations 2013 (UK), regs 8(4), (5), 14(4), (5), 20(4), (5), 26(4), (5), 32(5), (6).

[90] Bogdanor (2009), p. 67; Bevir (2010), p. 163.

[91] Courts and Tribunal Judiciary, https://www.judiciary.uk/about-the-judiciary/history-of-the-judiciary/

2.4 The Importance of the Method of Appointment and the Security of Tenure... 37

> surrender or limit their powers, the exclusive exercise of which by the Government of the day should have no place in a modern democracy ... and I purpose that the Government should consider relinquishing its residual role in the appointment of judges.[92]

In following in the footsteps of the CRA of the UK, the Constitution (Eighteenth Amendment) Act, 2010 was passed in Pakistan to insert Article 175(A) in the Constitution of Pakistan, 1973, providing for a new method of selecting candidates for appointment, among others, as the judges of the Supreme Court, which is the highest court of law in Pakistan, involving a Judicial Commission—the membership of which is stipulated by the Constitution itself. The Commission is chaired by the Chief Justice of Pakistan and is additionally composed of 8 members, namely, four senior-most judges of the Supreme Court, a retired Chief Justice or a former judge nominated by the Chief Justice, the Federal Minister for Law and Justice, the Attorney-General for Pakistan, and a senior advocate of the Supreme Court nominated by the Bar Council.[93]

It is evident that although the Constitution of Pakistan, as amended by the Eighteenth Amendment, provides for inclusion in the Judicial Commission of a member of the executive branch, present and past members of the judiciary constitute a majority in the Commission, thereby limiting the executive's opportunity to unduly influence the process of selecting judges. The Commission's recommendations for appointments to the Supreme Court are sent to a Parliamentary Committee comprising eight members with equal representation from both the ruling and opposition political parties for confirmation.[94] The Parliamentary Committee has the authority to not confirm the recommendation only if at least six out of eight members favour such an action.[95] However, any such non-confirmation of recommendation shall be accompanied by "reasons so recorded".[96] Thus, it is evident that under the new method prescribed by the Constitution of Pakistan for appointing judges of the Supreme Court, each of the three branches of government has been given a role to play. However, it is the senior members of the judiciary who have been given pre-eminence in the selection process of the judges as they are better placed than the other branches of the government to know about the suitability of the candidates in terms of experience or knowledge of law, ability to handle cases, firmness and fearlessness requisite for appointment as superior court judges, thereby obviating the possibility of patronage appointments to the highest court of the land.

India represents another example where multiple attempts have been made since the 1980s to promote greater transparency and accountability in the judicial appointments process. The Constitution of India, 1950, makes it mandatory for the President to consult the Chief Justice of India in appointing the judges of the Supreme

---

[92] Quoted in Ministry of Justice (2007), p. 5.

[93] Constitution of Pakistan, 1973 (Pakistan) art. 175A(2).

[94] Constitution of Pakistan, 1973 (Pakistan) art. 175A (8) and (9).

[95] Constitution of Pakistan, 1973 (Pakistan) art. 175A(12).

[96] Ibid.

Court[97]—the final court of appeal and the highest court of the land. The Constitution further provides that in appointing the judges of the Supreme Court, the President may consult "such of the judges of the Supreme Court, and of the High Courts" he deems necessary for making such appointments.[98] However, in appointing the judges of the High Courts of the States, the President is not only required to mandatorily consult the Chief Justice of India but also two other constitutional functionaries, namely, the Governor of the State concerned and the Chief Justice of the High Court concerned.[99] It is noteworthy that the Constitution does not accord primacy to the views of any of the three consultees, particularly that of the Chief Justice of India, in appointing the judges of the High Courts. Furthermore, it should be stressed here that the Constitution in the context of the appointment of judges of the Supreme Court and the High Courts has prescribed the requirement of consultation, as opposed to concurrence or consent, with the designated authorities including the Chief Justice. It is, therefore, evident from the above discussion that the Constitution of India rests the final decision regarding the appointment of judges with the executive as the opinion of the Chief Justice or any other functionaries in the matter has not been made binding on it.

However, the issue of safeguarding the independence of the judiciary from the executive came to the forefront following the unprecedented attack on the judiciary by the government of Mrs Indira Gandhi during the continuation of an emergency, which was invoked on 25 June 1975 on the nebulous ground of internal disturbance.[100] Strikingly, the emergency was proclaimed only 13 days after Justice Jagmohan Lal Sinha of the Allahabad High Court nullified Mrs Gandhi's election as a Member of Parliament (MP) due to her resort to corrupt practices. Justice Sinha's decision to invalidate Mrs Gandhi's election as an MP was also accompanied by an imposition of a six-year ban on "her holding elected public office".[101] Within 46 days of pronouncement of this courageous decision by Justice Sinha, on 10 August 1975, Mrs Gandhi persuaded the Parliament to pass the *Constitution (Thirty-Ninth Amendment) Act* inserting a new Article 329A in the Constitution of India, which precluded the authority of the courts "to resolve disputes relating to the election of any MP who subsequently became the Prime Minister or Speaker of the *Lok Sabha* [the lower house of the Indian Parliament] and abated any election petition relating to these functionaries which had been pending before any court (this referred to the Prime Minister's appeal before the Supreme Court)".[102] It is further noteworthy that this new Article provided that the election of any such person to the Parliament,

---

[97] Proviso to Article 124(2) of the Constitution of India, 1950. *Supreme Court Advocates-on-Record Association v. Union of India* (2) 4 SCC 1 (India).

[98] Constitution of India, 1950 (India) art 124(2).

[99] Constitution of India, 1950 (India) art. 217(1)

[100] Constitution (Thirty-Eighth Amendment) Act, 1975 (India) s 4.

[101] Bari (2017), p. 38.

[102] Ibid., p. 69, 70.

2.4 The Importance of the Method of Appointment and the Security of Tenure... 39

"which had previously been invalided by a court of law, would continue to be valid".[103]

However, the emergency regime of Mrs Gandhi went even further than simply persuading the Parliament to insert an amendment to the Constitution aimed at undermining the authority of the courts. Rather when Justice Hans Raj Khanna of the Indian Supreme Court delivered the sole dissenting judgment in the case of *Additional District Magistrate, Jabalpur v. Shivakant Shukla (Habeas Corpus Case)*,[104] he was victimized for not deferring to the wishes of the regime. In this context, it is noteworthy that Justice Khanna in his judgment in the *Habeas Corpus Case* disagreed with the majority view that a preventive detention order vitiated by *mala fides* cannot be challenged in a court of law due to the ouster of the court's jurisdiction under the Maintenance of Internal Security Act, 1971 and that the court could not enforce the fundamental rights to life and liberty under Article 21 of the Indian Constitution due to the suspension of these rights during the continuation of the emergency declared in June 1975.[105] Consequently, the regime in violation of the time-honoured of convention of appointing the senior-most judge of the Supreme Court as the Chief Justice of India, appointed Justice MH Beg as the Chief Justice in supersession of Justice Khanna—the senior-most judge of the Supreme Court.[106]

Following the revocation of the controversial proclamation of emergency, which was invoked to ensure Mrs Gandhi's survival in power, on 21 March 1977, the Indian Supreme Court through a series of cases have sought to exclude the say of the executive in the matter of judicial appointments in order to the uphold the independence of the judiciary. The cumulative effect of the Supreme Court's judgments in the cases of the *Supreme Court Advocates-on-Record Association v Union of India (the Second Judges' Case)*[107] and *Special Reference No. 1 of 1998 (the Third Judges' Case)*[108] is that the opinion of the Chief Justice of India should be given primacy over that of the executive in the matter of appointing judges as the former is best suited to know about the competence of the candidates. To this end, the Court interpreted the word "consultation" as used in Articles 124(2) and 217(1) of the Indian Constitution to mean "concurrence". The Court further interpreted the expression "consultation with the Chief Justice of India" to mean that the final opinion of the Chief Justice on the issue of recommending nominees to the executive for judicial appointment, should be formed after consultation with four of his colleagues, i.e. the four senior-most judges of the superior courts.[109] The Court has termed the system developed for obligating the Chief Justice of India to consult the senior-most judges before putting forward his recommendation to the President for

---

[103] Ibid., p. 70; Austin (2003), pp. 319–325.

[104] *Additional District Magistrate, Jabalpur v. Shivakant Shukla* [1976] AIR (SC) 1207.

[105] Ibid., p. 1234.

[106] Bari (2016), p. 51.

[107] *Supreme Court Advocates-on-Record Association v Union of India* 1991 Supp (1) SCC 574.

[108] *Special Reference No. 1 of 1998* (1998) 7 SCC 739.

[109] Ibid., p. 772, 763.

appointment to the bench, a "collegium". It should be pointed out here that the framers of the Indian Constitution did not intend to accord primacy to the opinion of the Chief Justice of India in the matter of appointment of judges and as such, they deliberately refrained from inserting the words "with the concurrence/consent of the Chief Justice" in Articles 124(2) and 217(1). In this context, the remarks of Dr BR Ambedkar, Chairman of the Constitution Drafting Committee, in the Indian Constituent Assembly are noteworthy:

> With regard to the question of concurrence of the Chief Justice, it seems to me that those who advocate that proposition seem to rely implicitly both on the impartiality of the Chief Justice and the soundness of his judgment. I personally feel no doubt that the Chief Justice is a very eminent person. But after all, the Chief Justice is a man with all the failings, all the sentiments and all the prejudices which we as common people have; and I think, to allow the Chief Justice practically a veto upon the appointment of Judges is really to transfer the authority to the Chief Justice which we are not prepared to vest in the President or the Government of the day. I therefore, think that is also a dangerous proposition.[110]

It should be further stressed here that the "collegium" system as developed by the judges is not provided for by the Constitution. In fact, the word "collegium" has not found a place anywhere in the text of the Constitution. Thus, it is evident that in order to safeguard judicial independence, the Indian Judiciary went beyond the letter of the Constitution by arrogating to itself the final say in the matter of appointing judges. As VR Krishna Iyer pertinently notes: "The ... Judges [in India]..., in a mighty seizure of power, wrested authority to appoint.... judges from the top executive to themselves by a stroke of adjudicatory self-enthronement."[111]

However, notwithstanding the objective underlying the development of the "collegium" system to promote the independence of the judiciary by introducing objectivity in the appointment process, the actual functioning of the system has been marred by allegations of it being cloaked in veils of secrecy, non-transparency and arbitrariness, which in turn resulted in competent candidates being overlooked for appointment.[112] As Justice Ruma Paul, a retired Supreme Court Judge who herself served as a member of the "collegium", noted:

> The process by which a judge is appointed to the High Court or elevated to the Supreme Court is one of the best kept secrets in the country. The "mystique" of the process, the small pool from which the selections were made and the "secrecy and confidentiality" ensured that the process may, on occasions, make wrong appointments and, lend itself to nepotism.[113]

Taking into account the above issues regarding the "collegium" system, successive governments in India have sought to reform the process concerning the appointment of the judges. First, the Government of India in 1990 introduced in the Lower House of the Parliament, a Bill, titled the Constitution (Sixty-Seventh Amendment) Bill,

---

[110] Law Commission of India (1979).

[111] Iyer (2003), p. 278.

[112] Ramkrishnaiah (2015), https://indianexpress.com/article/opinion/columns/rend-the-veil-of-secrecy/

[113] Paul (2013).

2.4 The Importance of the Method of Appointment and the Security of Tenure... 41

1990, seeking to constitute the National Judicial Commission and to make appointment to the Supreme Court and the High Courts on the basis of the Commission's recommendation. But the Bill lapsed with dissolution of that *Lok Sobha*.[114] Later in 2002, the Government introduced the Constitution (Ninety-Eighth Amendment) Bill to constitute a National Judicial Commission, by incorporating Chapter IVA in Part V of the Constitution, consisting of the Chief Justice of India as its Chairman, two senior-most Judges of the Supreme Court, the Union Minister for Law and Justice, and one eminent citizen to be nominated by the President in consultation with the Prime Minister. However, due the controversies regarding the composition and functions of the Commission, the second Bill also lapsed in 2003.[115] A revised version of the bill was introduced as the Constitution (One Hundred and Twentieth Amendment) Bill, 2013 in the Parliament in August 2013. However, this Bill also met the same fate as its predecessors due to the dissolution of the *Lok Sabha.*

Finally, on 14 August 2014, the Constitution (Ninety-Ninth Amendment) Act was enacted, which amended Articles 124 and 217 of the Constitution of India[116] by replacing the word "consultation" with the phrase "on the recommendation of the National Judicial Appointments Commission". It also inserted a new Article 124A in the Constitution, which provided that the National Judicial Appointments Commission (NJAC) would be composed of the Chief Justice of India, the next two senior-most judges of Supreme Court, the Union Minister of Law and Justice, and two "eminent persons" to be nominated by a committee consisting of the Prime Minister, the Chief Justice of India and the Leader of the Opposition in *Lok Sabha.*[117] Thus, it is evident that unlike the Judicial Commission of Pakistan, judges did not constitute a majority in the NJAC.

On the same day as the enactment of the Ninety-Ninth Amendment, the Indian Parliament also passed the National Judicial Appointments Commission Act, 2014. The NJAC Act regulated the appointment procedures and empowered the NJAC to enact regulations to carry on with its functions. Furthermore, the Act effectively permitted any two members of the commission to veto nominations.[118] Since the Constitution of India, as amended by the Ninety-Ninth Amendment, provided for inclusion of the Union Law Minister and two eminent persons to be nominated, among others, by the Prime Minister and the Leader of Opposition, it can be argued that the government of the day could influence the functioning of the selection process in an adverse manner by persuading the Law Minister and one of the "eminent persons' to veto any candidate it deemed unfriendly. This objectionable possibility

---

[114] 'National Commission to Review the Working of the Indian Constitution (2001), https://legalaffairs.gov.in/sites/default/files/(XII)Superior%20Judiciary.pdf

[115] Venkatesan (2003), https://frontline.thehindu.com/the-nation/article30217285.ece

[116] Constitution (Ninety-Ninth Amendment) Act, 2014 (India) ss. 3, 6.

[117] The two eminent person were to be nominated by a committee that will consist of Prime Minister, Leader of Opposition in the Lok Sabha (or the Leader of the single largest party in Opposition as the case maybe) and Chief Justice of India.

[118] National Judicial Appointments Commission Act, 2014 (India) s 5(2). *Supreme Court Advocates-on-Record Association v. Union of India* (2) 4 SCC at 357

coupled with the fact that the Constitution did not allow the senior members of the judiciary to constitute a majority in the NJAC meant that the functioning of the Commission was not adequately insulated from political pressure. Accordingly, the Indian legal fraternity considered the amendment and the NJAC Act an assault on the independence of judiciary—reminiscent of the dark days of the 1975 emergency. Consequently, Supreme Advocates-on-Record Association and plethora of Senior Advocates challenged the constitutionality of the Ninety-Ninth Amendment and the NJAC Act.

On 15 October 2015, the Supreme Court in *Supreme Court Advocates-on-Record Association v. Union of India* (hereinafter referred to as NJAC Case),[119] declared the Ninety-Ninth Amendment Act and NJAC Act *ultra vires* the Constitution of India. The majority advanced the following reasonings in support of its decision. First, the majority elevated the status of the "collegium" system, which was dispensed with by the Ninety-Ninth Amendment, to a basic structure of the Constitution by way of creative invocation. For the system ensured that the opinion of the Chief Justice of India, which was formed after consultation with the senior-most judges, had primacy over the executive on the crucial issue of appointing judges, which was conducive to preventing the intrusion of extraneous considerations, such as political favouritism, in the process. Second, the inclusion of the Union Minister of Law & Justice in the NJAC was considered to be a violation of the principle of separation of powers.[120] This argument is further bolstered by reference to the fact that the "government is the biggest litigant in India".[121] Therefore, allowing it to have a say in the appointment of judges would potentially create a conflict of interest.[122] Finally, the appointment of "eminent persons" as members of the NJAC coupled with their potential power to veto any nomination gave rise to the disturbing possibility of stifling the voice of the senior members of the judiciary in the Commission. Accordingly, the majority of the judges of the Supreme Court held that both the amendment and the NJAC Act undermined the independence of the judiciary—a basic structure of the Constitution which cannot be diminished by an amendment.

Although this judgment was hailed as a triumph of judicial independence, it should be stressed here that the Supreme Court decided to uphold the constitutionality of an extra-constitutional body, namely the collegium, which the Court itself had created to serve its own interests. As Justice Chelameswar, who delivered the lone dissenting judgment in the NJAC case, rhetorically noted:

> We, the members of the judiciary, exult and frolic in our emancipation from the other two organs of the State (Legislature and Executive). But have we developed an alternate

---

[119] *Supreme Court Advocates-on-Record Association v. Union of India* (2) 4 SCC 1 (India) (hereinafter referred to as NJAC judgement).

[120] Ibid., p. 369

[121] Rajagopalan (2018), https://www.livemint.com/Opinion/tWZ7dVM2608hVfdOyvjP0J/The-elephant-in-the-courtroom.html

[122] Ibid.

2.4 The Importance of the Method of Appointment and the Security of Tenure…

> constitutional morality to emancipate us from the theory of checks and balances, robust
> enough to keep us in control from abusing such independence?[123]

Arguably, the Ninety-Ninth Amendment and the NJAC Act would have had a better chance of surviving challenges to their constitutionality, had they: a) followed in the footsteps of the Pakistani Constitution, as amended by the Eighteenth Amendment, to allow the senior members of the Indian Judiciary to constitute a majority in the NJAC in an attempt to limit the scope for the executive to unduly influence the process of selecting judges; and b) not provided members of the NJAC the power to veto nominations, which could potentially have been exercised by the Law Minister in collaboration with either of the "eminent persons" to thwart the selection of a candidate deemed worthy by the senior members of the judiciary for appointment to the bench.

It is evident that in order to safeguard the independence and impartiality of the judiciary, entrusting effective and independent judicial commissions—wherein the senior members of the judiciary, including the head of the judiciary, will constitute a majority—with the power to select candidates on their merit and to subsequently recommend such meritorious candidates for judicial appointment, is the demand of modern times. Although the CRA, as discussed above, stipulates that candidates for judgeship should be appointed on "merit", it does not list the criteria that should be taken into account in determining such "merit". However, in this context, the criteria listed by the British Lord Chancellor a year prior to the enactment of the CRA, are instructive:

- "legal knowledge and experience;
- intellectual and analytical ability;
- sound judgment;
- decisiveness;
- communication and listening skills;
- authority and case management skills;
- integrity and independence;
- fairness and impartiality;
- understanding of people and society;
- maturity and sound temperament;
- courtesy; and
- commitment, conscientiousness and diligence."[124]

The objective of securing the appointment of candidates who possess the above qualities as judges, should not, however, be achieved by way of judicial activism, as has been done in India. Rather in order to ensure that the matter of appointment in the superior courts, does not result in politically biased judges or judges who feel beholden to the appointing authority, independent judicial appointments

---

[123] Singh (2018), https://www.livemint.com/Politics/DsUXbu4j6FWeYzZMnD7SAM/Justice-Jasti-Chelameswars-lasting-legacy-striking-a-note.html

[124] Sackville (2005), p. 133; Lavarch (1993), pp. 5–12; Evans & Williams (2006), pp. 21–22.

commissions should be set up through constitutional amendments. The recommendation of such commissions should be binding upon the executive. But it should be open to the executive to return the recommendation in any given case along with the information in its possession regarding the suitability of the candidates. If, however, commissions reiterate their recommendations after reconsideration, then the government should be bound to make the appointment.

2.4.2 The Importance of a Transparent Method of Removal of Judges

The principle of the independence of the judiciary implies that "judges are not dependent on Government in any way which might influence them in coming to decisions in individual cases."[125] In other words, individual judges should be independent of the political branches of government, especially the executive, so that they have "nothing to lose by doing what is right and little to gain by doing what is wrong."[126]

Consequently, it can be argued that there is nothing that can contribute more to the firmness and independence of the judiciary as security of tenure of the judges. For such security enables them to decide cases regardless of whether their decisions are in line with the desires of the political branches of government. Therefore, once appointed a judge should remain in office for a long term, preferably for life[127] or until he attains a specified age.[128] This argument is further bolstered by reference to the international standards on the independence of judges, such as the International Bar Association's Minimum Standards of Judicial Independence, 1982, which, among other things, stipulates that: "Judicial appointments should generally be for life, subject to removal for cause and compulsory retirement at an age fixed by law at the date of appointment."[129] A judge should be removable from office only for misconduct or incapacity, whether physical or mental, "that clearly renders ...[him] unfit to discharge ... [his] duties."[130] Such removal must of necessity be made a difficult process, involving careful consideration by more than one person. Otherwise, a judge would be vulnerable to the process being used against him by the

---

[125] Griffith (1977), p. 29.

[126] Quoted in Friedland (2001), p. 861.

[127] U.S. Constitution. art. III § 1 (stipulating that the "Judges, both of the supreme and inferior Courts, shall hold their Offices during good behavior.")

[128] Constitution of Australia, 1901 (Australia) s. 72 (stipulates that "[t]he appointment of a Justice of the High Court shall be for a term expiring upon his attaining the age of seventy years.")

[129] See above n 46, art. 22.

[130] Smit (2015), p. 79.

2.4 The Importance of the Method of Appointment and the Security of Tenure... 45

government of the day for "applying the law as… [he] saw it,"[131] thereby preventing him from acquiring the habit of independence requisite in his office.

Accordingly, the international norms concerning judicial independence advocate for a transparent method of removal of judges which is not susceptible to the influence of the political branches of the government. In this context, reference can be made, in the first instance, to the recommendation of the International Congress of Jurists, which was held in New Delhi in 1959, that "[t]he reconciliation of the principle of irremovability of the judiciary with the possibility of removal in exceptional circumstances necessitates that the grounds for removal should be before a body of judicial character assuring at least the same safeguards to the judge as would be accorded to an accused person in a criminal trial."[132] Furthermore, in the same vein, the Latimer House Guidelines for the Commonwealth, 1998, *inter alia*, provide that "[i]n cases where a Judge is at risk of removal, the Judge must have the right to be fully informed of the charges, to be represented at a hearing, to make full defence and to be Judged by an independent and impartial tribunal."[133] It is noteworthy that a majority of the Commonwealth jurisdictions invest either ad hoc or permanent disciplinary tribunals with the responsibility of inquiring into the facts alleged against a judge and of subsequently recommending, if proved, the removal of the concerned judge from office.[134]

The issue with ad hoc tribunals is that their composition is generally not specified by constitutions. Consequently, they provide the executive with the leeway to pack tribunals with loyalists, thereby enabling it to influence the functioning of tribunals. In order to substantiate this argument, reference can be made to the removal method prescribed by the Federal Constitution of Malaysia, which in Article 125(4) entrusts the *Yang di-Pertuan Agong*—the head of the State—with the authority to appoint the members of the tribunal constituted for investigating whether a judge of the Federal Court should be removed from office "on the ground of any breach of any provision of the code of ethics … or on the ground of inability, from infirmity of body or mind or any other cause," which has impeded his ability to properly "discharge the functions of his office."[135] The susceptibility of this removal method to executive manipulation was manifestly apparent during the judicial crisis of 1988. The crisis began when angered by some of the decisions of the superior judiciary, the Government led by Mahathir Mohamad persuaded the Parliament to amend Article 121 of the Constitution for depriving the courts of the judicial power of the Federation. Consequently, courts in Malaysia are to exercise only those powers granted to them by the Parliament. When the head of the judiciary—Lord

---

[131] *Chapter 3: Removal from office* (1), p. 524.

[132] International Commission of Jurists (1959), Committee IV, cl. 4.

[133] Smit, above n 130, p. xxi.

[134] See generally, Constitution of the Co-operative Republic of Guyana, 1980 (Guyana); Constitution of the Sovereign Democratic Republic of Fiji, 1990 (Fiji); Constitution of South Africa, 1996 (South Africa); Constitution of the Republic of Trinidad and Tobago, 1976; Constitution of India, 1950 (India); Constitution of Malaysia, 1957 (Malaysia).

[135] Constitution of Malaysia, 1957 (Malaysia), Art. 125(3).

President of the Supreme Court, Tun Salleh Abas—took a stand against these arbitrary actions aimed at limiting the independence of the judiciary,[136] Mahathir advised the *Yang di- Pertuan Agong* to remove the Lord President from office on account of misconduct.[137] Consequently, for the first time in the nation's history, the *Yang di- Pertuan Agong* appointed a tribunal under Article 125(3) of the Constitution to investigate the allegations of misconduct brought against the Lord President, who had been suspended pending the determination of the tribunal. It is striking that in exercise of the powers under Article 125(4) of the Constitution, the executive entrusted the person who stood to benefit the most from the removal of Lord President Abas, namely, Acting Lord President Tan Sri Abdul Hamid Omar, with the responsibility of heading the Tribunal.[138] Consequently, in accordance with the designs of the government of the day, the tribunal recommended the removal of Lord Abas from office.[139] On the basis of this recommendation, the *Yang di- Pertuan Agong* formally removed Tun Salleh Abas from the office of the Lord President. The judicial crisis of 1988—a crisis from which the nation never fully recovered—is considered a "watershed" moment in the judicial history of Malaysia which compromised "both the appearance and reality of judicial autonomy."[140]

By way of contrast, the establishment of a permanent disciplinary tribunal preserves the objectivity and fairness of the removal proceedings initiated against a judge of the superior court provided the constitution of a nation itself specifies the composition of the tribunal and confines the membership to senior members of the superior judiciary with a view to obviate the possibility for either the executive or legislature to influence the functioning of the tribunal. To this end, the provisions of the Constitution of Pakistan, 1973 deserve special attention. For Article 209 of the Constitution, in the first instance, establishes a Supreme Judicial Council for enquiring whether a judge of the superior judiciary is incapable of properly performing the duties of his office due to physical or mental incapacity or is guilty of misconduct.[141] Subsequently, it confines the membership of the Council to the senior members of the superior judiciary, namely, the Chief Justice of Pakistan, the two next most senior judges of the Supreme Court and the two most senior Chief Justices of High Courts.[142] Thus, it is evident that a permanent disciplinary tribunal meeting the

---

[136] Lord President Abas issued a statement stressing the importance of an independent judiciary. He also chaired a meeting of the judges of the Supreme Court in Kuala Lumpur, in which he persuaded the judges to send a joint letter to the *Yang di-Pertuan Agong*. This letter read: "All of us are disappointed with the various comments and accusations made by the honourable prime minister against the judiciary, not only outside but within the Parliament." Koshy, Ng, Habib, Fung, Hock & The (2008), https://www.thestar.com.my/news/nation/2008/04/18/events-that-led-to-judicial-crisis-of-88

[137] Tew (2016), p. 679.

[138] Ibid.

[139] Ibid.

[140] Ibid.

[141] Constitution of Pakistan, 1973 (Pakistan) art. 209(1) read together with art. 209(5) and (6).

[142] Constitution of Pakistan, 1973 (Pakistan) art. 209(2).

above requirements is more conducive to upholding the independence of the judiciary from the political branches of the government.

It should be stressed here that entrusting bodies of judicial character with the responsibility to select and discipline judges, would have a two-fold effect. First, it would give judges the confidence to decide cases in accordance with the dictates of law without fear or favour, thereby safeguarding their individual independence. Second, it enables such bodies "to view the collective needs of the institution or branch rather than look to individual interests"[143] while performing the task of selecting judges and conducting disciplinary proceedings against them, thereby furthering the independence of the judiciary as a whole.

2.5 Case Study: The Independence of the Judiciary in Pakistan

Although it has been 74 years since Pakistan secured its independence from Britain, the concept of democracy has not yet found a solid footing in the country. In fact, the nation's journey towards democracy has constantly been "derailed" due to the army's proclivity for capturing power through either proclamations of martial law or declarations of both constitutional and extraconstitutional emergencies.[144] In fact, the general election held in May 2013 marked the first ever peaceful transfer of power in Pakistan's history following a democratically elected government's completion of its five-year tenure. However, notwithstanding such stark realities, the only institution in Pakistan which has in recent times sought to realise its purpose, is the judiciary. This has, arguably, been possible due to the Constitution of Pakistan, 1973, securing the independence of the judiciary by prescribing, as pointed out earlier in Sects. 2.4.1 and 2.4.2, a transparent method of appointment of judges involving the Judicial Commission and guaranteeing the security of tenure of judges through, among other things, provisions concerning the Supreme Judicial Council. The beneficial impact of these guarantees on the independence of the judges was manifestly apparent: (a) in 2007 during the autocratic rule of General Pervez Musharraf; (b) in 2012 during rule of the Pakistan Peoples Party (PPP); and c) more recently in 2017 during the tenure of the government of Pakistan Muslim League (PMLN). First, in October 1999, General Musharraf—then the Chairman of the Joint Chiefs of Staff Committee and Chief of Army Staff—had seized power through the proclamation of an emergency, which was declared after suspending the Constitution of Pakistan, 1973.[145] Unlike his predecessors, who had usurped power through martial law, Musharraf sought to characterise his military adventurism as an emergency—albeit an extraconstitutional one—"to make the military interven-

---

[143] See above n 43, p. 379.

[144] See above n 101, pp. 39–56; Bari (2018), p. 68.

[145] See above n 101, pp. 51–52.

tion acceptable ... [to the people of Pakistan who had witnessed several Martial Law regimes in the past] and to give it a benign political appearance to the outside world".[146]

Although Musharraf managed to consolidate his grip on power by systematically annihilating the two major political parties of the country, namely PPP and PMLN, it was an independent judiciary—led by a courageous Chief Justice, Iftikhar Muhammad Chaudhry—which posed considerable threat to the former's desire of perpetuating power. For instance, the Supreme Court under the leadership of Chief Justice Chaudhry in *Watan Party and Pakistan Steel People's Workers Union et al v. Federation of Pakistan*,[147] declared the Musharraf regime's privatisation of the Pakistan Steel Mills Corporation, invalid.[148] For the Court held that the "indecent haste" in which the entire privatisation process was completed, casted serious "doubt on the transparency of the whole exercise".[149] Furthermore, the Supreme Court took *suo moto* notice of scores of enforced disappearances perpetrated by the Musharraf regime.[150] In fact, the Court under Justice Chaudhry's leadership had traced as many as 186 disappeared individuals between October 2006 and November 2007.[151]

The manner in which the Supreme Court held the regime accountable incensed Musharraf. Consequently, he asked Justice Chaudhry to resign. When he refused, Musharraf suspended him from office on 9 March 2007. Justice Chaudhry's suspension galvanised massive protests, which saw lawyers and human rights activists taking to the streets demanding his reinstatement.[152] Musharraf, ultimately, bowed down to popular pressure and reinstated Justice Chaudhry to office on 20 July 2007.[153] However, even after his reinstatement, Justice Chaudhry continued to hold the Musharraf regime to account. This gave Musharraf the convenient premise to proclaim yet another extraconstitutional emergency on 3 November 2007 after suspending the Constitution. But unlike the 1999 extraconstitutional emergency, which was used to crush Musharraf's political adversaries, the 2007 emergency was invoked to launch an unprecedented crackdown on the Judiciary. Strikingly, as many as 6 out of the 8 preambular paragraphs of the proclamation of emergency described the manner in which the Supreme Court had proved to be disloyal to his regime.[154] However, notwithstanding this, Chief Justice Chaudhry and his colleagues remained unfazed. For, notwithstanding the suspension of the Constitution

---

[146] Maluka (2004), p. 55.

[147] *Watan Party and Pakistan Steel People's Workers Union et al v. Federation of Pakistan* [2006] PLD (SC) 697.

[148] Ibid.

[149] See above n 101, p. 55.

[150] HRW (2011), https://www.hrw.org/report/2011/07/28/we-can-torture-kill-or-keep-you-years/enforced-disappearances-pakistan-security

[151] Amnesty International (2008), p. 5.

[152] See above n 101, p. 55.

[153] Ibid.

[154] Proclamation of Emergency, 2007 (Pakistan).

2.5 Case Study: The Independence of the Judiciary in Pakistan

of Pakistan, 1973, the Supreme Court, among other things, invalidated the 2007 proclamation of emergency for not being invoked in accordance with the terms of the Constitution. The Court further instructed all judges not to take a new oath of office to protect and defend the Provisional Constitutional Order, 2007, which was issued by Musharraf after the suspension of the regular Constitution.[155] However, such defiance of the Chief Justice and his colleagues led to them being placed under house arrest.[156]

When normalcy was finally restored after the election of a civilian government of the PPP on 31 March 2008, the Supreme Court under the leadership of Chief Justice Chaudhry continued to act independently and impartially. For instance, when Prime Minister Yousaf Raza Gilani refused to reopen fraud investigations against President Asif Ali Zardari, Chief Justice Chaudhry and his colleagues, on 26 April 2012, convicted the Prime Minister on contempt of court charges. Subsequently, on 20 June 2012, relying on Article 63 of the Constitution, which, among other things, disqualifies an individual convicted by a court from membership of the Parliament, Chief Justice Chaudhry held that Prime Minister Gilani had ceased to be the Prime Minister since 26 April 2012—the day on which he was convicted for contempt of court.[157] This was an unprecedented event in history of Pakistan as a sitting Prime Minister was ousted from office by the judiciary for non-compliance with its direction.

Five years later, on 28 July 2017, Prime Minister Nawaz Sharif suffered the same fate as Gilani, when he was also disqualified by the Supreme Court from holding the office of the Prime Minister. However, unlike Gilani, who was convicted for contempt of court due to his inability to comply with a direction of the highest court of the land, Sharif was removed from office on charges of corruption. The Court held that Sharif had "failed to disclose his un-withdrawn receivables constituting (overseas) assets" in the nomination papers that he filed prior to the 2013 general election and "had furnished false declaration under solemn affirmation".[158] Consequently, it held that Sharif was "not honest" and as such, he was "disqualified" to be a Member of Parliament (MP).[159] To this end, the Court relied on the terms of Article 62(1)(f) of the Constitution of Pakistan, 1973, which stipulates that MPs should, *inter alia*, be "righteous" and "honest".

It is manifestly evident from the above discussion that safeguarding the individual independence of the judges through the incorporation of meaningful guarantees in the Constitution of Pakistan, has enabled the judiciary to dispense justice according to the dictates of law and to, consequently, hold the powerful to account, thereby

---

[155] Proclamation of Emergency, 2007 (Pakistan).

[156] See above n 101, p. 55.

[157] Boone (2012), https://www.theguardian.com/world/2012/jun/19/pakistan-prime-minister-yousuf-gilani-disqualified

[158] Gul (2017), https://www.voanews.com/east-asia-pacific/pakistan-supreme-court-disqualifies-sharif-he-steps-down

[159] Ibid.

50   2 The Principle of Judicial Independence and Its Recognition in the Constitution…

realising Thomas Fuller's aspiration, as articulated nearly 400 years ago: "Be ye never so high, the law is above you."[160]

2.6   The Principle of Judicial Independence as Enshrined in the Constitution of Bangladesh, 1972

The independence of judiciary, which is the central principle underlying the administration of justice, succeeded to acquire the place of a cornerstone in the scheme of the 1972 Constitution of Bangladesh. It is, indeed, a fundamental feature of the Constitution. Although the Constitution, as pointed out earlier in Sect. 1.3, does not explicitly speak of vesting judicial power of the Republic in the Judiciary, it provides, *inter alia*, that "[t]he State shall ensure the separation of the judiciary from the executive organ of the State".[161] This constitutional provision emphasises the importance of protecting the judiciary from executive interference as an independent judiciary is a fundamental requirement for the existence of any society based on democratic values, such as respect for the rule of law and the human rights of individuals. Thus, the well-chosen words of democracy, rule of law, fundamental rights and freedom, equality and justice have, as pointed out earlier in Sect. 1.3, been articulated in the preamble of the Constitution as the fundamental aims of the State.

The Constitution also emphatically embraces the principle of independence of the individual judges by providing in Article 94(4) that "[s]ubject to the provisions of this Constitution, the Chief Justice and the other Judges shall be independent in the exercise of their judicial functions".[162] Furthermore, Article 35(3) of the Constitution provides that "[e]very person accused of a criminal offence shall have a right to a speedy and public trial by an independent and impartial court or tribunal established by law." It is evident that this provision guarantees a fundamental right to every accused person in Bangladesh to have a "speedy and public trial" by not only an "independent" judiciary but also by an "impartial" judiciary—meaning members of the judiciary should have neutrality of "mind or attitude in relation to the issues and the parties in a particular case".[163]

Consequently, all the members of the superior judiciary, including the Chief Justice of Bangladesh and the judges of both the divisions of the Supreme Court of Bangladesh, namely the Appellate Division and the High Court Division, are not only required to "solemnly swear (or affirm) to preserve, protect and defend the Constitution and the laws of Bangladesh" but also to swear to "faithfully discharge

---

[160] Ratcliffe (2016), https://www.oxfordreference.com/view/10.1093/acref/9780191826719.001.0001/q-oro-ed4-00003551

[161] Constitution of Bangladesh, 1972 (Bangladesh) art. 22.

[162] Constitution of Bangladesh, 1972 (Bangladesh) art. 94(4).

[163] *Valente v The Queen* [1985] 2 SCR 673, 685.

the duties of ... [their] office according to law" and to "do right to all manner of people according to law, without fear or favour, affection or ill-will".[164] This pattern of oath for the Chief Justice or judges of the Supreme Court emphasises that they are expected to hold the scales of justice even between the humblest of citizens and an all-powerful executive, without fear or favour—regardless of the consequences to themselves. In order to maintain the independence of the judges of the Supreme Court of Bangladesh, the framers of the Constitution also provide that the remuneration, privileges and other terms and conditions of service of a judge of the Supreme Court "shall not be varied to ... [his] disadvantage ... during his term of office".[165] The present laws which govern these matters are the Supreme Court Judges (Remuneration and Privileges) Ordinance, 1978 and the Supreme Court Judges (Leave, Pension and Privileges) Ordinance, 1982, as amended from time to time to the advantage, not disadvantage, of the judges of the Supreme Court.

Taking into account the above constitutional guarantee of the remuneration and privileges of judges, the Appellate Division of the Supreme Court of Bangladesh observed in *Commissioner of Taxes v. Justice S. Ahmed*[166] that salary of the Supreme Court judge is exempted from income tax and this position cannot be affected by notification issued under the Income Tax Act.[167] Furthermore, the Constitution of Bangladesh also gives the High Court Division and the Appellate Division of the Supreme Court "the power subject to law to make an order for the investigation of or punishment for any contempt of itself,"[168] e.g. for scandalising the court to bring its authority into disrepute, disobeying its orders and interfering with the due course of justice. In *Moazzem Hossain v. State,*[169] the Appellate Division of the Supreme Court of Bangladesh rightly observed that the power to punish for contempt has been given not for the protection of the individual judges from imputations, but for the protection of the public themselves from the mischief they will incur if the authority of the Supreme Court is impaired.[170] Thus, it is evident that the principle of independence of judiciary has been incorporated into the Constitution of Bangladesh as an integral and inseparable pillar. With regard to ascertaining the basic pillars of the Constitution, the observations made by Justice Shahabuddin Ahmad in the 1989 case of *Anwar Hossain Chowdhury and Others v. Bangladesh*[171] are noteworthy:

> There is no dispute that the Constitution stands on certain fundamental principles which are its structural pillars and if these pillars are demolished or damaged the whole Constitutional

---

[164] Constitution of Bangladesh, 1972 (Bangladesh) Third Schedule, Oaths and Affirmations, Chief Justice or Judges.

[165] Constitution of Bangladesh, 1972 (Bangladesh), art. 147(2) and (4)(e).

[166] *Commissioner of Taxes v. Justice S. Ahmed* 42 DLR (AD) (1990) 162.

[167] Ibid.

[168] Constitution of Bangladesh, 1972 (Bangladesh) art. 108.

[169] *Moazzem Hossain v. State* 35 DLR (AD) (1983) 290.

[170] Ibid.

[171] *Anwar Hossain Chowdhury and Others v. Bangladesh* 41 DLR (AD) (1989) 165.

edifice will fall down. It is by construing the Constitutional provisions that these pillars are to be identified.[172]

After referring to the provisions of certain Articles of the Constitution, including Article 94(4) which, as noted above, speaks of the independence of the judges of the Supreme Court in the exercise of their judicial functions, the learned Judge concluded that "[i]ndependence of the Judiciary [is] a basic structure of the Constitution".[173] Eleven years later in 2000, in the case of *Secretary, Ministry of Finance v. Md. Masder Hossain and Others*,[174] Justice Mustafa—then the Chief Justice of Bangladesh—in light, among others, of the provision contained in Article 94(4) of the Constitution of Bangladesh, held that:

> The independence of the judiciary, as affirmed and declared by Article[.] 94(4) ..., is one of the basic pillars of the Constitution and cannot be demolished, whittled down, curtailed or diminished in any manner whatsoever, except under the existing provisions of the Constitution. It is true that this independence .... is subject to the provisions of the Constitution, but we find no provision in the Constitution which curtails, diminishes or otherwise abridges this independence.[175]

However, unlike the constitutions of other commonwealth jurisdictions, such as the Constitution of Malaysia, 1957, which contain procedural safeguards restricting the discussion of the conduct of judges of the superior courts in the Parliament,[176] the Constitution of Bangladesh does not contain any provision whatsoever aiming at preventing the unsavoury discussion of the conduct of a judge of the Supreme Court, which may cause undue distress or embarrassment to the judge concerned, in the Parliament. Notwithstanding the constitutional silence, the Rules of Procedure of the Parliament contain provisions in this regard stipulating that question, motion or resolution which contains reflection on the conduct of any judge of the Supreme Court shall not be admissible.[177] But the enforcement of this provision depends

---

[172] Ibid., p. 262.

[173] Ibid., p. 259.

[174] *Secretary, Ministry of Finance v. Md. Masder Hossain and Others* 52 DLR (AD) (2000) 82.

[175] Ibid., p. 103.

[176] See for example, the Constitution of Malaysia, 1957, in Article 127 stipulates that the conduct of a judge of the Federal Court, the Court of Appeal or a High Court shall not be discussed in either House of Parliament except on a substantive motion of which notice has been given by not less than one quarter of the total number of members of that House and shall not be discussed in the Legislative Assembly of any State.

[177] Rules 53, 63 and 133, Rules of Procedure of the Parliament, 1973. Rule 53 (2) provides that "In order to be admissible a question must ...", inter alia, "(xviii) .... not ask for information on a matter which is under adjudication by a Court of Law having jurisdiction in any part of Bangladesh;" "(xx) .... (a) contain any reflection on the conduct .... of the Judges of the Supreme Court." Rule 63, which deals with restrictions on the right to make adjournment motions, provides: "The right to make an adjournment motion under rule 61 shall be subject to the following restrictions, namely: .... xi) the motion shall not deal with any matter which is under adjudication by a Court of Law having jurisdiction in any part of Bangladesh; and xii) the motion shall not contain a reflection on the conduct .... of a Judge of the Supreme Court of Bangladesh." Rule 133 provides that "No resolution shall be admissible which ..." *inter alia*, "iv)" do "not relate to any matter which is

2.6 The Principle of Judicial Independence as Enshrined in the Constitution... 53

generally on the neutrality, boldness and uprightness of the Speaker of the Parliament.[178]

Having discussed the general provisions concerning the principle of judicial independence in the Constitution of Bangladesh, the extent to which the Constitution seeks to guarantee such a principle through provisions concerning the method of appointment and the security of tenure of the judges, will be examined in the remaining chapters of the book. For, as is evident from the discussion in Sects. 2.4 and 2.5, the guarantees of suitable method of appointment and security of tenure of judges not only have the beneficial impact of safeguarding the independence of the individual judges but also of the judiciary as a whole.

---

under adjudication by a court of law having jurisdiction in any part of Bangladesh"; v) do "not contain a reflection on .... a Judge of the Supreme Court."

[178] In the past, following the pronouncement of the judgment of the *Anwar Hossain Case* in 1989 by the Appellate Division of the Supreme Court of Bangladesh, the then Leader of the Opposition strongly protested and questioned the rational and justification of the decisions given by the Supreme Court. Following a remark of the then Chief Justice of Bangladesh made in 1999, the then Home Minister made some unkind remarks about the judiciary in the Parliament and contradicted the Chief Justice by saying that the judges of the Supreme Court were also responsible for increased violence and terrorism in the country for releasing the notorious criminals on bail. But the Speaker did not stop them on either of the occasions from making indecent remarks about the Chief Justice of Bangladesh and other Judges of the Supreme Court. Their remarks were also not expunged from the proceedings of the Parliament. The then Prime Minister on 2 August 2000 in an interview with the BBC attacked the judiciary in line with its home minister. Furthermore, in a meeting held in Dhaka on 18 April 2000 the speakers, including half a dozen of ministers and state ministers of the Party in power, made outrageous and audacious remarks about certain judges of the Supreme Court as they felt embarrassed in hearing the Murder Case (death reference) of Sheikh Mujibur Rahman. After the meeting, they went so far as to bring out a procession brandishing lethal sticks, warning that they had simply exhibited sticks this time, but these would be used in the future (against the judges of the Supreme Court). Ultimately three petitions were filed seeking the drawing up of contempt of court proceedings against the Prime Minister. The common allegations in these applications were that on 26 July 2000, Sheikh Hasina, in an interview with BBC, made objectionable and contemptuous statements that both the lower courts and the High Court Division had become the sanctuary of corrupt and accused persons; that whenever they approach the Court, they were released on bail after which they again commit murders; that both, the lawyers seeking bail and the courts granting bail, should be held accountable. Justice Mozammel Hoque of the High Court Division on 24 October 2000, disposed of all three applications (the case is reported as *Mainul Hosein & others v Sheikh Hasina*, 53 DLR (2001) 138) with a note that *'the Hon'ble Prime Minister shall be more careful and respectful in making any statement or comment with regard to the Judiciary or the judges or the Courts of Bangladesh in future'*. 53 DLR ((2001) 138, at p. 142, para. 10.) In doing so, he noted that the Court was taking into consideration: a) the greater interest of the country; b) protection of the prestige and dignity of the executive; and c) avoidance of any possible political unrest over a sensitive issue. He further stressed the necessity to prevent confrontation between the executive and the judiciary, and to maintain and preserve harmonious coordination and cooperation between these two important organs of the State.

References

(2015) Chapter 3: Removal from office, *Commonwealth Law Bulletin 41*(4), 524.

African Charter on Human and Peoples' Rights. (1981). OAU Doc CAB/LEG/67/3 21 (27 June 1981).

Agresto, J. (1984). *The supreme court and constitutional democracy* (p. 25). Cornell University Press.

American Convention on Human Rights. (1969). 1144 UNTS 123 (22 November 1969).

Amnesty International. (2008). *Denying the Undeniable: Enforced disappearances in Pakistan'*. Available at https://www.amnesty.org/download/Documents/ASA330182008ENGLISH.pdf

Austin, G. (2003). *Working a democratic constitution: A history of the Indian experience* (pp. 319–325). Oxford University Press.

Bacon, F. (1612). *Essay on judicature.*

Baderin, M. A., & Ssenyonjo, M. (2016). Development of international human rights law before and after the UDHR. In M. Ssenyonjo (Ed.), *International human rights law: Six decades after the UDHR and beyond* (p. 3). Routledge.

Bari, M. E. (2014). The natural death of the supreme judicial commission of Bangladesh & the consequent patronage appointments to the bench: Advocating the establishment of an independent judicial commission. *International Review of Law, 1*, 15.

Bari, M. E. (1993). Importance of an independent judiciary. *Dhaka University Studies Part-F, 4*, 10.

Bari, M. E. (2016). Supersession of the senior-most judges in Bangladesh in appointing the chief justice and the other judges of the appellate division of the supreme court: A convenient means to a politicized bench. *San Diego International Law Journal, 18*(1), 51.

Bari, M.E. (2017). *States of emergency and the law: The experience of Bangladesh* (pp. 38, 39–56). Routledge.

Bari, M. E. (2018). The incorporation of the system of non-party caretaker government in the constitution of Bangladesh in 1996 as a means of strengthening democracy, its deletion in 2011 and the lapse of Bangladesh into tyranny following the non-participatory general election of 2014: A critical appraisal. *Transnational Law and Contemporary Problems, 28*(1), 68.

Bevir, M. (2010). *Democratic governance* (p. 163). Princeton University Press.

Bogdanor, V. (2009). *The new British constitution* (p. 67). Hart Publishing.

Boone, J. (2012). *Pakistan's Prime Minister Yosuf Raza Gilani disqualified by Supreme Court.* Available at https://www.theguardian.com/world/2012/jun/19/pakistan-prime-minister-yousuf-gilani-disqualified

Bryce, J. (1921). *Modern democracies* (Vol. II, pp. 384–385). The Macmillan Company.

Burger, W. (1972). *Address to the American Bar Association, San Francisco.* Reported in Vital Speeches cited in Kirby, J. (2005). *Independence of the legal profession: Global and regional challenges.* Presidents of Law Association in Asia Conference, . Available at http://www.hcourt.gov.au/speeches/kirbyj/kirbyj_20mar05.html

Campbell, E., & Lee, H. P. (2001). *The Australian judiciary* (p. 95). Cambridge University Press.

Convention for the Protection of Human Rights and Fundamental Freedoms. (1950). 213UNTS 221. Available at https://treaties.un.org/doc/Publication/UNTS/Volume%20213/volume-213-I-2889-English.pdf

Courts and Tribunals Judiciary. *History of the judiciary.* Available at https://www.judiciary.uk/about-the-judiciary/history-of-the-judiciary/

Dakolias, M., & Thachuk, K. (2000). Attacking corruption in the judiciary: A critical process in judicial reform. *Wisconsin International Law Journal, 18*, 361.

Dawson, R. M. (1954). *The government of Canada* (p. 486). University of Toronto Press.

Douglas, W. O. (1956). *From Marshal to Mukharjee: Studies in American and Indian constitutional law* (p. 345). Tagore Law Lectures.

Evans, S., & Williams, J. (2006). *Appointing Australian Judges: A new model* (pp. 21–22). Judicial Conference of Australia – Colloquium.

References

Frankfurter, F. (1957). The supreme court in the mirror of justice. *University of Pennsylvania Law Review, 105*, 796.

Friedland, M. L. (2001). Judicial independence and accountability in Canada. *Advocate, 59*, 861.

Gibbs, H. (1987). The appointment and removal of judges. *Federal Law Review, 17*, 142.

Green, G. (1985). The rationale and some aspects of judicial independence. *Australian Law Journal, 59*, 135.

Griffith, J. A. G. (1977). *The politics of the judiciary* (p. 29). Fontana.

Gul, A. (2017). *Pakistan Supreme Court disqualifies Sharif. In He steps down.* Available at https://www. voanews.com/east-asia-pacific/pakistan-supreme-court-disqualifies-sharif-he-steps-down

Hamilton, A. (1948). The Federalist No. 78. In A. Hamilton, J. Madison, & J. Jay (Eds.), *The federalist or the new constitution* (pp. 396–397). Basil BlackwelL.

International Bar Association. (1982). *Minimum Standards of Judicial Independence* (art. 1(b), (c)).

International Commission of Jurists. (1961). *African Conference on the Rule of Law* Art. III. Available at https://www.icj.org/wp-content/uploads/1961/06/Africa-African-Conference-Rule-of-Law-conference-report-1961-eng.pdf

International Congress of Jurists. (1959). *Report of Committee IV, The Judiciary and the Legal Profession under the Rule of Law, Clause I*. Available at https://www.icj.org/wp-content/uploads/1959/01/Rule-of-law-in-a-free-society-conference-report-1959-eng.pdf

International Covenant on Civil and Political Rights. (1966). UNTS 999 UNTS 171 (16 December 1971).

Iyer, V. R. K. (2003). *Judiciary: A reform agenda* (p. 278). Eastern Books.

Josan, H. K., & Shah, S. K. (2002). Internet monitoring of federal judges: Striking a balance between independence and accountability. *Hofstra Labour & Employment Law Journal, 20*, 175.

Karlan, P. S. (1999). Two concepts of judicial independence. *Southern California Law Review, 72*, 558.

Koshy, S., Ng, C. L. Y., Habib, S., Fung, C., Hock, T. E., & Teh, J. (2008). *Events that led to judicial crisis of, 88*. Available at https://www.thestar.com.my/news/nation/2008/04/18/events-that-led-to-judicial-crisis-of-88

Larkin, F. J. (1997). The variousness, virulence, and variety of threats to judicial independence. *Judges' Journal, 36*, 7.

Laski, H. J. (2015). *A grammar of politics* (p. 542). Routledge.

Lavarch, M. (1993). *Judicial appointments – Procedure and criteria*. Attorney General Department, Canberra.

Law Association for Asia and the Pacific (LAWASIA). (1995). *The Beijing statement of the principles of the independence of the judiciary in the LAWASIA Region* (art. 3 (a), 11, 36).

Law Commission of India. (1979). *Report on the method of appointment of judges*. Available at http://lawcommissionofindia.nic.in/51-100/report80.pdf

Lienhard, A. (2008). The Swiss federal supreme court: A constitutional assessment of control and management mechanisms. *International Journal of Court Administration, 1*, 2.

Maluka, Z. K. (2004). Reconstructing the constitution for a COAS president: Pakistan 1999–2002. In B. Craig (Ed.), *Pakistan on the brink: Politics, economics and society* (p. 55). Lexington Books.

Meeting of Commonwealth Law Ministers. (1996 April 15–19). Available at https://read.oecd-ilibrary.org/commonwealth/governance/1996-meeting-of-commonwealth-law-ministers-and-senior-officials/commonwealth-law-ministers-statement-on-prevention-of-corruption_9781848596054-18-en#page1

Ministry of Justice. (2007). *The Governance of Britain: judicial appointments* 5. Consultation Paper Code No CP 25/07.

Montreal Declaration. (1983). *Universal declaration on the independence of justice* (art. 2.02, 2.11, 2.41).

National Commission to Review the Working of the Indian Constitution. (2001). *A consultation paper on superior judiciary*. Available at https://legalaffairs.gov.in/sites/default/files/(XII)Superior%20Judiciary.pdf

56 2 The Principle of Judicial Independence and Its Recognition in the Constitution...

Paul, R. (2013). *Fifth V.M. Tarkunde Lecture*. In S. Paul (Ed.), *Choosing hammurabi: Debates on judicial appointments*. Lexis Nexis.

Quoted in Sturgess, G. & Chubb, P. (1988). *Judging the world: Law and politics in the world's leading courts* (p. 149). Butterworths.

Rajagopalan, S. (2018). *The elephant in the courtroom*. Available at https://www.livemint.com/Opinion/tWZ7dVM2608hVfdOyvjP0J/The-elephant-in-the-courtroom.html

Ramkrishnaiah, D. (2015). *Rend the veil of secrecy*. Available at https://indianexpress.com/article/opinion/columns/rend-the-veil-of-secrecy/

Ratcliffe, S. (2016). *Oxford essential quotations* (4th ed.), https://www.oxfordreference.com/view/10.1093/acref/9780191826719.001.0001/q-oro-ed4-00003551

Roosevelt, F. (1937). *Fireside chat*. Available at http://www.presidency.ucsb.edu/ws/?pid.15381

Sackville, R. (2005). Judicial appointments: A discussion paper. *Journal of Judicial Administration, 14*, 133.

Sackville, R. (2006). The judicial appointments process in Australia: Towards independence and accountability. *Journal of Judicial Administration, 128*, 130.

Singh, Aditi. (2018). *Justice Jasti Chelameswar's lasting legacy striking a note of dissent.*. Available at https://www.livemint.com/Politics/DsUXbu4j6FWeYzZMnD7SAM/Justice-Jasti-Chelameswars-lasting-legacy-striking-a-note.html

Smit, J. V. Z. (2015). *The appointment, tenure and removal of judges under commonwealth principles: A compendium and analysis of best practice* (p. 79). Bingham Centre for the Rule of Law.

Stephen, N. (1985). Judicial independence- A Fragile Baston. In S. Shetreet & J. Deschenes (Eds.), *Judicial independence: The contemporary debate* (p. 531). Martinus Nijhoff.

Taipale, E. -J.. (1980). Judicial independence from the lawyer's point of view. In *Report of the symposium on the independence of judges and lawyers* (p. 118).

Tew, Y. (2016). On the uneven journey to constitutional redemption: The Malaysian judiciary and constitutional politics. *Washington International Law Journal, 25*, 679.

The Commonwealth Latimer House Guidelines. (1998). *Independence of judiciary art*. II.

UN Special Rapporteur on the Independence of Judges and Lawyers. (2004). *Civil and political rights, including the questions of independence of the judiciary, administration of justice, impunity* [28]. E/CN.4/2004/60 (31 December 2003). Available at https://documents-dds-ny.un.org/doc/UNDOC/GEN/G04/100/26/PDF/G0410026.pdf?OpenElement

UN Transparency Joint Initiative. (2002). *Bangalore principles of judicial conduct*. Available at https://www.unodc.org/pdf/crime/corruption/judicial_group/Bangalore_principles.pdf

United Nations. (1985). *Basic principles on the independence of the judiciary article 1*. GA/RES/40/32 & GA/RES/40/146 (29 November & 13 December 1985). Available at https://www.ohchr.org/EN/ProfessionalInterest/Pages/IndependenceJudiciary.aspx

Universal Declaration of Human Rights. (1948). GA Res 217A (III), UN Doc A/810 at 71(10 December 1948). Available at http://hrlibrary.umn.edu/instree/b1udhr.htm

Venkatesan, V. (2003). *Judiciary: A flawed mechanism*. Available at https://frontline.thehindu.com/the-nation/article30217285.ece

Chapter 3
The Method of Appointment of the Judges of the Supreme Court Under the Constitution of Bangladesh, 1972

3.1 Introduction

It may be recalled from the discussion in Sect. 2.3 that the method of appointment of judges is one of the crucial factors for safeguarding their independence. For a suitable method of appointment goes a long way in securing the appointment of fair judges, who, in the words of Socrates, are required to do four things, namely "to hear courteously, to answer wisely, to consider soberly, and to decide impartially".[1] An erroneous appointment of an individual of doubtful competence as a judge on the basis of political or personal favouritism is bound to produce irreparable damage not only to the fair administration of justice, but also to the public's faith in the administration of justice. Accordingly, Justice Pandian of the Indian Supreme Court rightly observed in *Supreme Court Advocates-on-Record Association v. Union of India*,[2] that if the appointee "bears a particular stamp for the purpose of changing the cause of decisions bowing to the diktat of his appointing authority then the independence of the judiciary cannot be secured".[3] Thus, governments have the utmost duty to ensure that individuals of the highest calibre are appointed as judges of the superior courts.

It might be recalled from the discussion in Sect. 2.4.1 that the method of appointing judges of the superior courts by the head of the state, is most commonly followed in common law countries. As a common law country, Bangladesh has also adopted the constitutional method of investing the head of the state with the responsibility to appoint the judges of the highest court of law, namely the Supreme Court (SC), which is composed of two divisions—the Appellate Division (AD) and the

---

[1] Dictionary of Familiar Quotations (1988), p. 75; David (2013), p. 871.

[2] *Supreme Court Advocates-on-Record Association v. Union of India* (1993) 4 SCC 441.

[3] Ibid. p. 525.

© The Author(s), under exclusive license to Springer Nature Singapore Pte Ltd. 2022
M. E. Bari, *The Independence of the Judiciary in Bangladesh*,
https://doi.org/10.1007/978-981-16-6222-5_3

High Court Division (HCD).[4] The Constitution of Bangladesh, 1972, contains provisions concerning the appointment of three kinds of judges of the superior courts, namely, the Chief Justice of Bangladesh, the judges of the AD and the HCD. This Chapter will first examine the provisions of the Constitution relating to the appointment of the Chief Justice of Bangladesh and the judges of the AD. Second, the constitutional provisions concerning the appointment of the regular as well as the additional judges of the HCD will be discussed. Third, it will be shown that the Constitution originally imposed an obligation on the President—the ceremonial head of state—to consult the Chief Justice in appointing the judges of the SC. This obligation to consult the Chief Justice, however, was first dispensed with by the Constitution (Fourth Amendment) Act, 1975 so as to invest the executive with unfettered discretion in the process of appointing judges. Although this constitutional obligation to consult the Chief Justice was restored in May 1976 for a year and a half, it remained suspended for nearly 34 years from November 1977 till July 2011. Furthermore, the judiciary's interpretation of the President's obligation to consult the Chief Justice will also be discussed. Finally, this chapter will shine light on the establishment in March 2008 of the Supreme Judicial Commission (now defunct) to recommend suitable candidates to the executive for appointment as judges of the HCD and the AD.

3.2   The Appointment of the Chief Justice of Bangladesh

Before discussing the method of appointing the Chief Justice of Bangladesh, it is apposite to discuss, in the first place, the manner in which the Chief Justice of the highest court is appointed in different countries of the world. The methods followed in various jurisdictions for appointing the Chief Justice can be grouped into the following four categories:

1. Appointment by the head of the state:

    (a) unilaterally as in Ireland, Kenya, Sri Lanka, and Sudan[5];
    (b) on the advice of the Prime Minister, as in Malta and Western Samoa[6];

---

[4] Constitution of Bangladesh, 1972 (Bangladesh) art. 9(1).

[5] BUNREACHT NA HÉIREANN [Irish Constitution], 1937 (Ireland) art. 35(1) ("The Judges of the Supreme Court shall be appointed by the President."); Constitution of Kenya, 2010 (Kenya) art. 166(1)(a) ("The President shall appoint-the Chief Justice … in accordance with the recommendation of the Judicial Service Commission…"); Constitution of the Democratic Socialist Republic of Sri Lanka, 1978 (Sri Lanka) art. 107(1) ("The Chief Justice …*[shall, subject to the provisions of Article 41C, be appointed by the President by warrant under his hand]."); Constitution of the Republic of Sudan, 1998 (Sudan) art. 104(1) ("The President of the Republic shall appoint the Chief Justice and his deputies according to the law").

[6] Constitution of Malta, 1964 (Malta) art. 95(6) ("The judges of the Superior Courts shall be a Chief Justice and such number of other judges…") art. 96(1) ("The judges of the Superior Courts shall be appointed by the President acting in accordance with the advice of the Prime Minister.");

3.2 The Appointment of the Chief Justice of Bangladesh

(c) on the advice of the Prime Minister after consultation with the Attorney General or the leader of the opposition, as in Fiji, and Trinidad and Tobago, respectively[7];

(d) on the advice of the Prime Minister after consulting the Conference of Rulers, as in Malaysia[8];

(e) on the advice of the Cabinet, as in Greece[9];

(f) with the consent of the Parliament, as in South Korea and Puerto Rico[10];

(g) on obtaining the agreement of the leader of the opposition, often called the "Minority Leader," as in Guyana[11];

(h) on the proposal or recommendation of, or in consultation with, an independent selection body such as judicial council or national judicial commission or judicial service commission/constitutional council or high council of justice, as in Armenia, Poland, Saudi Arabia, Spain, Namibia, Nepal, and Nigeria[12];

Constitution of the Independent State of Western Samoa, 1960 (West Samoa) art. 65(2) ("The Chief Justice of the Supreme Court shall be appointed by the Head of State, acting on the advice of the Prime Minister.")

[7] Constitution of the Republic of Fiji, 2013 (Fiji) arts. 98, 106 ("The Supreme Court consists of the Chief Justice, who is the President of the Supreme Court—The Chief Justice is appointed by the President on the advice of the Prime Minister following consultation by the Prime Minister with the Attorney-General."); Constitution Of The Republic Of Trinidad And Tobago, 1976 (Trinidad and Tobago) art. 102 ("The Chief Justice shall be appointed by the President after consultation with the Prime Minister and the Leader of the Opposition.")

[8] See Laws of Malaysia Federal Constitution, 1957 (Malaysia) art. 122B (incorporating all amendments up to 2006) (stating that the Chief Justice of the Federal Court shall be appointed by the Head of the State acting on the advice of the Prime Minister, after consulting the Conference of Rulers.)

[9] 1975 SYNTAGMA [SYN.] [Constitution] 90(5) (Greece) ("Promotion to the post of President or Vice President of the Supreme Administrative Court, of the Supreme Civil and Criminal Court and of the Court of Audit shall be effected by presidential decree issued on the proposal of the Cabinet, by selection from among the among the members of the respective supreme court, as specified by law.")

[10] 1948 DAEHANMINKUK HUNBEOB [HUNBEOB] [Constitution], 1948 (S. Korea) art. 104(1) ("The Chief Justice of the Supreme Court is appointed by the President with the consent of the National Assembly."); Puerto Rico Constitution, 1952 (Puerto Rico) art. V, § 8 ("Justices of the Supreme Court shall not assume office until after confirmation by the Senate and shall hold their offices during good behaviour.")

[11] Constitution of the Co-Operative Republic of Guyana, 1980 (Guyana) art. 127(1) ("[T]he Chief Justice shall be appointed by the President acting after the consultation with the Minority Leader.")

[12] See Constitution of The Republic of Armenia 1995 (Armenia) art. 95, § 3. (providing that the President of the Court of Appeals shall be appointed on the proposal of the Judicial Council); KONSTYTUCJA RZECZYPOSPOLITEJ POLSKIEJ Z DNIA 2 KWIETNIA, [Constitution of the Republic of Poland], 1997 (Poland) art. 144, sec. 3(1) ("The First President of the Supreme Court shall be appointed by the President of the Republic from a2mongst candidates proposed by the General Assembly of the Judges of the Supreme Court"); See Basic Law of the Government, 1992 (Saudi Arabia) art. 52 (Saudi Arabia) (stipulating that the appointment of judges, including the Chief Justice, by Royal Decree upon a proposal from the Higher Council of Justice); See CONSTITUCIÓN ESPAÑOLA, *Boletín Oficial del Estado*, n.123(2), 1978 (Spain) (providing that

60   3   The Method of Appointment of the Judges of the Supreme Court...

   (i) in consultation with the senior judges of the superior courts, as in India.[13]

2. Appointment by the parliament upon proposal or nomination or recommendation by the head of the state, as in Croatia, Ethiopia, and Russia[14];
3. Election of the Chief Justice by the judges of the Supreme Court, as in Belgium,
   Denmark, and Ukraine[15];
4. Election of the Chief Justice by the parliament upon nomination or proposal or
   recommendation by the head of the state, as in Georgia, Hungary, Rwanda,
   Serbia, and Montenegro.[16]

---

the President of the Supreme Court shall be appointed by the King at the proposal of the General
Council of the judicial branch); See Constitution of the Republic of Namibia, 1990 (Namibia) art.
82(1) (stating that the appointment of the Judge-President of the High Court shall be "made by the
President on recommendation of the Judicial Service Commission."); *see* NĒPĀLAKŌ
SANVIDHĀNA [Constitution of Nepal], 2015 (Nepal) art. 129(2) (providing that the President
shall appoint the Chief Justice of Nepal on the recommendation of the Constitutional Council);
Constitution of Nigeria, 1999 (Nigeria) art. 231(1) ("The appointment of a person to the office of
Chief Justice of Nigeria shall be made by the President on the recommendation of the National
Judicial Council subject to confirmation of such appointment by the Senate.")

[13] *See* Constitution of India, 1950 (India) art 124(2) (providing that every judge of the Supreme
Court shall be appointed by the President after consultation with "Judges of the Supreme Court and
of the High Court in the States as the President may deem necessary for the purpose").

[14] *See* USTAV REPUBLIKE HRVATSKE [Constitution of the Republic Of Croatia], 1990 (Croatia)
art. 119 (amended 2010) (providing that the Chief Justice of the Supreme Court shall be "appointed
by the Croatian Parliament at the proposal of the President of the Republic with a prior opinion of
the general session of the Supreme Court of the Republic of Croatia and of the authorized committee of the Croatian Parliament."); Constitution of Ethiopia, 1995 (Ethiopia) art. 81(1) ("The
President and Vice-President of the Federal Supreme Court shall, upon recommendation by the
Prime Minister, be appointed by the House of Peoples' Representatives."); *see* KONSTITUTSIIA
ROSSIISKOI FEDERATSII [KONST. RF], 1993 (Russia) art. 128, § 1 (stipulating that the judges
of the Supreme Court of the Russia Federation shall be appointed by the Federal Council following
nomination by the President of the Russian Federation); DRUK-GI CHA-THRIMS-CHEN-MO,
2008 (Bhutan) art. 21(4) ("The Chief Justice of Bhutan shall be appointed from among the Judges
of the Supreme Court or from among eminent jurists in consultation with the National Judicial
Commission."); South African Constitution, 1996 (SA) art. 174(3) (stating that the President, after
consulting the Judicial Service Commission, appoint the Chief Justice of the Supreme Court of
Appeal.)

[15] *See* Constitution of Belgium, 1994 (Belgium) art. 151, § 5 (providing that the Court of Cassation
and the High Courts' choose within themselves their Presidents and Vice-Presidents);
GRUNDLOVEN [Constitution Of Denmark], 1953 (Denmark) LOV NR. 59(2) ("The High Court
of the Realm shall elect a President from among its members."); *See* КОНСТИТУЦІЯ УКРАЇНИ
[Constitution of Ukraine], 2004 (Ukraine) art. 128 (stating that the Chairman of the Supreme Court
of Ukraine is elected to office by the Plenary Assembly of the Supreme Court of Ukraine by secret
ballot.)

[16] See SAKARTVELOS K'ONSTITUTSIA [Constitution of Georgia], 1995 (Georgia) art. 90(2)
(providing that the President of the Supreme Court of Georgia shall be elected by the Parliament
by the majority of the number of the members of Parliament on the current nominal list upon the
submission of the President of Georgia); *see* A MAGYAR KÖZTÁRSASÁG ALKOTMÁNYA
[Constitution of the Republic of Hungary], 2011 (Hungary) art. 24(8) (stating that the Parliament
shall elect the President of the Supreme Court based on the recommendation and vote made by the
President of the Republic); Constitution of the Republic of Rwanda, 2003 (Rwanda) art. 147 ("The

3.2 The Appointment of the Chief Justice of Bangladesh

Therefore, it is evident that there are four broad modalities prevalent in different jurisdictions for appointing the Chief Justice. A large number of countries have adopted the specific method of appointment of the Chief Justice by the head of the state on the basis of proposal or recommendation of or in consultation with an independent judicial or advisory body. This method is followed by the procedure to appoint the Chief Justice by the head of the state on the advice of the prime minister or cabinet or on the agreement of the leader of the opposition. Since the Chief Justice symbolises and epitomises the independence of the judiciary, his appointment cannot be left to the exclusive discretion of the executive, as doing so would pave the way for the intrusion of political considerations into the process. Accordingly, only a handful of countries, namely Ireland, Kenya, Sri Lanka, and Sudan, have bestowed upon the head of the state the exclusive power to appoint the head of the judiciary.

In Bangladesh, the Chief Justice, designated by the Constitution as "the Chief Justice of Bangladesh,"[17] is the head of the Bangladeshi Judiciary and the paterfamilias of the judicial fraternity. The office of Chief Justice is, therefore, the most dignified and exalted post in the judiciary of Bangladesh, being ranked fourth in the Warrant of Precedence.[18]

Arguably, the appointment of the Chief Justice is of critical importance in the administration of justice for retaining public confidence in the impartiality, credibility, and reliability of the highest court of the land. The citizens of the country must be assured that the Chief Justice is not appointed because he shares the political and social philosophy of the party in power, as the Chief Justice is also required to adjudicate the lawfulness of the actions of the executive. This, therefore, necessitates a mechanism, independent of government control, for the appointment of the Chief Justice, that takes into account well-defined objective criteria. As to the importance of the selection and appointment of the Chief Justice for ensuring the independence of the judiciary, the observations of Justice Saiduzzaman Siddiqui, made in *Asad Ali v. Federation of Pakistan*[19] are noteworthy:

> The selection of a person to the high office of the Chief Justice ... is a pivotal appointment for maintaining the independence of judiciary and for providing a free and unobstructed access to impartial and independent Courts/Tribunals to the ordinary citizens ... guaranteed under ... the Constitution.[20]

President of the Supreme Court is elected by the Senate ... from two candidates in respect of each post proposed by the President of the Republic after consultation with the cabinet and the Supreme Council of the Judiciary); See USTAV REPUBLIKE SRBIJE [Constitution of Serbia], 2006 (Serbia) art. 73(10) (stipulating that the National Assembly shall elect the president of the Supreme Court); see Constitution of Montenegro, 2006 (Montenegro) art. 124 (stating that the President of the Supreme Court shall by elected and dismissed from duty by the Parliament at the joint proposal of the President of Montenegro, the speaker of the Parliament and the Prime Minister.)

[17] Constitution of Bangladesh, 1972 (Bangladesh) art. 94(2).

[18] BANGLAPEDIA (2015), http://en.banglapedia.org/index.php?title=Warrant_of_Precedence

[19] *Malik Asad Ali v. Federation of Pakistan*, (1998) 50 PLD (SC) 161.

[20] *Malik Asad Ali v. Federation of Pakistan*, (1998) 50 PLD (SC) 161, 189.

These realities were indeed ignored and disregarded in 1972 when the Constitution of Bangladesh in Article 95(1) provided that "[t]he Chief Justice shall be appointed by the President". Thus, the power to appoint the Chief Justice was an executive power vested in the President, who, as the constitutional head, was duty-bound to exercise this power under Article 48(3) "in accordance with the advice of the Prime Minister". Later, however, the Constitution (Twelfth Amendment) Act of 1991 freed the President from the obligation to consult the Prime Minister in appointing the Chief Justice of Bangladesh.[21]

Consequently, the President of Bangladesh is given a blank cheque of unfettered discretion to appoint the Chief Justice of Bangladesh. This discretion ignores the benefit of shared responsibility: responsibility preferably shared between the President and a selection committee consisting of majority members from the superior judiciary, in order to prevent a politically motivated appointment for improper motives.

It is noteworthy that there are no specific qualifications listed in the Constitution for the appointment of the Chief Justice. Therefore, the qualifications laid down in the Constitution for the appointment of judges of the HCD and the AD of the SC are equally applicable in case of appointment of the Chief Justice of Bangladesh. As to the criteria for selecting the judges of SC, the Constitution originally provided:

(2) A person shall not be qualified for appointment as a judge unless he is a citizen of Bangladesh and–
a) has for not less than ten years been an advocate of the Supreme Court; or
b) has, for not less than ten years, held judicial office or an advocate in the territory of Bangladesh and has, for not less than three years, exercised the power of a District Judge.[22]

The Constitution, thus, provided for the appointment of judges to the SC both from the bench and the bar. Under the original provision, only a citizen of Bangladesh, not a foreigner, could be appointed as a judge of the SC, provided he fulfilled one of the three qualifications mentioned above.

Ordinarily, an advocate who has practised before the subordinate courts in Bangladesh for a period of 2 years may be enrolled as an Advocate of the SC[23] and would, subsequently, be eligible for appointment as a judge of the SC after practicing before the Court for a period of not less than 10 years. In 1977, the provisions for appointing an advocate having the experience of practising before the subordinate courts for not less than 10 years and of exercising the powers of a district judge for not less than 3 years, was done away with by an amendment to the Constitution.[24] Furthermore, that same amendment replaced the requirement of acting as a district judge with the stipulation of serving as a judicial officer for at least 10 years for

---

[21] Constitution of Bangladesh, 1972 (Bangladesh) art 48(3) ("In exercise of all his functions, save only that of appointing the Prime Minister pursuant to clause (3) of art. 56 and the Chief Justice pursuant to clause 1 of art. 95, the President shall act in accordance with the advice of the Prime Minister.")

[22] Constitution of Bangladesh, 1972 (Bangladesh) art 95(2).

[23] Bangladesh Legal Practitioners and Bar Council Order, 1972 (Bangladesh) art. 21(2).

[24] Second Proclamation Order No. I of 1977 (Bangladesh).

3.2 The Appointment of the Chief Justice of Bangladesh

appointment as a judge of the SC. Therefore, under the existing arrangement of the Constitution, an Advocate having 10 years standing practise before the SC or a judicial officer having not less than 10 years of experience shall be qualified for an appointment to the highest court of the nation.

It is noticeable that the Constitution does not prescribe any guidelines as to the academic qualification, legal knowledge, reputation, integrity or impartiality necessary for the selection of the advocates and judicial officers as judges of the SC. Consequently, any Advocate of the SC having no standing practise, e.g., someone who only kept his enrolment updated by paying the prescribed fees without going to the Court or those having no experience of handling crucial cases, but rather only moved simple matters like bail or stay petitions, can be appointed as a judge of the SC. In the same vein, the Constitution is silent as to the criteria, e.g., seniority, disposal of cases in an efficient manner, fairness and impartiality, maintenance of good relationship with colleagues and the bar, which should be kept in mind in appointing a judicial officer as a judge of the SC. Thus, any judge of a subordinate court who has served the court for at least 10 years without being appointed as a district judge—the head of a District Court—can theoretically be appointed as a judge of the SC.[25] However, no one below the rank of a district judge has so far been appointed as a judge of the SC.

In 1977, clause (c) was added to Article 95(2) of the Constitution empowering the Parliament to prescribe by law any other qualifications as alternatives to the 10-year requirement as a SC Advocate or a judicial officer for appointment as a judge of the SC.[26] However, no such law has, to date, been enacted.

It should be stressed here that in addition to providing for the appointment of a regular Chief Justice, the Constitution in Article 97 speaks of the appointment of an Acting Chief Justice as a stop-gap arrangement for a shorter period. Unlike the Constitution of India, 1950, which, in Article 126, has empowered the President to appoint any judge of the Supreme Court irrespective of seniority as acting Chief Justice "when the office of the Chief Justice of India is vacant" or when the Chief Justice is unable to perform his duties "by reason of absence or otherwise," the Constitution of Bangladesh in Article 97 unequivocally states that President should follow the mechanical rule of seniority in appointing the Acting Chief Justice of Bangladesh when a vacancy arises in the office or when the Chief Justice is unable to perform his functions due to absence, illness or any other cause. The expression "[i]f the office of the Chief Justice becomes vacant" used in Article 97 does not refer to the vacancy which occurs on account of the normal retirement of the incumbent Chief Justice, rather it refers only to the vacancy caused by sudden death, resignation, illness or any other unforeseen reasons. In the case of an unexpected vacancy, the Constitution of Bangladesh provides that the President will appointment an

---

[25] In this context, it is noteworthy that for the appointment of a district judge, a judicial officer requires at least 10 years of experience including 3 years' experience as a joint district judge or both as a joint district judge and additional district judge. See Bangladesh Civil Service Recruitment (1995 Amendment) Rules, 1981 Ordinance No. 087 (Bangladesh) pt. XXII.

[26] Second Proclamation Order No. I of 1977 (Bangladesh).

Acting Chief Justice from amongst the judges of the AD solely on the basis of seniority, which negates the possibility of a patronage appointment.

However, the Constitution, strikingly, does not contain any provision specifying that the senior-most judge of the AD shall receive appointment as the regular Chief Justice of Bangladesh. Such an omission stands in stark contrast to the constitutional arrangement in Pakistan. For the Constitution of Pakistan, 1973, as amended by the Constitution (Eighteenth Amendment Act), 2010, in Article 175A(3) stipulates that "the President shall appoint the most senior Judge of the Supreme Court as the Chief Justice of Pakistan," thereby precluding the possibility of appointing the head of the judiciary on political considerations. Consequently, in the absence of any such provision in the Constitution of Bangladesh, it can strongly be argued that any Advocate of the SC or any judicial officer having fulfilled the qualifications laid down in Article 95(2) of the Constitution can directly be appointed as the Chief Justice of Bangladesh.

Thus, the appointment of the Chief Justice has been left at the pleasure of the President, who is not supposed to know the judicial track record of the judges of the AD, e.g., their performance in handling and conducting cases including cases of constitutional importance, their keen intellect, legal acumen, integrity, and reputation. In fact, it is the Ministry of Law, Justice, and Parliamentary Affairs that initiates the proposal through the Prime Minister, recommending the senior-most judge of the AD for the appointment as the Chief Justice, whenever vacancy occurs in that office. The President ordinarily approves the proposal. It should be stressed here that the convention of appointing the senior-most judge of the AD as the Chief Justice was developed to obviate the possibility of extraneous considerations being taken into account in the pivotal appointment of the Chief Justice. According, this convention was consistently observed in Bangladesh until June 2003, with the exception of an abortive attempt made by the former President H M Ershad in January 1990.

After the retirement of Chief Justice Badrul Haider Chowdhury, President Ershad appointed the senior-most Judge of the AD, Justice Shahabuddin Ahmed, as the Acting Chief Justice under Article 97 of the Constitution, instead of appointing him as the regular Chief Justice.[27] This appointment evoked sharp reactions from the Supreme Court Bar Association (SCBA).[28] The SCBA demanded an immediate return to the tradition of appointing the senior most Judge of the AD to the office of the Chief Justice of Bangladesh.[29] After 13 days, Justice Shahabuddin Ahmed was appointed as the sixth regular Chief Justice of the country.[30]

The instances of violation of the convention of seniority in appointing the Chief Justice of Bangladesh since June 2003, will be discussed in detail in Chap. 4 of this Book.

---

[27] Bari (2016), p. 43.

[28] Ibid.

[29] Ibid.

[30] Ibid.

3.3 The Provisions of the Constitution of Bangladesh, 1972, Concerning the Appointment of Judges of the AD of the SC of Bangladesh

The AD is the higher division of the SC that hears and determines appeals against judgment, decrees, orders, and sentences of the HCD, the lower division of the Court.[31] The judges, along with the Chief Justice, appointed to the AD sit only in that division.[32] The Constitution invests the President of the country with the power of ascertaining the number of the judges of the SC on the advice of the Prime Minister.[33] Accordingly, the number of judges to be appointed in the AD was initially fixed at five, which was later in 2002 increased to seven during the regime of the BNP (2001–2006).[34] Finally, when the current government of the Bangladesh Awami League (BAL) came to power in January 2009, the then President Zillur Rahman increased the number of judges in the AD from seven to 11 in pursuance of Article 94(2) of the Constitution.[35] However, President Rahman did not specify any reasons for increasing the number of judges, such as the necessity of speedy disposition of cases in order to reduce backlog. Strikingly, there is also neither any provision in the Constitution of Bangladesh nor any constitutional convention requiring the President to consult the Chief Justice, who is the most competent and well-equipped person to articulate his objective opinion after discussing the matter with his colleagues, i.e., the senior-most judges of the Court, and after taking into account the number of cases pending before the AD, before raising the number of posts in the AD.

With regard to the appointment of the judges of the SC, Article 95(1) of the Constitution of Bangladesh provides that "[t]he ... judges [of the Supreme Court] shall be appointed by the President after consultation with the Chief Justice". After consulting the Chief Justice, the President is required under Article 48(3) of the Constitution to exercise his power of appointing judges of both the divisions of the SC in accordance with the advice of the Prime Minister. It is evident that this procedure resembles the British method of appointing judges of the higher judiciary which was prevalent until the enactment of the Constitutional Reforms Act, 2005 (CRA). As prior to the enactment of the CRA, the Prime Minister used to recommend names to the Crown for appointment as judges after consulting with the Lord Chancellor—then the head of the judiciary.[36]

It is noteworthy that in the Subcontinent, Bangladesh is not the first nation to have adopted the method of appointment of judges of superior courts after

---

[31] Constitution of Bangladesh, 1972 (Bangladesh) art. 103(1).

[32] Constitution of Bangladesh, 1972 (Bangladesh) art 94(3).

[33] Constitution of Bangladesh, 1972 (Bangladesh) art. 94(2) and 48(3).

[34] Bari (2014), p. 8.

[35] The Daily Star (2009), http://www.thedailystar.net/newDesign/news-details.php?nid=96998

[36] The Lord Chancellor used to sit as the Chief Justice in the Judicial Committee of the House of Lords.

consultation with the Chief Justice. Rather it is the Constitution of India of 1950, which, for the first time, provided for this stipulation. Article 124(2) of the Constitution provides that the President of India shall consult the Chief Justice along with "such of the Judges of the Supreme Court and of the High Court in the States as the President may deem necessary" in appointing the judges of the Supreme Court. Subsequently, the 1956 and 1962 Constitutions of Pakistan, which were abrogated in 1958 and 1969 respectively, adopted the Indian method by providing for the appointment of judges of the Supreme Court by the President after consultation with the Chief Justice, with the modification that the President was given the discretion to not consult such of the judges of the Supreme Court and of the High Courts in the States.[37]

This method of appointing judges of the SC in consultation with the Chief Justice, as incorporated into the Constitution of Bangladesh, is very much in line with the suggestion of the International Congress of Jurists, namely, that there should be "some degree of cooperation (or at least consultation) between the judiciary and the authority actually making the appointment".[38] Since the President, as a layman, can have no knowledge about the legal acumen, legal expertise, independence and firmness, ability to handle cases and personal conduct of advocates or subordinate judicial officers, the requirement of consulting the Chief Justice who would have expert knowledge about the ability, competency and suitability of an advocate or a judicial officer for judgeship, was originally provided for ensuring the selection of the most appropriate person for appointment. However, as will be made evident in the forthcoming discussion, this requirement remained deleted from the Constitution for 34 years until July 2011 for enabling the President to exercise unfettered discretion in appointing the judges of the highest court of law.

Apart from fulfilling the general qualification requirements as laid down in Article 95(2) of the Constitution, e.g., citizenship of Bangladesh and either experience as an Advocate of the SC for not less than 10 years or experience as a judicial officer for not less than 10 years as mentioned earlier in Sect. 3.2, there is no other pre-requisite provided for either by the Constitution or by any other law. Therefore, theoretically it is possible that any advocate or judicial officer, who fulfils the prescribed Constitutional requisites, can directly be appointed as a judge of the AD without being a judge of the HCD. But in practice, no such advocate or judicial officer, except HCD judges, has yet been appointed directly as a judge of the AD. Rather a convention has developed to provide flesh to clothe the dry bone of the Constitution to the effect that the appointment of judges to the AD shall be made

---

[37] Constitution of Pakistan, 1973 (Pakistan) art. 149, § 1 (1956) (provided that "the Chief Justice of Pakistan shall be appointed by the President and the other judges of the Supreme Court shall be appointed after consultation with the Chief Justice."); Article 50, § 1 of the Pakistan Constitution, like article 149 of the 1956 constitution, provided: "The Chief Justice of the Supreme Court shall be appointed by the President, and the other Judges shall be appointed by the President after consultation with the Chief Justice." PAKISTAN CONST. art. 50, § 1 (1962).

[38] International Congress of Jurists (1959), https://www.icj.org/wp-content/uploads/1959/01/Rule-of-law-in-a-free-society-conference-report-1959-eng.pdf

3.4 The Constitutional Provisions Concerning the Appointment of the Judges... 67

from amongst the judges of the HCD on the basis of seniority. The development of this convention was a safeguard against the possibility of intrusion of extraneous considerations in appointing the judges of the AD. However, this convention has also been transgressed at regular intervals by successive governments since 13 August 1976. Light will be shed on these instances of the contravention of the principle of seniority in appointing the judges of the AD in Chap. 4 of this Book.

3.4 The Constitutional Provisions Concerning the Appointment of the Judges of the HCD of the SC

The Constitution of Bangladesh, 1972 provides for the appointment of two types of judges, i.e., regular and additional judges, to the HCD—the lower division of the SC which has both original and appellate jurisdictions and powers. Since the coming into force of the Constitution in December 1972, judges have initially been appointed to the HCD as additional judges for a period of 2 years and have, subsequently, generally been appointed as regular judges.[39] Thus, additional judgeship has become a gateway for entering the cadre of permanent judgeship of the HCD. Since an additional judge is appointed initially for a period of 2 years, which can be extended for "a further period" and the judge concerned can be appointed as a regular judge, it cannot be said that he is appointed on probation for ascertaining "if he is fit to be a permanent judge."[40] For, unlike an employee on probation, whose employment can be terminated during the probationary period, the service of an additional judge cannot ordinarily be terminated before the expiration of his term.

It was the British Government in India, which governed the Indo-Pak-Bangladesh Subcontinent for nearly two hundred years until August 1947, which for the first time introduced the system of appointing additional judges to the High Courts in the Subcontinent under the Indian High Courts Act, 1911,[41] the Government of India Act, 1915,[42] and the Government of India Act, 1935.[43] Although the Constitution of

---

[39] Constitution of Bangladesh, 1972 (Bangladesh) art. 98.

[40] *S.P. Gupta v Union of India*, 1981 Supp SC 87 at 347 (as per Justice Gupta).

[41] Indian High Courts Act, 1911 (British India) s. 3 (empowered the Governor-General-in-Council to appoint from time-to-time persons to act as Additional Judges of any High Court for such period not exceeding 2 years as may be required.)

[42] Section 101 of the Government of India Act, 1915 (British India) Clause (i) of the proviso to subsection (2) (authorised the Governor-General-in-Council to appoint persons to act as additional judges of any High Court for such period not exceeding 2 years as may be required).

[43] Government of India Act, 1935 (British India) s. 222(3) (provided for the appointment of Additional Judges thus: "If by reason of any temporary increase in the business of any High Court or by reason of arrears of work in any such Court, it appears to the Governor-General that the number of the Judges of the Court should be for the time being increased, the Governor-General (in his discretion) may, subject to the foregoing provisions of this chapter with respect to the maximum number of Judges, appoint persons duly qualified for appointment as Judges of the Court for such period not exceeding 2 years as he may specify.")

India, 1950, did not originally contain any provision regarding the appointment of additional judges,[44] the Constitution (Seventh Amendment) Act, 1956 incorporated into the Constitution the provisions concerning the appointment of such judges.[45] However, when Pakistan enacted its first Constitution in 1956, there was no provision concerning appointment of additional judges to the High Courts and, as such, judges of the High Courts were appointed permanently. But the provisions providing for the appointment of additional judges even against permanent vacancies were incorporated in the second Constitution of Pakistan, which was enacted in 1962 and, subsequently, found a way in the nation's current Constitution, which was enacted in 1973.[46]

It may be recalled here that Article 95(1) of the Constitution of Bangladesh, 1972 provides that the judges of the SC "shall be appointed by the President after consultation with the Chief Justice". Thus Article 95(1) deals with the appointment of regular judges to both the HCD and the AD of the SC after consultation between two very high dignitaries, namely, the President and the Chief Justice of Bangladesh. On the other hand, Article 98 of the Constitution deals with the appointment of the additional judges to the HCD and *ad hoc* judges to the AD of the SC. As Article 98 provides:

> Notwithstanding the provisions of Article 94, if the President is satisfied that the number of the judges of a division of the Supreme Court should be for the time being increased, the President may appoint one or more duly qualified persons to be additional judges of that division for such period not exceeding two years as he may specify, or if he thinks fit, may require a judge of the High Court Division to sit in the Appellate Division for any temporary period:

> Provided that nothing in this article shall prevent a person appointed as an additional judge from being appointed as a judge under article 95 or as an additional judge for a further period under this article.

Thus, unlike the Indian Constitution, as amended in 1956, which provides for two specified situations, namely, temporary increase either in the business of a High

---

[44] The Constitution of India did not originally provide for the appointment of additional judges due to the apprehension that such judges on their return to the Bar, upon expiration of their term, would be given "a pre-eminence over their colleagues and embarrass[...] the subordinate Judges who were at one time under their control and thus instead of helping justice they [would] act as a hindrance to free justice." See *S.P. Gupta v Union of India* 1981 Supp SCC 87 at 235.

[45] Constitution (Seventh Amendment) Act, 1956 (India) amended Constitution of India's article 224 (substituted) provides that "(1) If by reason of any temporary increase in the business of a High Court or by reason of arrears of work therein, it appears to the President that the number of the judges of that Court should be for the time being increased, the President may appoint duly qualified persons to be Additional Judges of the Court for such period not exceeding 2 years as he may specify."

[46] Constitution of Pakistan, 1962 (Pakistan) art. 96 provided that an additional Judge could be appointed against a permanent vacancy or when a High Court Judge was absent or was unable to perform the functions of his office due to any other cause or for any reason it is necessary to increase the number of judges of a High Court for a period not exceeding 2 years. These provisions have been reproduced in Article 197 of the 1973 Constitution of Pakistan.

3.4 The Constitutional Provisions Concerning the Appointment of the Judges... 69

Court or in arrears of work therein, in which the President can exercise the power of appointing additional judges,[47] the Constitution of Bangladesh does not spell out any specific reason for the appointment of additional judges to the HCD of the SC. Rather it has left the matter of increasing the number of judges to the subjective satisfaction of the President, which in turn leaves the door wide open for him to increase the number for packing the HCD with judges who share the same political ideology.

The words "for the time being", as used in Article 98 of the Constitution of Bangladesh, clearly indicate that the appointment of additional judges to the HCD by increasing the number of posts, would be for a short period or to deal with a temporary situation. However, the provision contained in proviso to Article 98 for appointment of an additional judge as a regular judge or his extension "for a further period," may generate the legitimate expectation that he would not have to go back to the bar on the expiration of his term. Rather he would either get appointment as a permanent judge or reappointed as an additional judge for a further period. However, it should be mentioned here that successive governments have honoured, save in rare cases, the expectations they have generated in the minds of additional judges.

It should be stressed here that the qualification required for appointment as both permanent and additional judges of the HCD, as mentioned earlier, are the same and their status, with the exception that an additional judge can only hold office for the period specified in the warrant of his appointment, as well as functions are the same. Consequently, it seems unjustified to continue the practice of treating Article 98 as a gateway through which every HCD judge is required to pass before being appointed as a permanent judge. An additional judge appointed for 2 years would constantly be worried about being reappointed either "for a further period" or on a permanent basis, and would, consequently, be more inclined towards favouring the executive in cases where the latter is a party. Accordingly, the Montreal Declaration on the Independence of Justice, 1983, states that the system of appointment of additional judges "is inconsistent with judicial independence" and, as such, calls for such appointments to be gradually phased out.[48]

---

[47] Constitution of India, 1950 amended Article 224 (substituted) provides that '(1) If by reason of any temporary increase in the business of a High Court or by reason of arrears of work therein, it appears to the President that the number of the judges of that Court should be for the time being increased, the President may appoint duly qualified persons to be Additional Judges of the Court for such period not exceeding 2 years as he may specify.'

[48] Montreal Declaration (1983), art. 2.20.

3.5 Dispensation of the Constitutional Requirement of "Consultation with Chief Justice" in the Appointment of Judges of the SC

It should be stressed that the Constitution of Bangladesh originally stipulated not only in Article 95(1) but also in Article 98 the requirement of consultation with the Chief Justice of Bangladesh by the President as an imperative necessity in the matter of appointment of judges to the SC. For the Chief Justice is best suited and equipped to select the most suitable amongst the available candidates for appointment as judges of the SC by objectively assessing their legal expertise, soundness, legal experience, professional attainment, ability to handle cases, ability to analyse and articulate, personal integrity, judicial temperament and firmness.

It should be noted here that during the British rule in the Indian Subcontinent, there was no specific provision in any law obligating the Crown to consult the Chief Justice in appointing judges of the Federal Court and the High Courts and as such, the Crown had absolute discretion in the matter. This practice of vesting unfettered discretion in the hands of the Crown to appoint judges in British India stood in stark contrast to the practice prevalent at the time in the UK, as pointed earlier in Sect. 3.3, of appointing judges in consultation with the head of the judiciary—the Lord Chancellor. Accordingly, when India secured its independence from British rule, it adopted, as pointed earlier in Sects. 2.4.1 and 3.3, a constitutional scheme of appointing judges of the superior courts by the executive after consultation with the constitutional functionaries, including the Chief Justice of India, who are best placed to give expert opinion on the suitability of candidates. Furthermore, Indian Supreme Court has, as discussed earlier in Sect. 2.4.1, held that the opinion of the Chief Justice should be given primacy over that of the executive in the matter of appointment of judges. However, unlike the Constitution of India, the 1972 Constitution of Bangladesh only placed an obligation on the President to consult one constitutional functionary, namely, the Chief Justice of Bangladesh, in appointing the judges of both the HCD and the AD. But it neither accorded primacy to the views of the Chief Justice of Bangladesh nor were his views made binding on the executive.

Notwithstanding the beneficial impact of the constitutional provision requiring the President to consult the Chief Justice before appointing the judges of the SC, this requirement remained deleted from the Constitution for nearly 34 years. An attempt will now be made to shed light on some of the key developments during this period.

3.5.1 Deletion of the Constitutional Requirement of Consultation with the Chief Justice by the Constitution (Fourth Amendment) Act, 1975

The Constitution (Fourth Amendment) Act, which was passed by the Parliament on 25 January 1975 during the tenure of the first elected government of the Awami League (1973–1975), is considered as the most far-reaching amendment to the Constitution of Bangladesh.[49] For it diminished the liberal character of the Constitution to cement then Prime Minister Sheikh Mujibur Rahman's grip on power. To this end, the Fourth Amendment, *inter alia,*

(a) replaced parliamentary democracy with a presidential form of government[50] modelled on the American pattern without, however, the checks and balances underpinning that system;

(b) proclaimed that Prime Minister Sheikh Mujibur Rahman (hereafter Mujib) had ascended to the office of the "President of Bangladesh as if [he was] elected to that office under the Constitution as amended by this Act [the Constitution (Fourth Amendment) Act]"[51];

(c) concentrated virtually all the powers of the Republic in the hands of the President, including the power to withhold assent to a bill passed by the Parliament[52] and to declare Bangladesh a one-party State[53]—a power which was exercised on 25 February 1975 to transform Bangladesh into a one-party dictatorship[54]; and

(d) invested the President with the unilateral and absolute power to appoint and remove the judges of the SC.[55]

In an attempt to confer unfettered power on the President to appoint both permanent and additional judges of the SC, the Fourth Amendment dispensed with the former's obligation to consult the Chief Justice before making such appointments under Articles 95(1) and 98 of the Constitution. Thus, this amended method of appointing judges was identical to the method of appointment of the judges of the Federal Court prevalent during the British rule in India as provided for by the Government of India Act, 1935. As the Government of India Act, 1935 provided: "every Judge of the Federal Court shall be appointed by His Majesty by warrant under the Royal Sign Manual."[56] Thus, like the Crown during the British rule in India, the President

---

[49] Bari (2017), pp. 173–175.

[50] Constitution (Fourth Amendment) Act, 1975 (Bangladesh) s. 4.

[51] Constitution (Fourth Amendment) Act, 1975 (Bangladesh) s. 35.

[52] Constitution (Fourth Amendment) Act, 1975 (Bangladesh) s. 12.

[53] Constitution (Fourth Amendment) Act, 1975 (Bangladesh) s. 23.

[54] See above n 49, p. 176.

[55] Constitution (Fourth Amendment) Act, 1975 (Bangladesh) s. 15.

[56] Government of India Act, 1935 (India) s. 200(2),

of Bangladesh was given the unconstrained power to make judicial appointments. As to the implication of this sort of arrangement, Dr. BR Ambedkar said in the Indian Constituent Assembly: "[it is] dangerous to leave the appointments to be made by the President, without any kind of reservation or limitation, that is to say, merely on the advice of the executive of the day."[57] For the President cannot generally be expected to be aware of the judicial qualities of the candidates nor can it be guaranteed that political or personal favouritism will not motivate his judgment while making the appointments.

Thus, the abolition of constitutional requirement of consultation with the Chief Justice arguably left the door too wide-open for President Mujib to appoint judges on extraneous considerations. Since he could not be expected to have the knowledge about the candidates' legal acumen and suitability for appointment to the superior courts, he was more likely to measure their fitness in terms of political allegiance rather than judicial qualities. This apprehension gained further momentum after he declared Bangladesh to be a one-party party state on 25 February 1975. These developments had the disastrous impact of resulting in the appointment of obedient and spineless judges, which is the antithesis of the concept of an independent judiciary, as epitomised in the Constitution of Bangladesh as a fundamental characteristic, thus: "the Chief Justice and the other judges shall be independent in the exercise of their judicial functions."[58] In this context, the observations of Justice Md Joynal Abedin in *Bangladesh and Justice Syed Md Dastagir Hossain and others v. Md Idrisur Rahman*[59] are noteworthy:

> Since the fourth amendment of the Constitution, amongst others, affected one of the basic structures of the Constitution by destroying the independence of judiciary by eliminating the process of consultation in the matter of appointment of Judges in the superior Judiciary it is considered as invalid but for some unavoidable reason it could not have been set aside.[60]

It seems that the learned judge made reference to "unavoidable reason" in his observations in light of the fact that the Fourth Amendment has never been challenged before the SC as most of the changes introduced by the Amendment were dispensed with by the first Martial Law Regime (1975–1979).

---

[57] Quoted in *Supreme Court Advocates-on-Record Association v Union of India* (1993) 4 SCC 441, p. 563.

[58] Constitution of Bangladesh, 1972 (Bangladesh) art. 94(4).

[59] *Bangladesh and Justice Syed Md Dastagir Hossain and others v. Md Idrisur Rahman* 38 CLC (AD) 2009.

[60] *Bangladesh and Justice Syed Md Dastagir Hossain and others v. Md Idrisur Rahman* 38 CLC (AD) 2009 [64].

3.5.2 Restoration of the Constitutional Requirement of Consultation with the Chief Justice and Deletion of this Requirement Again by the First Martial Law Regime (1975–1979)

Bangladesh witnessed the declaration of Martial Law for the first time in its history on 15 August 1975, immediately after the assassination of President Mujib. It is pertinent to stress here that Martial Law was declared at a time when the nation was already under a state of emergency declared on 28 December 1974.[61] It seems that Martial Law was declared as a precautionary measure as the emergency powers were not considered sufficient to contain any potential threat to the newly established regime. Since the Constitution of Bangladesh does not make any reference whatsoever to the concept of Martial Law in its text, it can be strongly argued that this declaration of Martial Law in Bangladesh was, indeed, an extra-constitutional act. Pertinently, unlike the 1956 and 1962 Constitutions of Pakistan, which had been abrogated after Proclamations of Martial Law in 1958 and 1969 respectively, the 1972 Constitution of Bangladesh was neither abrogated nor suspended by the 1975 Martial Law administration. But the Constitution ceased to exist as the supreme law of the nation as it was made subordinate to the First Proclamation, which was issued on 20 August 1975, and to Martial Law Regulations or Orders issued by the regime from time to time.

Although the 1972 Constitution of Bangladesh only invests the Parliament, not the President, with the power to amend any provision of the Constitution, the President assumed, on 19 September 1975, the power to issue Orders on any subject provided for by the Constitution through the promulgation of the Proclamation (First Amendment) Order, 1975 (Proclamation Order No I of 1975). Accordingly, he amended the Constitution from time to time by issuing Proclamations (Amendments) Orders.

Consequently, Justice AM Sayem, who had assumed the offices of the President and the Chief Martial Law Administrator in November 1975,[62] issued the Second Proclamation (Seventh Amendment) Order on 28 May 1976, which provided that "[t]he .... judges shall be appointed by the President after consultation with the Chief Justice".[63] Thus the constitutional stipulation of consultation with the Chief Justice in appointing the permanent judges of the SC, which, as pointed out above in Sect. 3.5.2, was omitted by the regime of the Awami League, was restored by the Martial Law administration. However, it is noteworthy that the Martial Law regime did not restore the requirement of consultation with the Chief Justice in Article 98 of the Constitution. Thus, the President retained the unfettered discretion to appoint

---

[61] See above n 49, p. 177.

[62] Ibid., p. 135.

[63] Second Proclamation (Seventh Amendment) Order, 1976 (Second Proclamation Order No IV of 1976) (Bangladesh) art. 4.

additional judges to the HCD. But the constitutional stipulation of consultation with the Chief Justice in the matter of appointing permanent judges was destined to remain in force only for a year and a half. As General Ziaur Rahman (hereafter Zia), who had replaced AM Sayem as the Chief Martial Law Administrator on 29 November 1976 and subsequently as the President on 21 April 1977, issued the Second Proclamation (Tenth Amendment) Order on 27 November 1977, which restored the method of appointment as had been introduced by the Constitution (Fourth Amendment) Act, 1975. For it provided that the "[t]he .... judges [of the Supreme Court] shall be appointed by the President."[64] This provision was, subsequently, ratified by the Constitution (Fifth Amendment) Act, which was passed by the Parliament on 6 April 1979.

Thus, the President was once again freed from the constitutional obligation of consulting the Chief Justice, who was in the best possible position to assess the fitness of the candidates most likely to succeed on the bench, in appointing judges of the SC. Since the President cannot be expected to intimately know about the judicial qualities of the members of the bar and the bench and, as such, may be influenced by political considerations, it is striking that his power to appoint judges was not circumscribed by adequate constitutional safeguards to ensure that appointments would only be made when the need arises in the bench.

Although the requirement for consultation with the Chief Justice in Article 95 of the Constitution of Bangladesh was once again omitted in 1977, the then Chief Justice of Bangladesh, Justice Kemaluddin Hossain, claimed in a public lecture delivered in Dhaka that President Zia had established the convention in 1978 of consulting the Chief Justice before appointing judges to the SC.[65] Later, Justice Hossain further claimed that while it was true that not all of his recommendations had been accepted by President Zia for appointment to the bench, it was equally true that none was appointed as a judge of the SC by the President without his concurrence.

3.5.3 The Method of Appointment of Judges Under the Second Martial Law Regime (1982–1986)

Bangladesh returned to democratic rule on 6 April 1979 at the initiative of President Zia when the Martial Law, which had been declared on 15 August 1975, was withdrawn. But this return to democracy was short-lived. For Zia was assassinated on 30 May 1981 by a handful of members of the armed forces.[66] Following his assassination, General HM Ershad, then the Chief of Army Staff, emphatically ruled out the

---

[64] Second Proclamation (10th Amendment) Order, 1977 (Second Proclamation Order No I of 1977) (Bangladesh) art. 2.

[65] Hossain (1986), p. 45.

[66] See above n 49, pp. 38–40; Bari & Dey (2020), p. 487.

3.5 Dispensation of the Constitutional Requirement of "Consultation with Chief... 75

possibility of the imposition of yet another Martial Law as, according to him, "democracy… [had] found firm roots in the soil of Bangladesh".[67] However, Ershad had a complete change of heart within a matter of few months. As on 24 March 1982, he overthrew the democratically elected government of the Bangladesh Nationalist Party (BNP)—the party founded by Zia—in a bloodless coup and imposed Martial Law throughout the nation. The declaration of Martial Law was followed by the suspension of the Constitution of Bangladesh. Ershad first assumed the office of the Chief Martial Law Administrator with the absolute power of promulgating Martial Law Orders and Regulations dealing practically with every organ of the government. Although he seized "the entire executive and legislative authority"[68] by eroding the concept of separation of powers envisaged by the Constitution, he did not immediately assume the office of the President. Instead, Justice AFM Ahsanuddin Chowdhury was sworn in as the 9th President of Bangladesh on 27 March 1982 on the degrading and ignominious condition that he would "not exercise any power or perform any function without the advice and approval of the Chief Martial Law Administrator".[69]

Although the Proclamation of Martial Law, which was issued on 24 March 1982, provided that the judges of the SC including the Chief Justice would continue to function,[70] it did not contain any provision whatsoever regarding the appointment of judges of the Court. But the Proclamation (First Amendment) Order, which was issued on 11 April 1982, empowered the Chief Martial Law Administrator (CMLA), not the President of the Country, to appoint the "Chief Justice and other Judges of the Supreme Court .... from among Advocates of the Supreme Court or Judicial officers". Although the CMLA was given the power of appointing judges of the SC from among advocates of the highest court or judicial officers irrespective of their length of experience in contravention of constitutional provisions (i.e. at least 10 years of standing practise as an Advocate of the SC or at least 10 years' experience as a judicial officer),[71] no advocate of the SC or judicial officer having less than 10 years' experience was appointed by the Second Martial Law regime as a judge.[72] It should be stressed here that, unlike Justice Kemaluddin Hossain, who had claimed that President Zia had established the convention of consulting the Chief Justice before making appointments to the bench, none of the three Chief Justices who had served during Ershad's 8-year rule, claimed the continuance of the convention of consulting the Chief Justice before making such appointments. This does not come as a surprise. Ershad could hardly be expected to observe the convention of consulting the Chief Justice in appointing the judges of the SC as he, in stark contrast to the

---

[67] *Asian Recorder* (1982), p. 16519 (corrected page 101435).

[68] Proclamation (First Amendment) Order I of 1982 (Bangladesh).

[69] Proclamation (First Amendment) Order I of 1982 (Bangladesh) art. 2(6).

[70] Proclamation of Martial Law, 1982 (Bangladesh) clause 9.

[71] Constitution of Bangladesh, 1972 (Bangladesh) art. 95(2).

[72] Interview with the then Deputy Secretary, Ministry of Law, Justice and Parliamentary Affairs (1 September 2008).

precedent set by the 1975 Martial Law Regime, after the declaration of Martial Law in March 1982: (a) suspended the 1972 Constitution of Bangladesh,[73] and (b) usurped as the Chief Martial Law Administrator not only the legislative but also the executive authority, which should have been given to the President, including the power to appoint the Chief Justice, permanent and additional judges of the SC "from among Advocates of the Supreme Court or judicial officers"[74] irrespective of their length of experience, which contravened the constitutional requirement of appointing judges from among the Advocates of the SC having at least 10 years standing practise or judicial officers having not less than 10 years' experience.

On 11 December 1983, Ershad finally replaced his appointee, Justice Chowdhury, as the President allegedly to pave the way for the transition from Martial Law to democracy and, as a natural consequence of this change, the CMLA was substituted by the President as the appointing authority of the judges of the SC.[75] Thus Ershad followed in the footsteps of General Zia-ul-Haq, who had first assumed the office of the CMLA in Pakistan upon seizure of power in July 1977 apparently to demonstrate that he was not power hungry but later in September 1978 took over as the President.

3.5.4 Breach of the Convention of Consulting the Chief Justice in 1994 in Appointing the Judges of the SC

Notwithstanding the existence of a convention of consulting the Chief Justice before making appointments to the bench by the President, which according to Justice Kemaluddin Hossain had been established in 1978, a controversy erupted over the appointment of nine additional judges to the HCD on 2 February 1994. For Justice Shahabuddin Ahmed—the then Chief Justice—claimed the next day, on 3 February 1994, in his address to the Bar at the Annual Conference of Bar Council that he had been "Mr Nobody" in the matter of the appointment of the said nine judges, thereby implying that he was not consulted in the process. The breach by the executive of the convention of consulting the Chief Justice in appointing the said nine additional judges,[76] infuriated the bar. The Conference adopted a resolution unanimously disapproving the appointment of these judges and demanded the cancellation of the relevant gazette notification. Furthermore, the Chief Justice was requested not to administer oath to the newly appointed judges. Moreover, "on 3rd of February, a Full Court Meeting consisting of all the judges of both the Divisions of ... [the

---

[73] Proclamation (First Amendment) Order I of 1982 (Bangladesh)

[74] Proclamation (First Amendment) Order I of 1982 (Bangladesh).

[75] The Proclamation Order No. III of 1983 (Bangladesh).

[76] Justice Md. Abdul in *Bangladesh and Justice Syed Md. Dastagir Hossain v Md. Idrisur Rahman, Advocate*, held that: 'This convention was however breached by the executive in 1994 when 9 Additional Judges were appointed to the High Court Division without consultation with the Chief Justice.' 38 CLC (AD) 2009, at para 182.

3.5 Dispensation of the Constitutional Requirement of "Consultation with Chief...

Supreme Court] unanimously resolved authorising the Chief Justice not to administer oath to the newly appointed judges".[77] Accordingly, the Chief Justice, after consultation with all other judges of the SC, deferred the administration of oath of office to the newly appointed nine judges for 2 days so that the President and the Prime Minister could be approached to resolve the matter. A delegation of senior and prominent members of the Supreme Court Bar met with the then President Abdur Rahman Biswas, and Prime Minister Begum Khaleda Zia and requested them not to violate the convention of consulting the Chief Justice in the matter of appointment of judges of the SC established by their late leader, President Zia. The government responded by cancelling the earlier Gazette Notification regarding the appointment of the nine judges. On 9 February 1994, the President appointed nine additional judges of the HCD after consulting the Chief Justice, dropping two of the original nine names—one of them was the then Law Secretary who hailed from the village of the Chief Justice—and replacing them with two new names, namely Md Hamidul Haque and MM Ruhul Amin. The new notification for the first time spoke about the appointment of the judges of the HCD by the President in consultation with the Chief Justice, thereby officially recognising the convention of consultation with the Chief Justice.[78]

However, it seems that the restoration of constitutional stipulation of consulting the Chief Justice by President Sayem in 1976 and the subsequent creation of a convention of consultation with the Chief Justice in 1978, were unknown to Justice Syed Amirul Islam of the SC of Bangladesh as he observed in June 2001 in *SN Goswami Advocate v. Bangladesh*[79]:

> This is not true that there is consistent practice and convention regarding consultation with the Chief Justice in the matter of appointment of Judges of both the Division. It is untrue and a misstatement of fact. It was true up to 1974 and since 1975 when the 4th Amendment came into force the process of consultation was done away [with] and since then until February 1994 no consultation was made with the Chief Justice while making appointment of Judges in both the Divisions .... after the 4th Amendment of the Constitution the President never consulted the Chief Justice. The Executive on their own appointed the judges.[80]

Although Justice Islam, within only a year, became aware and enlightened about the convention of Presidential consultation with the Chief Justice in appointing judges, he remained unaware of the restoration of the constitutional requirement of

---

[77] Justice Amirul Islam in *State v Chief Editor, Manabjamin*, 31 CLC (HCD) (2002), Part 2, para 222 http://clcbd.org/judgments/18-criminal-law/3806-state-vs-chief-editor-manabjamin-and-others-2002-31-clc-hcdpart-two.html (accessed on 10 December 2010).

[78] Notification S/R.O. No. 54- Law/94, Ministry of Law, Justice and Parliamentary Affairs (People's Republic of Bangladesh), Justice Section-4, 9 February 1994.

[79] *SN Goswami Advocate v Bangladesh* 55 DLR (2003) 392.

[80] Ibid., pp. 344–5.

78   3   The Method of Appointment of the Judges of the Supreme Court...

consultation with the Chief Justice for a brief period in 1976. As he observed in 2000 in the case of the *State v. Chief Editor, Manabjamin & Others*[81]:

> [B]ut it is, revealed that even after the Fourth Amendment the judges were, appointed in consultation with the Chief Justice of Bangladesh even during the Martial Law Regime though the matter of consultation was not reflected in the notification .... until February 1994.[82]

3.5.5   Judicial Interpretation of the Requirement of "Consultation with the Chief Justice" in Bangladesh

Upon achieving independence from British rule, it is the Constitution of India, 1950, which, as pointed out earlier in Sect. 2.4.1, for the first time, provided for the appointment of judges of the superior courts after consultation, among others, with the Chief Justice of India. The Indian Supreme Court, as pointed out earlier in Sect. 2.4.1, interpreted the word consultation, as used in Articles 124(2) and 217(1) of the Constitution of India, 1950, in a number of cases to mean "concurrence". This rather creative interpretation of the term "consultation" in turn enabled the Court to construe the expression "consultation with the Chief Justice of India" to mean that the final opinion of the Chief Justice on the issue of recommending nominees to the executive for judicial appointment, which should be formed after consultation with the "four senior-most puisne Judges of the Supreme Court,"[83] shall be binding on the President.[84] Thus the Supreme Court of India did not keep itself confined to the four corners of the Constitution and had re-written the provisions of Articles 124(2) and 217(1) in order to appropriate the final say in the appointment of judges of the superior courts, supposedly to safeguard the over-arching concept of judicial independence.

Following the example of the 1950 Indian Constitution, the Constitution of Pakistan, 1973 also originally provided for the appointment of Supreme Court judges by the President after consultation with the Chief Justice, with the modification that the Chief Justice had discretion whether or not to consult the judges of the Supreme Court and of the High Courts in the States. In 1996, the Supreme Court of Pakistan examined the meaning and scope of "consultation" by the President in

---

[81] Justice Amirul Islam in *State v Chief Editor, Manabjamin* 31 CLC (HCD) (2002), Part 1 & 2 < http://clcbd.org/judgments/18-criminal-law/3805-state-vs-chief-editor-manabjamin-and-others-2002-31-clc-hcdpart-one.html> & < http://clcbd.org/judgments/18-criminal-law/3806-state-vs-chief-editor-manabjamin-and-others-2002-31-clc-hcdpart-two.html>. The case is also reported in 57 DLR (2005) 359.

[82] Justice Amirul Islam in *State v Chief Editor, Manabjamin* 31 CLC (HCD) (2002), Part 2, para 222 http://clcbd.org/judgments/18-criminal-law/3806-state-vs-chief-editor-manabjamin-and-others-2002-31-clc-hcdpart-two.html

[83] *In re* special reference 1 of 1998 AIR 1999 SC 1, 739.

[84] *In re* special reference 1 of 1998 AIR 1999 SC 1, 772, 763

3.5 Dispensation of the Constitutional Requirement of "Consultation with Chief...

Al-Jehad Trust & Others v. Federation of Pakistan.[85] Chief Justice Sajjad Ali Shah, in delivering the majority judgment, observed that although consultation is different from consent, the expert opinions of the Chief Justices of the High Courts about the advocates who regularly appeared before their courts, must be given due weight as to the fitness and suitability of those advocates for appointment as judges.[86] He held that these opinions were entitled to be accepted in the absence of very sound reasons to be recorded in writing by the President. He further held that consultation as envisaged in the 1973 Constitution of Pakistan was supposed to be "effective, meaningful, purposive, consensus-oriented," leaving no room for complaint of arbitrariness or unfair play.[87] Thus, the Supreme Court of Pakistan, without making any attempt to rewrite the provisions of the Constitution, gave a realistic and sensible interpretation to the word "consultation" to serve the constitutional purpose of selecting and appointing the most suitable and meritorious candidates as judges of the superior courts.

In Bangladesh, the requirement of consultation, as discussed above in Sects. 3.5.1 and 3.5.2, with the Chief Justice of Bangladesh in the matter of appointment of judges, was omitted from the Constitution in the 1970s. However, the convention of consulting the Chief Justice in appointing judges of the Supreme Court, as mentioned earlier in Sect. 3.5.2, was established by President Zia in 1978. The nature, scope and binding force of the conventional consultation with the Chief Justice was examined by the SC in a number of cases since June 2001.

In 2001, in *SN Goswami, Advocate v. Bangladesh,*[88] Justice Syed Amirul Islam held that the conventional consultation between the President and the Chief Justice did not have any binding force as it was not a rule of law and could not have primacy.[89] However, next year, in the case of *State v. Chief Editor, Manabjamin,*[90] Justice Islam had a complete change of heart. For in this case, Justice Islam observed that the Chief Justice was required to form his opinion in the matter of appointment of judges in the meeting of the Full Court of the Supreme Court.[91] Furthermore, like the majority view in the Indian case of *Supreme Court Advocates-on-Record v Union of India,*[92] he held that the opinion of the Chief Justice formed in the meeting of the Supreme Court must have "primacy and be binding on the Executive".[93] In doing so, Justice Islam did not keep in mind the fact that, unlike the Indian Constitution, the requirement of consultation with the Chief Justice at the time was not mentioned in the Constitution of Bangladesh and as such conventional

---

[85] *Al-Jehad Trust & Others v. Federation of Pakistan* (1996) PLD (SC) 324.

[86] Ibid., p. 329.

[87] Ibid., pp. 364–365.

[88] *SN Goswami, Advocate v. Bangladesh* (2003) 55 DLR 332.

[89] Ibid., p. 345.

[90] *State v. Chief Editor, Manabjamin* 31 CLC (HCD) (2002).

[91] Ibid., [247–248].

[92] *Supreme Court Advocates-on-Record v Union of India* (1993) 4 SCC 441.

[93] *State v. Chief Editor, Manabjamin* 31 CLC (HCD) (2002) at 247–248.

80 3 The Method of Appointment of the Judges of the Supreme Court...

consultation could not be interpreted in the same manner as that of constitutionally mandated consultation. It is further noteworthy that contrary to the decision of the AD of the SC in *Kudrat-E-Elahi v. Bangladesh* and of the opinion of noted jurist, Thomas M Cooley, Justice Islam entered into an uncalled-for academic discussion of an important constitutional issue like consultation with the Chief Justice in appointing judges of the SC as that was very *lis mota* for the case. In this context, it is pertinent to note here that the SC in *Kudrat-E-Elahi Panir v Bangladesh*[94] observed:

> the... decision.... made on hypothetical facts... as a rule, the Courts always abhor. The Court does not answer merely academic question but confines itself only to the point/points which are strictly necessary to be decided for the disposal of the matter before it. This should be more so when Constitutional questions are involved and the Court should be ever discreet in such matters. Unlike a civil suit, the practice in Constitutional cases has always been that if the matter can be decided by deciding one issue only no other point need be decided.[95]

To the same effect, Thomas M. Cooley more forcefully noted:

> the courts.... will not go out of their way to find such topics [i.e. constitutional questions]. They will not seek to draw in such weighty matters collaterally nor on trivial occasions. It is both more proper and more respectable to a coordinate department to discuss constitutional questions only when that is very *lis mota*. Thus presented and determined, the decision carries a weight.... In any case, therefore, where a constitutional question is raised, though it may be legitimately presented by the record, yet if the record also presents some other and clear ground upon which the court may rest its judgment, and thereby render the constitutional question immaterial to the case ... [the court will take that course and leave the question of constitutional power to be passed upon] until a case arises which cannot be otherwise disposed of, and which consequently renders a decision upon such question necessary.[96]

However, ultimately in March 2009, the AD of the SC in *Bangladesh and Justice Syed Md Dastagir Hossain v. Md Idrisur Rahman, Advocates and others*[97] set aside the observation of Justice Islam that in the matter of appointment of judges to the superior judiciary, the opinion of the judiciary expressed through the Chief Justice of Bangladesh had primacy, calling the decision "not ... a sound proposition of law".[98]

In *Md Idrisur Rahman, Advocate and others v. Secretary, Ministry of Law, Justice and Parliamentary Affairs, Government of the People's Republic of Bangladesh*,[99] Judge Md Abdur Rashid of the three-member Special Bench of the HCD of the SC laid down 12 norms and processes for appointment and non-appointment of the judges of the SC as "[e]xistence of guidelines or norms of general application

---

[94] *Kudrat-E-Elahi v. Bangladesh* (1992) 44 DLR (AD) 319.

[95] Ibid., para [107].

[96] Cooley (1878), p. 163.

[97] *Bangladesh and Justice Syed Md Dastagir Hossain v. Md Idrisur Rahman, Advocates and others* 38 CLC (AD) 2009.

[98] Ibid., [75].

[99] *Md Idrisur Rahman, Advocate and others v Secretary, Ministry of Law, Justice and Parliamentary Affairs, Government of the People's Republic of Bangladesh* 37 CLC (HCD) 2008.

3.5 Dispensation of the Constitutional Requirement of "Consultation with Chief... 81

excludes any arbitrary exercise of discretionary powers".[100] Of these 12 norms, six were relating to consultation with the Chief Justice of Bangladesh by the President in the matter of appointment of regular judges of the HCD and AD, and four were concerning consultation in the context of appointment or non-appointment of an additional judge of the HCD. The six guidelines as to the import and scope of consultation with the Chief Justice in the matter of appointment of regular judges of the SC were as follows:

(ii) the opinion of the Chief Justice of Bangladesh in the matter of appointment of Judges to the Supreme Court is entitled to have the primacy;

(iii) in case of appointment to the High Court Division, the Chief Justice shall consult with two senior most Judges of the Appellate Division and equal number of Judges of the High Court Division to form his opinion and he shall also consult senior members of the Supreme Court Bar and the Attorney-General; and in the case of appointment of Judges to the Appellate Division, he shall consult with three senior-most Judges of the Appellate Division to form his opinion;

(iv) the President or the Government shall have no right to directly initiate the process for appointment of Judges to the Supreme Court bypassing the Chief Justice of Bangladesh but the President/ Government shall have the right of suggesting the names of suitable candidates for consideration of the Chief Justice for appointment to the Supreme Court;

(v) the non-appointment of anyone recommended, on the ground of unsuitability, must be for good reasons, disclosed and conveyed to the Chief Justice with the reasons, materials and information to enable him to reconsider and withdraw his recommendation. If the Chief Justice after consultation with the above Judges in respect of particular appointments in the Division concerned, does not find it necessary to withdraw and again recommended, then the President must adhere to such recommendation;

(vi) the President as a rule shall accept the recommendation of the Chief Justice for appointment of Judges. If the recommendation of the Chief Justice for appointment or non-appointment of any person as a Judge either to the High Court or the Appellate Division could not be accepted by the Government, it cannot outright, reject such recommendation and go ahead with appointment of persons of its own choice. The Government in such case shall send the recommendation back to the Chief Justice for reconsideration on the reasons supported by materials and information conveyed by the Government;

(vii) after consideration of the reasons of the Government along with the materials and the information conveyed, the Chief Justice may withdraw his recommendation. But if he again recommends the same recommendation after consultation with the aforesaid senior-most Judges of the Appellate Division for appointment, the Government shall be obliged to complete the process of appointment.[101]

The following four norms dealt with the import of consultation in the frame of reference to appointment or non-appointment of an additional judge of the HCD:

(viii) appointment or non-appointment of an Additional Judge as Judge under Article 95 of the Constitution by the executive disregarding the recommendation of the Chief Justice violates the Constitution;

---

[100] Ibid., [94].

[101] Ibid., [152].

(ix) when the executive may not accept such recommendation of the Chief Justice for reasons to be recorded, it may request the Chief Justice for reconsideration on the materials and information conveyed;

(x) the Chief Justice shall then reconsider the case on the materials and information furnished, and if after such reconsideration, he again recommends for appointment or non-appointment, the executive would be left with no choice but to complete the process of appointment of such an Additional Judge on the basis of such recommendation;

(xi) after successful conclusion of the period under Article 98, an Additional Judge acquires legitimate expectation and he becomes entitled to be considered for appointment under Article 95 of the Constitution in the absence of positive valid reason(s) to be recorded by the Executive.[102]

Thus, unlike the decisions, as discussed earlier in Sect. 2.4.1, of the Indian Supreme Court in the *Second and Third Judges' Cases*, Justice Rashid in the case of *Idrisur Rahman* observed that the Chief Justice was required to form his opinion for the appointment of judges to the HCD by consulting not only the two senior-most judges of each of the two Divisions of the SC, but also the Attorney-General and one or more members of the "broad band" of the Supreme Court Bar.[103] While the Chief Justice was required to expand the zone of consultees beyond the fellow judges of the SC in the formation of his opinion as to the appointment of HCD judges, he was required to constitute his opinion for the appointment of judges to the AD of the SC by only consulting three senior-most judges of the AD to stifle his individual voice.[104] It should be stressed here that unlike the Indian Supreme Court, which interpreted consultation with the Chief Justice as mentioned in Articles 124(2) and 217(1) of the Constitution of India, the Supreme Court of Bangladesh interpreted consultation with the Chief Justice, a requirement which had deliberately been deleted twice from Articles 95(1) and 98 of the Constitution of Bangladesh—first on 25 January 1975, and then again on 27 November 1977. Thus, there was hardly any scope for giving such a wide connotation to *ex gratia* or conventional consultation with the Chief Justice of Bangladesh by the President as developed in 1978.

Although Justice Joynul Abedin of the AD in *Bangladesh and in Justice Syed Md Dastagir Hossain's Case*, rightly struck down those 12 norms or guidelines as they had not been construed by the provisions of Article 95 and 98 of the Constitution,[105] Justice Abdul Matin disapproved of 10 out of 12 norms in delivering the majority judgment of the Court.[106] Justice Matin disapproved of norm iii, which provided that the Chief Justice was to form his opinion on the appointment of judges to the AD in consultation with a collegium of judges and to, subsequently, form his opinion on the appointment of judges to the HCD in consultation with a collegium including

---

[102] Ibid.

[103] Ibid.

[104] Ibid.

[105] *Bangladesh and Justice Syed Md Dastagir Hossain v. Md Idrisur Rahman, Advocates and others* 38 CLC (AD) 2009, [92].

[106] Ibid., [232–239].

not only judges,[107] but also the Attorney General and one or two members of the Supreme Court Bar.[108] Like Justice SP Bharucha of the Indian Supreme Court, who, in the Third Judges' Case, for the first time used the word "collegium" consisting of four senior-most puisne judges of the Supreme Court with which the Chief Justice was required to consult in the formation of his opinion, Justice Matin for the first time described the system of formation of opinion by the Chief Justice, as described in norm iii, a collegium of judges.[109] But he disapproved of the concept of collegium by making reference to its non-existence in the Constitution or convention and to the non-satisfactory functioning, as discussed earlier in Sect. 2.4.1, of the collegium system in India.[110] It was held that the opinion of the Chief Justice should be given due weightage in the area of legal acumen and suitability of the candidates for appointment as judges to the SC, while the opinion of the President should be dominant in the area of antecedents of the candidates. Thus, he advocated for a consensus-oriented approach to "find out the most suitable (candidates) available for appointment."[111] This interpretation of consultation by the AD of the SC of Bangladesh to the effect that the opinion of the Chief Justice with regard to higher judicial appointments shall not be binding on the President, seems to be a fair, appropriate, and a balanced interpretation of the word "consultation".

3.6 Restoration of the Requirement of "Consultation with the Chief Justice" in the Constitution of Bangladesh in July 2011

The current government of the Bangladesh Awami League (BAL), which had for the first time in January 1975 omitted the phrase "consultation with the Chief Justice" from the Constitution of Bangladesh in connection with the appointment of judges, restored the original stipulation of Presidential consultation with the Chief Justice in appointing the regular judges of the SC under Article 95(1), through the enactment of the Constitution (Fifteenth Amendment) Act, 2011. But the requirement of consultation with the Chief Justice by the President when appointing additional judges of the HCD has not been restored in Article 98 of the Constitution. It will be made evident in Chap. 4 of this Book that this requirement was not restored deliberately so as to enable the BAL executive to make patronage appointments to the bench.

---

[107] Ibid., p. 50.

[108] Ibid., p. 235.

[109] Ibid.

[110] Ibid.

[111] Ibid., [256].

3.7 The Establishment of the Supreme Judicial Commission in Bangladesh to Recommend Candidates for Appointment as Judges to the SC

Since the number of judges to be appointed in the HCD and AD of the SC of Bangladesh, as pointed out above in Sect. 3.4, has been kept indeterminate,[112] it is to be determined by the President on the advice of the Prime Minister. Although the AD has the strength of judges determined by the President from time to time, there is no such strength for the HCD. Thus, the number of judges varies at the pleasure of the executive. If the President is satisfied that the number of judges of a Division should be increased for the time being, then under Article 98 of the Constitution, the President may appoint additional or *ad hoc* judges to that Division for a period of 2 years. This is, indeed, a departure from the constitutional pattern followed elsewhere. For instance, the Constitution of Puerto Rico, 1952 stipulates that "the number of Justices [of the Supreme Court] may be changed only by law upon request of the Supreme Court".[113] Consequently, the absence of any such provision in the Constitution of Bangladesh has enabled successive governments to take advantage of this lacuna to pack the SC with judges with political allegiance on the hope that these judges would support their actions, omissions, and legislation, if and when challenged.

When the government of the BAL succeeded the Bangladesh Nationalist Party (BNP) government in 1996, there were 37 judges in the HCD and five judges in the AD, including the Chief Justice of Bangladesh. During their five-year rule, the number of judges in the HCD was increased from 37 to 56, although the number of judges in the AD remained the same. The BAL government appointed 40 additional judges to the HCD.[114] In October 2001, the BNP came to power and the next year it raised the number of judges in the AD from five to seven.[115] When the BNP Government relinquished power in October 2006, the number of judges in the HCD was 72 and it had appointed a total of 45 judges.[116] In order to prevent the politically-motivated appointments that took place allegedly during the previous two regimes and "to select and recommend competent persons for appointment as judges of the SC,"[117] President Iajuddin Ahmad, on 16 March 2008, issued the Supreme Judicial Commission Ordinance providing for the establishment of a

---

[112] Constitution of Bangladesh, 1972 (Bangladesh) art. 94(2) (provides that "the Supreme Court shall consist of the Chief Justice, to be known as the Chief Justice of Bangladesh, and such number of other Judges as the President may deem it necessary to appoint to each division").

[113] Constitution of Puerto Rico, 1952 (PU) art. 5, s 3.

[114] Asian Human Rights Commission (2008), http://www.humanrights.asia/news/ahrc-news/AHRC-STM-201-2008/?searchterm

[115] U.S. Dept. State (2003), https://2009-2017.state.gov/j/drl/rls/hrrpt/2003/27944.htm

[116] The Daily Star (2008), https://www.thedailystar.net/news-detail-61184. After 2004, the B.N.P Government did not appoint any additional judges to the High Court Division; See above n 34, p. 9.

[117] The Supreme Judicial Commission Ordinance, 2008 (Bangladesh) preamble.

3.7 The Establishment of the Supreme Judicial Commission in Bangladesh... 85

Supreme Judicial Commission for selection and recommendation of names to the President for appointment as additional and regular judges of the HCD and as judges of the AD of the SC. The Ordinance was issued during the tenure of the non-party caretaker government (NPCG).

In this context, it should be mentioned here that the mechanism of NPCG was inserted in the Constitution of Bangladesh through the Constitution (Thirteenth Amendment) Act in 1996 due to the distrust that exists between the two main political parties, i.e., the BNP and the BAL, over the issue of conducting a free, fair and impartial general election under the supervision of a political government. In fact, the nation's electoral history has been marred by numerous instances of the incumbent government resorting to various forms of electoral malpractices, such as ballot stuffing, "voter intimidation" and disruptions of the registration of voters, for manipulating the outcome of the election in its favour.[118] Accordingly, the Constitution, as amended by the Thirteenth Amendment, stipulated that a NPCG, headed by the last retired Chief Justice and additionally composed of 10 advisers appointed by the President among eminent citizens of the nation, would be constituted after the dissolution of the Parliament[119] with the principal mandate of providing "all possible aid and assistance" to the Election Commission for holding the general election "fairly and impartially".[120] It was expected that the NPCG due to its neutral character would have no motivation to manipulate the outcome of general elections, thereby uphold the democratic right of the citizens of the country to vote in free, fair and impartial elections[121] and to, consequently, "effect change of government in a peaceful manner."[122]

3.7.1 Composition of the Supreme Judicial Commission

The Supreme Judicial Commission Ordinance, 2008, which was originally issued in March 2008, provided that the Commission would be headed by the Chief Justice of Bangladesh and would additionally be composed of the Minister of Law, Justice and Parliamentary Affairs, the two senior-most judges of the AD, the Attorney General of Bangladesh, two Members of Parliament (MPs)—one nominated by the Leader of the House and the other by the Leader of the Opposition in Parliament— President of the Supreme Court Bar Association, and Secretary, Ministry of Law, Justice and Parliamentary Affairs, as the members of the Commission.[123] Thus among the members of the Commission, the six non-judicial members constituted

---

[118] Bari (2018), p. 31.

[119] Constitution of Bangladesh, 1972 (Bangladesh) former art 58C(2).

[120] Constitution of Bangladesh, 1972 (Bangladesh) former art 58D(2).

[121] See above n 118, p. 57.

[122] Ibid., p. 72.

[123] The Supreme Judicial Commission Ordinance, 2008 (Bangladesh) sec. 3(2).

the majority. Since the Commission was established to guarantee a cautious, professional, and non-political search for the best persons for judgeships of the SC, based on first-hand knowledge about each of the candidate's keen intellect, legal acumen, integrity, suitability of character, and temperament as an advocate and a judicial officer, the provisions for inclusion into it two members of a political body like the Parliament, a minister, who is a politician belonging to the ruling party, and a civil servant, as members, could hardly serve the purpose of selecting and recommending the best candidates for appointment as judges. Although both the President of the Supreme Court Bar Association and the Attorney General—the principal law officer of the nation—are pre-eminently suited to evaluate the competence of Advocates of the SC for appointment as judges, their inclusion in the Commission could not be said to be conducive to prevent patronage appointments. For they remain under the influence of either the party in power or opposition political parties and, as such, are highly politically charged.

Furthermore, out of the nine members of the Commission, only three were judges, namely, the Chief Justice and two senior-most judges of the AD of the SC, which manifested the domination of the six non-judicial members in the selection process. Accordingly, it can be argued that the government of the day was given significant leeway to influence the process for selecting and recommending judges, thereby frustrating the purpose underlying the establishment of the Commission, i.e., securing the appointment of the most qualified and appropriate persons as judges. But only 3 months after the promulgation of the Ordinance, on 16 June 2008, the Supreme Judicial Commission (Amendment) Ordinance, 2008, was issued to introduce changes in the composition of the Commission. The provisions concerning the appointment of two MPs and of the Secretary of the Ministry of Law as Commission members were deleted, and a provision was added to include two senior-most judges of the HCD of the SC as members of the Commission. Thus, under the new arrangement, the Commission would consist of the Chief Justice as its Chairman, and 8 ex-officio members, namely, the Minister of Law, three senior-most judges of the AD—an increase from the previous arrangement—two senior-most judges of the HCD, the Attorney General, and the President of the Supreme Court Bar Association.[124]

Thus, the President of Bangladesh was not given any authority to appoint any eminent person, jurist or judge of the SC, who were perceived as being close to the government of the day, as a member of the Commission. More importantly, the senior members of the judiciary were given a majority in the Commission, which was, indeed, conducive to the selection of suitable candidates for appointment as judges. The senior members of the judiciary, who were six in number in the Commission, could reasonably be expected to have expert knowledge of candidates' acumen and suitability for appointment to the bench. If the other three members of the Commission, i.e., the Law Minister, the Attorney General, and the President of the Supreme Court Bar Association (if the Bar President has political

---

[124] The Supreme Judicial Commission Ordinance, 2008 (Bangladesh) sec. 2.

3.7 The Establishment of the Supreme Judicial Commission in Bangladesh... 87

allegiance to the party in power), made an abortive attempt in the meeting of the Commission in deference to the wishes of the government for filling the vacancies in the SC, then the majority in the Commission could thwart such an attempt.

3.7.2 Selection Process

The Supreme Judicial Commission of Bangladesh was not given any discretion to advertise on the Commission's website or in any other medium to fill any vacancies in the SC. Thus, any citizen having the experience of practising before the SC for a period not less than 10 years or any judicial officer having not less than 10 years' experience could not apply directly for selection as a judge of the SC. The Commission was required to consider the names of the candidates proposed by the Law, Justice, and Parliamentary Affairs Ministry (Law Ministry).[125] The Law Ministry could propose a minimum of three and a maximum of five names for each judicial vacancy to the Commission for its consideration.[126] It is obvious that candidates sharing ideological views of the party in power had better prospects of getting nominated by the Law Ministry. However, if the Commission considered it necessary to take into account the names of the additional candidates, it could make such a request to the Law Ministry or, it could select any competent person outside of the names proposed by the Law Ministry.[127] Of course, such a candidate, if selected and recommended, would have the least chance of getting appointed because he or she would lack political patronage.

Thus, lack of plurality of sources for proposing candidates from outside the Law Ministry for judicial appointment was a serious drawback of the system. However, as opposed to the previous system of appointing the judges of the SC, which had been cloaked in secrecy and was devoid of any transparency, the Supreme Judicial Commission was allowed to follow a transparent process in selecting the candidates by conducting interviews of the candidates at its discretion.[128] In spite of these changes, the Supreme Judicial Commission Ordinance of Bangladesh did not contain any provision regarding screening of the antecedents of the candidates by the Anti-Corruption Commission, Police Forces, or Tax Ombudsman of Bangladesh with respect to candidates' educational qualifications, tax payment records, credit, history as to arrest and conviction, or integrity.

---

[125] The Supreme Judicial Commission Ordinance, 2008 (Bangladesh), s. 6(1).

[126] Ibid., s. 6(2).

[127] Ibid., s. 6(3).

[128] Ibid., s. 5(7).

3.7.3 Functions and Selection Criteria

The authority of the Commission was confined only to selecting and recommending candidates for appointment of regular and additional judges to the HCD and of regular judges to the AD of the SC. But the Commission was not given the jurisdiction to recommend candidates for appointment as the Chief Justice of Bangladesh. It was also not given any authority to discuss anything about the disposal of cases and improving the performance of the SC judges. The Supreme Judicial Commission Ordinance provided for different sets of criteria for the Commission to consider before recommending candidates for the appointment of additional judges to the HCD and of judges to the AD. The Commission was required to consider the candidates' educational qualifications, professional skills, efficiency, seniority, honesty, and reputation, along with other ancillary matters, when recommending candidates for appointment as additional judges of the HCD.[129] On the other hand, for recommending any judge of the HCD for appointment to the AD, his seniority, judicial skills, integrity and reputation, and other subsidiary matters were to be taken into account by the Commission.[130]

3.7.4 Selection Meeting of the Commission

The Supreme Judicial Commission of Bangladesh was required to sit at least once every 6 months.[131] But the Chairman of the Commission, the Chief Justice, would immediately convene a meeting of the Commission if he was requested to consider candidates for appointment as judges of the SC by the competent authority, i.e. the Law Ministry under the Rules of Business.[132] It was stressed in the Supreme Judicial Commission Ordinance that the Commission would first strive to make a unanimous decision, perhaps taking into account the importance of appointing the most qualified and suitable persons as judges to maintain the quality of the Bench. If that was not possible, the decision of a majority of the members present would prevail.[133] The presence of five members would constitute a quorum, and a decision to recommend names for appointment could be made by a majority of the members present, which meant that a decision of the Commission could have been based on the support of three members if only five members attended the meeting.[134] However, the Ordinance did not mention that the quorum would include the Chairman. Rather, it was provided that when there was an equality of votes, the Chairman of the

---

[129] Ibid., s. 5(6).

[130] Ibid., s. 5(5).

[131] Ibid., s. 4(5).

[132] Ibid., s. 4(6).

[133] Ibid., s. 4(7).

[134] Ibid., proviso s. 4(4).

Commission or the person presiding over the meeting could exercise a casting vote.[135]

It should be stressed here that the three non-judicial members of the Commission, namely, the Law Minister, Attorney General and President of the Supreme Court Bar Association, were allowed to attend its meeting as members of the Commission for selecting and recommending the HCD judges for appointment to the vacant posts in the AD. But the senior-most judges of the HCD, who were Members of the Commission, were precluded from taking part in its meeting without assigning any reason whatsoever, e.g. if they were being considered for selection and, as such, were being precluded from participation in the meeting to avoid any conflict of interest.[136] The Commission was required to select and recommend two candidates for each vacancy in the SC without the requirement of any mention of the order of preference,[137] perhaps to give a free hand to the appointing authority in selecting either of the two candidates proposed.

3.7.5 Consideration of Report by the President

The Supreme Judicial Commission of Bangladesh was required to send its recommendation for whom to appoint to judicial vacancies to the Law Ministry for forwarding to the President.[138] Ordinarily, the President would appoint the judges of the SC in accordance with the recommendation of the Commission.[139] In case, the President did not agree with the recommendation of the Commission, he would send the recommendation back for its reconsideration.[140] After receipt of any request from the President for reviewing any recommendation, the Commission would promptly reconsider the recommendation and would send to the President either its modified recommendation or its earlier recommendation with recorded reasonable grounds.[141] The President was given the right to ignore and reject the recommendation of the Commission by recording appropriate reasons.[142]

Thus, the power of the President to accept or reject the candidates recommended by the Commission at his pleasure defeated the very objective of establishing the Commission for appointing persons of the highest calibre, character, professional skill and integrity as judges (i.e., the right type of judges) to the SC.

---

[135] Ibid. s. 4(6).

[136] Ibid., s. 4(9).

[137] Ibid., s. 5(2).

[138] Ibid., s. 7.

[139] Ibid., s. 9(1).

[140] Ibid., s. 9(2).

[141] Ibid., s. 9(3).

[142] Ibid., s. 9(4).

3.8 Validity of the Supreme Judicial Commission Ordinance

The ordinance-making power of the President of Bangladesh—conferred on him by Article 93 of the Constitution, which gives him power to carry out legislative functions—is a relic of the Colonial legislation, i.e., Government of India Act, 1935,[143] and is of the nature of an emergency power to meet "circumstances" that "render it necessary to take immediate action" when "the Parliament is not in session" to secure the immediate enactment of necessary legislation. Apart from the time and circumstances, there are other limitations on the ordinance-making power of the President, who is the sole judge of the necessity of issuing an ordinance as Article 93 contains the words "if the President is satisfied". The President cannot promulgate an ordinance making any provision "which could not lawfully be made under [the Bangladeshi] Constitution by Act of Parliament" or "which alter[s] or repeal[s] any provision of [the] Constitution."[144] Although the ordinance-making power of the President should be exercised sparingly, there has always been a tendency on the part of successive governments to resort to such a power more frequently than seems necessary and desirable.

However, the Supreme Judicial Commission Ordinance was issued, as pointed out above, in March 2008 during the tenure of the third NPCG, which was established in January 2007 for holding free and fair general elections. This government was required to discharge its function as an interim government and, as such, to carry out routine day-to-day works of the government in addition to its main function of assisting and aiding the Election Commission. Hence, it could not make any policy decision unless it was indispensably necessary for the discharge of its constitutional functions.[145]

The promulgation of the Supreme Judicial Commission Ordinance cannot be accepted as a valid piece of legislation within the framework of the Constitution due to the following grounds:

(a) Unlike Article 115 of the Constitution of Bangladesh, which empowers the President to make rules that he is required to follow when exercising his power to appoint subordinate judicial officers and magistrates exercising judicial functions, Articles 95(1) and 98, which deal with appointment of regular and additional judges of the SC respectively, do not provide for the enactment of any mechanism, such as the Supreme Judicial Commission, for selecting candidates for appointment to judicial vacancies in the SC by the President.

(b) Unlike the Constitutions of Algeria, France, Italy, Namibia and Rwanda,[146] the Constitution of Bangladesh does not even empower the legislative authorities to

---

[143] Government of India Act, 1935 (United Kingdom) ch. IV, s. 42(1).

[144] Constitution of Bangladesh, 1972 (Bangladesh) art 93(1).

[145] Constitution of Bangladesh, 1972 (Bangladesh) former art 58D(1).

[146] Constitution of Democratic Republic of Algeria, pt. 2, ch. III, art. 155; Constitution of France, 1958 (France) Title VIII, art. 65; Constitution of Republic of Rwanda, 2003 (Rwanda) Title IV, ch. 5, art. 158.

3.8 Validity of the Supreme Judicial Commission Ordinance

enact laws or promulgate ordinances regulating the organisation, powers, and functioning of the Supreme Judicial Commission. Article 95(2)(c) of the Constitution of Bangladesh only empowers the Parliament to pass laws providing for an alternative requisite qualification for judges appointed to the SC (e.g., a distinguished jurist), and an ordinance could only be promulgated in this regard. Instead, the Supreme Judicial Commission Ordinance laid down different selection criteria, such as educational qualification, professional skill, seniority, honesty and reputation for HCD judgeship, and seniority, judicial skill, integrity and reputation for appointment as judges to the AD.

Therefore, it can be argued that the Supreme Judicial Commission Ordinance, 2008, was not promulgated within the parameters of Articles 95, 98 and 65 of the Constitution of Bangladesh and, as such, is *ultra vires* the Constitution.

In 2008, the constitutional validity of the Supreme Judicial Ordinance, 2008, was challenged in *Idrisur Rahman v. Bangladesh*[147] on the following grounds, that: (a) the Constitution of Bangladesh has not empowered the President to promulgate an Ordinance prescribing a mode of selection and recommendation of persons for the appointment of judges of the SC, (b) there existed no circumstances that required immediate action by the President to promulgate the Ordinance, and (c) during the period of the NPCG, which had the mandate as an interim government to carry out routine functions, the President could not promulgate an Ordinance involving a policy decision not urgently necessary for the discharge of the routine functions of the NPCG. The majority decisions of Justices Nazmin Ara Sultana and Md Ashfaqul Islam found only the provisions of Section 9(4) of the Supreme Judicial Commission Ordinance, which empowered the President to reject the amended or the earlier recommendations of the Commission after recording the reasons thereof, unconstitutional because they were inconsistent with the provision of the Constitution and convention concerning the appointment of the judges of the SC.[148] Furthermore, such a provision was very much inconsistent with the objective of promulgating the Ordinance and, as such, rendered the entire exercise of the Supreme Judicial Commission meaningless, futile, and ineffective. They were of the opinion that several judicial appointments to the SC by the previous regime of the BNP were based on political considerations, which rendered the promulgation of the impugned Ordinance urgently necessary for the formation of the Supreme Judicial Commission to select the most suitable persons for appointment as judges of the SC and for making these appointments fair, beyond any controversy, and acceptable to all in order to maintain public confidence in the SC.[149]

On the other hand, Justice Md Abdur Rashid, who was in the minority, held that any law prescribing the mode or procedure for appointment of judges to the highest court cannot be independent of the Constitution. The President, therefore, cannot arrogate a power to make an Ordinance for selection of persons for appointment of

---

[147] *Idrisur Rahman v. Bangladesh* 37 CLC (HCD) (2008)

[148] Ibid., [168], [194].

[149] Ibid., [150].

judges to the SC on the fallacy of complementing and supplementing the constitutional provisions or conventions when that power is not conferred upon him by the Constitution. Such a law, if felt necessary, could only be incorporated into the Constitution by the Parliament by promulgating an amendment to the supreme law, i.e., the Constitution of Bangladesh, as it has been done in the United Kingdom in 2005. Justice Rashid, therefore, held that the entire Supreme Judicial Commission Ordinance was *ultra vires* the scheme and spirit of the Constitution and, as such, unconstitutional.[150]

It appears that the minority view of Justice Rashid is more convincing in view of the following facts: (a) since 1978, the President had established the convention of consulting the Chief Justice when appointing judges to the SC; (b) the Constitution does not provide for any provision to enact a law stipulating the establishment of a Supreme Judicial Commission; and (c) there hardly existed any circumstance which required immediate action for promulgating the impugned Ordinance for appointment of judges of the SC.

The actual functioning of the Commission following its establishment, the manner in which its life was brought to an end, and the aftermath of the "natural death" of the Commission, will be discussed in detail in Chap. 4 of this Book.

References

(1982). *Asian recorder*, 16519 (corrected page 101435).

(1988). *Dictionary of familiar quotations* (p. 75). Tophi Books.

Asian Human Rights Commission. (2008). *Bangladesh, government contests the reappointment of judges in Supreme Court*. Available at http://www.humanrights.asia/news/ahrc-news/AHRC-STM-201-2008/?searchterm

BANGLAPEDIA. (2015). *Warrant of precedence*. Available at http://en.banglapedia.org/index.php?title=Warrant_of_Precedence

Bari, M. E. (2016). Supersession of the Senior-Most Judges in Bangladesh in Appointing the Chief Justice and the Other Judges of the Appellate Division of the Supreme Court: A Convenient Means to a Politicized Bench. *San Diego International Law Journal, 18*(1), 43.

Bari, M. E. (2014). The natural death of the Supreme Judicial Commission of Bangladesh & the consequent patronage appointments to the bench: Advocating the establishment of an Independent Judicial Commission. *International Review of Law, 1*(8), 9.

Bari, M. E. (2018). The incorporation of the system of non-party caretaker government in the constitution of Bangladesh in 1996 as a means of strengthening democracy, its deletion in 2011 and the lapse of Bangladesh into tyranny following the non-participatory general election of 2014: A critical appraisal. *Transnational Law and Contemporary Problems, 28*(1), 59.

Bari, M. E. (2017). *States of emergency and the law: The experience of Bangladesh* (pp. 38–40, 76, 117, 173–175). Routledge.

Bari, M. E., & Dey, P. (2020). The anti-defection provision contained in the constitution of Bangladesh, 1972, and its adverse impact on parliamentary democracy: A case for reform. *Wisconsin International Law Journal, 37*(3), 487.

---

[150] Ibid., [100], [111], and [116].

References

Cooley, T. M. (1878). *A treatise on the constitutional limitations which rest upon the legislative power of the states of the American union* (p. 163). Little, Brown, and Company.

David, S. H. (2013). Four things: Socrates and the Indiana judiciary. *Indiana Law Review, 46*, 871.

Hossain, K. U. (1986). *Independent judiciary in developing countries* (p. 45). Speech delivered at the Justice Ibrahim Memorial Lecture Series, University of Dhaka.

International Congress of Jurists. (1959). *Report of committee IV, the judiciary and the legal profession under the rule of law, clause II.* Available at https://www.icj.org/wp-content/uploads/1959/01/Rule-of-law-in-a-free-society-conference-report-1959-eng.pdf

Montreal Declaration. (1983). *Universal declaration on the independence of justice* (art. 2.03).

The Daily Star. (2008). *10 New HC judges to be appointed.* Available at https://www.thedailystar.net/news-detail-61184

The Daily Star. (2009). *SC Appellate Division gets 5 more judges.* Available at http://www.thedailystar.net/newDesign/news-details.php?nid=96998

U.S. Department of State. Bureau of Democracy, Human Rights, and Labor. (2003). *Country reports on human rights practices: Bangladesh.* Available at https://2009-2017.state.gov/j/drl/rls/hrrpt/2003/27944.htm

Chapter 4
The Intrusion of Extraneous Considerations in the Appointment of the Chief Justice and the Other Judges of the Supreme Court of Bangladesh

4.1 Introduction

A suitable method of appointment of judges, as discussed earlier in Sects. 2.4.1 and 2.5, involving a body of judicial character wherein senior members of the judiciary constitute a majority, as stipulated, for instance, by the Constitution of Pakistan, 1973, enables judges to decide cases according to their oath of office without submitting to any kind of pressures. However, notwithstanding the effectiveness of such a method of appointment, the Constitution of Bangladesh, 1972, has not, as discussed earlier in Chap. 3, been amended to incorporate a similar kind of method of appointment of judges. Rather, the Constitution entrusts the executive with the authority to appoint judges of the superior courts, thereby allowing wide scope for the appointment of judges on extraneous considerations. In the absence of any provision in the Constitution either obligating the President to consult a selection committee consisting, for instance, of the senior-most judges of the judiciary before appointing the Chief Justice of Bangladesh—the head of the Bangladeshi judiciary—or stipulating any specific qualifications for the appointment of the Chief Justice, a convention of appointing the senior-most judge of the Appellate Division (AD)—the higher Division of the Supreme Court (SC)—as the Chief Justice was developed to ensure that extraneous considerations did not play any part in making such a pivotal appointment. A similar convention of appointing the senior-most judges of the High Court Division (HCD)—the lower Division of the SC—as judges of the AD was also developed to act as a check against patronage appointments.

However, no effective safeguards, as pointed out earlier in Sect. 3.4, are contained in the Constitution of Bangladesh to prevent patronage appointments to the HCD. Although a Supreme Judicial Council was established in March 2008 to

---

A significantly edited and truncated version of this chapter has been published in a refereed journal. For details, see Bari, M.E. (2016). Supersession of the Senior-Most Judges in Bangladesh in Appointing the Chief Justice and the Other Judges of the Appellate Division of the Supreme Court: A Convenient Means to a Politicized Bench. *San Diego International Law Journal* 18(1), 45–74.

© The Author(s), under exclusive license to Springer Nature Singapore Pte Ltd. 2022
M. E. Bari, *The Independence of the Judiciary in Bangladesh*,
https://doi.org/10.1007/978-981-16-6222-5_4

select and recommend suitable candidates for appointment as judges of the SC, the life of this Commission was purposefully brough to an end by the current government of the Bangladesh Awami League (BAL) following its ascension to power in January 2009.

This chapter will, first, discuss the violation of both the conventions of appointing the senior-most judge of the AD as the Chief Justice and of appointing the senior-most judges of the HCD as the judges of the AD. Second, light will be shed on the fact that the absence of a constitutional obligation to consult the Chief Justice in appointing the additional judges of the HCD under Article 98 of the Constitution, has enabled the executive to pack the bench with loyalists. Finally, the manner in which the journey of the Supreme Judicial Commission, which was established in 2008 through the promulgation of an Ordinance, to recommend the best candidates to the President for appointment as the judges of the HCD and the AD was calculatedly brought to an end, and the aftermath of the "natural death" of the Commission, will be discussed. This Chapter will make it manifestly evident that the weaknesses of the constitutional provisions concerning the appointment of the judges of the superior judiciary in Bangladesh have allowed succeeding generations of executives, particularly the current one, to politicize the bench, thereby undermining its reputation in the eyes of the litigants as a fair and impartial arbitrator of disputes.

4.2 Contravention of the Convention of Seniority in Appointing the Chief Justice of Bangladesh

The convention or tradition of appointing the senior-most judge of the AD as the Chief Justice of Bangladesh had consistently been followed by successive governments until June 2003. However, since then, it has been violated by the regimes of the Bangladesh Nationalist Party (BNP)– Jamaat-e-Islami Alliance (2001–2006), the Non-Party Caretaker Government (2006–2008), and the BAL (2009-to-date). An attempt will now be made to critically examine these instances of supersessions.

4.2.1 Supersession during the Regime of the BNP-Jamaat Alliance (2001–2006)

The convention of seniority was first violated on 23 June 2003, by the regime of the BNP-Jamaat Alliance when Justice KM Hasan was appointed as the Chief Justice of Bangladesh in supersession of two of his fellow colleagues, Justices Md Ruhul Amin and Md Fazlul Karim. It should be pointed out that both Justices Amin and Karim had been elevated to the AD superseding Justice Hasan, the senior-most judge of the HCD, by ignoring the recommendation of the Chief Justice.[1] The Government justified the supersession of Justices Amin and Karim in appointing the Chief Justice by terming it as a corrective measure aimed at redressing the earlier injustice that had been perpetrated by the BAL Government against Justice Hasan.

The next violation took place after the retirement of Chief Justice Hasan on 26 January 2004, when Justice JR Mudassir Husain was appointed as the Chief Justice of Bangladesh on 27 January 2004, in supersession of the same two judges—Justices Amin and Karim—who had also superseded him in getting appointed to the AD.[2] This supersession was also justified in the same vein as it had been done on the previous occasion.

However, contrary to the justifications put forward by the regime, it seems the objective behind these supersessions was to secure the appointment of Justice Hasan as the head of the Non-Party "Care-taker" Government (NPCG), which, in pursuance of the Constitution, would have been formed in October 2006 following the dissolution of the Parliament. The argument that Justices Amin and Karim were overlooked for appointment as the Chief Justice on two separate occasions with a view to secure Justice Hasan's appointment as the Chief Adviser of the next NPCG gains further momentum by reference to the fact that immediately following the retirement of Justice Hasan, the retirement age of SC judges was raised by the regime from 65 to 67 through the enactment of the Constitution (Fourteenth Amendment) Act, 2004.[3] This manoeuvre ensured that Justice JR Mudassir Husain would continue as the Chief Justice beyond the general election scheduled for January 2007, thereby making Justice Hasan the first option to head the NPCG in his capacity as the last retired Chief Justice of the country. Thus, it is evident that the ruling party went to great lengths to ensure that Justice Hasan was constitutionally destined to head the next NPCG, perhaps on the belief that he due to his past ties with the party would be willing to unduly influence the outcome of the election in its favour.[4]

---

[1] The Daily Star (2003) (explaining how Justice KM Hasan had been superseded twice by the Awami League Government during 1996–2001: first on January 9, 2000, in elevating Justice Rabbani and Justice Ruhul Amin, and again on May 15, 2001 in elevating Justice Md. Fazlul Karim to the AD. Staff Correspondent), http://archive.thedailystar.net/2003/06/23/d3062301033.htm

[2] Bari (2016), p. 44.

[3] Constitution of Bangladesh, 1972 (Bangladesh) art. 96(1).

[4] Justice K.M. Hasan had served as the International Affairs Secretary of the BNP in 1979 and was subsequently appointed as an Ambassador to Iraq by President Ziaur Rahman. During the first regime of the BNP KM Hasan was involved in BNP Politics in 1979. The Daily Star (2006), http://archive.thedailystar.net/2006/09/21/d6092101022.htm

98   4 The Intrusion of Extraneous Considerations in the Appointment of the Chief Justice...

4.2.2 Supersession during the Non-Party "Care-Taker" Government (2007–2008)

It is pertinent to note here that the prospect of Justice KM Hasan heading the NPCG which would have been formed in October 2006, after the completion of the BNP government's term in office, persuaded the BAL to resort to violent protests, which brought the nation to a complete standstill. Consequently, Justice Hasan declined to accept the position of the Chief Adviser.[5] However, Justice Hasan's refusal to head the NPCG paved the way for President Iajuddin Ahmed, who was elected to the office of the President on a BNP ticket, to assume the position of the Chief Adviser of the NPCG on 29 October 2006, in addition to the responsibilities of the Presidency. However, there is no evidence to suggest that President Ahmed took on this additional responsibility after meaningfully exhausting all other constitutional options for appointing the head of the NPCG.[6] Furthermore, the ascension of President Ahmed, who could hardly be expected to carry out his functions impartially due to his affiliation with the BNP, to the office of Chief Adviser cast serious doubts on the competency of the newly formed NPCG to supervise a free and fair general election, thereby frustrating the very objective underlying the insertion of the system of NPCG into the Constitution. Consequently, the BAL once again resorted to violence—but this time to compel the NPCG led by Ahmed to prove its neutrality.[7] However, the enormity of the BAL's violent campaign gave the Army the convenient premise to intervene. The Army pressurised President Ahmed, on 11 January 2007, to not only proclaim a state of emergency on account of "internal disturbance" but also to step down as the head of the NPCG.[8] Subsequently, on 12 January

---

[5] Bari (2017), p. 186.

[6] The four alternative constitutional options available to President Iajuddin for appointing the Chief Adviser were as follows: First, the *Constitution of Bangladesh* in former art 58C(3) provided that in the event of the reluctance of the last retired Chief Justice to hold the office of Chief Adviser, 'the President shall appoint as Chief Adviser the person who among the retired Chief Justices of Bangladesh retired next before the last retired Chief Justice'.

Secondly, in the event of the unwillingness or unavailability of the last two retired Chief Justices to assume the office of the Chief Adviser, the *Constitution of Bangladesh* in former art 58C(4) provided that 'the President shall appoint as Chief Adviser the person who among the retired Judges of the Appellate Division retired last.'

Thirdly, if the immediate past Judge of the Appellate Division of the Supreme Court was not available or willing to accept the position of the Chief Adviser, the Constitution in former art 58C(4) stipulated that 'the President shall appoint as Chief Adviser the person who among the retired Judges of the Appellate Division retired next before the last such retired Judge'. Finally, if no such Judge of the Appellate Division was available or willing to assume the office of the Chief Adviser, the next constitutional option for the consideration of the President was to search for under former art 58C(5) of the Constitution a consensus candidate after consultation, 'as far as practicable with the major political parties' for appointment as the Chief Adviser. See Bari (2018), p. 59.

[7] Ibid., 60.

[8] See above n 5, p. 186.

4.2 Contravention of the Convention of Seniority in Appointing the Chief Justice...

2007, the Army installed a new NPCG with its preferred candidate—Fakhruddin Ahmed—as the Chief Adviser.[9] However, Ahmed's appointment was also made without the exhaustion of the constitutional provisions governing the appointment of the Chief Adviser of the NPCG.

During the tenure of the NPCG led by Fakhruddin Ahmed, President Iajuddin Ahmed on 25 May 2008, appointed Justice MM Ruhul Amin as the 16th Chief Justice of Bangladesh in supersession of the senior-most judge of the AD, Justice Fazlul Karim.[10] Thus, it is evident that despite being the senior-most judge of the AD, Justice Karim was overlooked for appointment as the Chief Justice thrice over a span of just 5 years.

The President of the Supreme Court Bari Association (SCBA), Barrister Shafique Ahmed, expressed his dissatisfaction and disapproval of such supersession:

> Although supersession has also taken place in appointing Chief Justice and Appellate Division Judges during the past governments, the Bar has never accepted such supersession ... such supersession has led the people concerned to apprehend political ill-detention of the government.[11]

Consequently, the SCBA broke its tradition of welcoming the new Chief Justice when it refrained from felicitating Justice Amin on his assuming the Chief Justice on 1 June 2008.[12]

4.2.3 Supersession during the Present BAL Government (2009- to Date)

The military-backed NPCG, which, as discussed above in Sect. 4.2.2, was installed on 12 January 2007, did not immediately proceed to honour its constitutional mandate of assisting the Election Commission in conducting a free and fair general election for facilitating peaceful transfer of power to a government duly elected by people in exercise of their democratic right to vote. Instead, it deferred the polls indefinitely and made a number of policy decisions, including the reconstitution of the Anti-Corruption Commission and the prosecution of the top leadership of the two major political parties of the nation, including the BAL and the BNP, on charges of corruption on the plea of "cleansing the prevalent corruption in politics".[13] Since the Constitution of Bangladesh, as amended by the Constitution (Thirteenth Amendment) Act, 1996, did not authorise the NPCG to make "any policy decision" unless it was indispensably necessary for the discharge of its "routine functions",[14]

---

[9] See, above n 6, p. 61.

[10] See above n 2, p. 45.

[11] Quoted in ibid.

[12] Ibid., p. 46

[13] See above n 5, pp. 187–188.

[14] Constitution of Bangladesh, 1972 (Bangladesh) former art. 58D (1).

these measures undertaken by the military-backed NPCG cannot be justified as being necessary for the discharge of its functions. Consequently, it seems that these measures were taken to fulfil the Army's aspiration of formally capturing power. However, the foreign dignitaries, who had initially induced the Army to intervene to break the political deadlock over the issue of the appointment of the Chief Adviser of the NPCG, signalled its unwillingness to support Bangladesh's lapse into a military dictatorship.[15] Subsequently, the NPCG announced that a general election would be held on 29 December 2008.

In the election, the BAL-led grand alliance won the right to form a government after winning three-fourths of the 300 parliamentary seats.[16] Since entering office in January 2009, the present BAL government has violated the principle of seniority in appointing the Chief Justice on three occasions: first in December 2009, second in September 2010 and finally in February 2018.

On 23 December 2009, President Zillur Rahman appointed Justice Md Tafazzul Islam as the Chief Justice of Bangladesh in supersession of the senior-most judge of the AD, Justice Mohammad Fazlul Karim.[17] Thus, Justice Karim became the victim of supersession for the fourth time. It is ironic that the then-President of the SCBA who, as pointed out above in 4.2.2, in May 2008 had criticized and disapproved the appointment of Justice Amin as the Chief Justice of Bangladesh during the regime of the NPCG in supersession of Justice Karim, had a complete change of heart as the Minister for Law, Justice and Parliamentary Affairs of the regime of the BAL. As he proposed Justice Islam's appointment as the Chief Justice of Bangladesh, thereby ignoring the same senior judge.

The President again violated the principle of seniority on 26 September 2010, when he appointed Justice ABM Khairul Haque as the 19th Chief Justice of the country ahead of his two senior colleagues in the AD, namely, Justices Abdul Matin and Shah Abu Nayeem Mominur Rahman.[18] It seems that the regime appointed Justice Haque in supersession of his two senior colleagues, as he had:

(a) been appointed as an additional and regular judge of the HCD in 1998 and 2000 respectively by the then BAL government;
(b) upheld a lower court's verdict imposing death penalty on 15 individuals accused of killing *Bangabandhu* Sheikh Mujibur Rahman (the father of the current Prime Minister, Sheikh Hasina), as one of the members of the Death-Reference Bench of the HCD;
(c) delivered, as a judge of the HCD, the judgment declaring the *Constitution (Fifth Amendment) Act, 1979*, which was passed to ratify and confirm all the actions that the first Martial Law Regime (1975–1979) had taken following Sheikh Mujibur Rahman's assassination, unconstitutional; and

---

[15] See, above n 6, p. 64; See above n 5, 191.

[16] See, above n 6, p. 65.

[17] The Daily Star (2009c), https://www.thedailystar.net/news-detail-117925

[18] Mondal (2010), http://www.thedailystar.net/news-detail-157772

4.2 Contravention of the Convention of Seniority in Appointing the Chief Justice...

(d) been elevated to the AD in July 2009 by the present BAL regime.[19]

In light of these factors, it initially appeared that the regime appointed Justice Haque as the Chief Justice as he was deemed to have better imbibed "its gospel" to head the NPCG, which would have been formed in January 2014 after the BAL had concluded its term in office, and to, subsequently, manipulate the outcome of the election in its favour.[20] This objectionable possibility in turn persuaded the President and the Secretary-General of the SCBA to term the "appointment as politically motivated," which had the dreadful impact of tarnishing "the image of the apex court".[21] It is pertinent to stress here that the two superseded judges of the AD considered it dignified to go on leave.[22]

However, in appointing a judge who was ranked third in the seniority list as the Chief Justice, the Government had a more fatal plan in mind, i.e., securing the invalidation of the Thirteenth Amendment, which inserted the Chapter on NPCG in the Constitution of Bangladesh. For such a declaration of unconstitutionality would have enabled the BAL regime to supervise the general election scheduled for January 2014. This plan came to fruition in the case of *Abdul Mannan Khan v. Bangladesh (Thirteenth Amendment Case).*[23] This case involved an appeal against the decision of the HCD in *M Saleem Ullah v. Bangladesh,*[24] which upheld the validity of the incorporation of the provisions concerning the NPCG into the Constitution by the Thirteenth Amendment. In this context, it is pertinent to mention here that in *M. Saleem Ullah,* the petitioners challenged the constitutionality of the Thirteenth Amendment on the basis that it had destroyed a basic structure of the Constitution of Bangladesh, namely, the concept of democracy, by providing for the constitution of a "non-elected and unrepresentative" government, i.e., the NPCG, during the interim period between the dissolution of the Parliament and a general election.[25] However, the HCD in delivering its judgment duly took notice of the troubling electoral history of the nation, which ultimately led to the incorporation of the Chapter on NPCG in the Constitution of Bangladesh in 1996. The Court particularly took notice of the fact that successive political governments in their caretaker capacity had resorted to widespread electoral malpractices to improperly influence the outcome of election in their favour, thereby depriving people of their democratic right to elect governments of their choice and undermining in the process the concept of democracy as woven into the fabric of the Constitution as one of its basic features.[26] This in turn necessitated the incorporation of the mechanism of NPCG in

---

[19] See above n 2, p. 47; The Daily Star (2010b), http://www.thedailystar.net/news-detail-156149

[20] See above n 6, p. 70.

[21] See above n 18.

[22] Ibid.

[23] *Abdul Mannan Khan v. Bangladesh (Thirteenth Amendment Case)* Civil Appeal No. 139 of 2005 with Civil Petition for Leave to Appeal No. 596 of 2005.

[24] *M Saleem Ullah v Bangladesh* (2005) 57 DLR (HCD) 171.

[25] Ibid., pp. 185–186.

[26] Ibid., pp. 176, 180–181.

the Constitution, which succeeded in giving effect to peoples' right to elect governments truly representative of their will by supervising general elections that were "widely acclaimed both at home and abroad as free, fair and independent".[27] Accordingly, the HCD upheld the constitutionality of the Thirteenth Amendment. In this context, it is pertinent to quote the observations of Justice Mirza Hussain Haider:

> With such amendment [the Constitution (Thirteenth Amendment) Act, 1996], free will of the people for exercising their fundamental right of casting vote in the general election, has contributed to the establishment of democracy in its true meaning [sic]. As such, the people of Bangladesh with such amendment came up with a popular slogan... [I will vote for whom I wish]. Thus, it appears that the people have accepted the concept of non-party caretaker Government which has given the real meaning to the term "Democracy" and the democratic process as a whole. The crisis this created in the political arena in practicing democracy, has been solved. Consequently, the general election namely 7th and 8th general elections, for the parliament have been held under the new system and the democratic government elected by the people on exercising their rights freely, fairly and impartially have been running the country for their full terms... It appears that the 13th Amendment Act has actually strengthened and improved the system of holding free, fair and impartial elections by which the people can exercise their fundamental rights freely in electing the government. Thus, it cannot be said to have affected the basic feature of the Constitution [namely, the concept of democracy].[28]

Thus, it is evident from the above observations that the HCD upheld the validity of the Thirteenth Amendment in view of the fact that, instead of affecting or destroying a basic structure or feature of the Constitution, namely, the concept of democracy, the incorporation of the Chapter on NPCG in the Constitution had further strengthened democracy by facilitating free and fair general elections.

However, on appeal, Justice Khairul Haque in delivering the majority judgment in *Abdul Mannan Khan v. Bangladesh*,[29] prospectively declared the Thirteenth Amendment concerning the NPCG unconstitutional[30] notwithstanding its effectiveness, as discussed above, in promoting democracy in Bangladesh. Strikingly, Justice Haque did not issue a full judgment detailing the precise reasoning for reaching such a consequential conclusion. Instead, he issued a "short order", which was merely one-page long, on 10 May 2011—only 8 days before the expiration of his term as the Chief Justice of the nation.[31] However, it is noteworthy that the short order did recommend that the general elections scheduled for 2014 and 2019 should be held under the supervision of NPCGs. This recommendation was, indeed, contradictory to the declaration of the Thirteenth Amendment as being *ultra vires* the Constitution. But Justice Haque sought to justify such a recommendation on the basis of the "old age principles", namely, *quod alias non est licitum, necessitas*

---

[27] Ibid., p. 180.

[28] Ibid., pp. 196–197.

[29] *Abdul Mannan Khan v Bangladesh*, Civil Appeal No. 139 of 2005 with Civil Petition for Leave to Appeal No. 596 of 2005.

[30] Bangladesh Law House (2011a), http://bdlawhouse.blogspot.com.au/2011/06/sc-sets-aside-caretaker-govt-system.html

[31] Ibid.

4.2 Contravention of the Convention of Seniority in Appointing the Chief Justice...

lecitum facit (necessity makes lawful what is otherwise considered unlawful) and *salus populi suprema lex* (the safety of the people is considered the supreme law).[32] It can be strongly argued that the invocation of these principles in the short order was in essence an acknowledgment of the political crisis that had long plagued the nation's electoral process and that ultimately persuaded the politicians to broker a bipartisan solution, namely, the incorporation of the mechanism of NPCG in the Constitution. Consequently, it would have been more appropriate for the AD led by Justice Haque to abstain from reaching such a sweeping decision of invalidating the concept of NPCG through the invocation of the political question doctrine, which is a well-settled principle that certain issues are so politically charged that they are not "justiciable or amenable to judicial review"[33] and, as such, should be more properly left to the discretion of the political branches of the government.[34] It seems that Justice Haque's invocation of the old age principles to justify his incongruous recommendation that only the general elections scheduled for 2014 and 2019 should be held under the supervision of NPCGs was made to keep the door wide open for himself to head the next NPCG. As he would have been the last retired Chief Justice before the 2014 general election.

The short order of Justice Haque had a profoundly adverse impact on the political landscape of the country. The government of BAL conveniently overlooked his recommendation of retaining the system of NPCG for the supervision of next two general elections. Rather, the regime focused solely on the declaration of the Thirteenth Amendment as being *ultra vires* the Constitution. Subsequently, without considering it prudent to wait for the release of the full judgment to contemplate on the reasoning put forward by the court for invalidating the Amendment, the BAL within 53 days of the publication of the short order, on 3 July 2011, used its overwhelming majority in the Parliament to get the Constitution (Fifteenth Amendment) Act, 2011 passed, which repealed the Chapter on the NPCG from the Constitution.[35]

It should be pointed out here that the BAL's election manifesto, which was termed by the party as the "Charter for Change" and was published ahead of the 2008 general election, neither contained any proposal for improving the system of NPCG nor for the deletion of the system from the Constitution.[36] Thus, it is evident that the people were not given any opportunity whatsoever to express either their approval or disapproval on the pivotal issue of repealing the system of NPCG from the Constitution—a system which had facilitated their exercise of the right to vote in free and fair general elections to elect governments truly representative of their will. It seems that the omission of the system of NPCG from the Constitution with unprecedent haste without even eliciting any public opinion was aimed at realizing the BAL's parochial ambition of perpetuating its grip on power. Since the incorpora-

---

[32] Ibid.

[33] Dyzenhaus (2006), p. 19.

[34] See Marbury v. Madison, 5 U.S. (1 Cranch) 137, 165–66 (1803).

[35] Constitution (Fifteenth Amendment) Act, 2011 (Bangladesh) s 21.

[36] The Daily Star (2008a), http://www.thedailystar.net/news-detail-66898

tion of the system of NPCG into the Constitution had enabled the electorate to espouse anti-incumbent sentiment and to never return the incumbent party to power, the BAL considered the system as the principal obstacle to its desire of retaining power permanently. Consequently, through the omission of the system of the NPCG, the BAL had ensured that it would be responsible for supervising the next general election.

The BAL conducted a "virtually voter-less and one-sided" election in January 2014.[37] For, in the first place, the BNP, the principal opposition party, and its allies boycotted the election over their concern that it would be rigged in the absence of a neutral caretaker regime overseeing the electoral process. Second, due to opposition boycott, the BAL and its allies had managed to win 154 seats out of the total 300 unopposed, thereby masterminding the simple majority required to retain power even before a single vote was cast.[38] Strikingly, the BAL's desire to retain power resulted in 48 million registered voters in these 154 electorates being deprived of their right to vote.[39] Following elections in the remaining 146 seats, wherein "only around 20 percent" of the registered voters turned out to vote, the BAL had managed to win a total of 234 seats on its own.[40] Subsequently, the BAL persuaded General HM Ershad's Jatiya Party (JP), which was one of its principal allies in the Grand Alliance that it had formed before the general election in 2008 and had won 34 seats, to act as the opposition in the Parliament. However, the credibility of the JP as an effective opposition was undermined by the fact that three of its lawmakers were made cabinet ministers while its head, Ershad, received appointment as the special envoy to the Prime Minister with the rank and status of a cabinet minister.[41] Thus, it is manifestly evident that the 2014 general election produced a Parliament that was not only devoid of any real opposition but was also subservient to the BAL executive. In fact, it was the first and only Parliament in the world where members of the opposition were also members of the executive branch.

It should be pointed out here that Justice Haque wrote the full judgment of the Court invalidating the Thirteenth Amendment unconstitutional more than a year after he had retired as the Chief Justice of Bangladesh. The judgment was, subsequently, published on 16 September 2012—18 months after the deletion of the system of NPCG from the Constitution. Paradoxically, this judgment was devoid of any reference to the earlier recommendation contained in the "short order" underscoring the necessity of conducting the general elections of 2014 and 2019 under the supervision of the NPCGs. Rather, the judgment prescribed that the future general elections should be held under the supervision of caretaker governments comprising

---

[37] See above n 6, p. 75.

[38] Ibid., p. 76.

[39] Barry (2014), https://www.nytimes.com/2014/01/06/world/asia/boycott-and-violence-mar-elections-in-bangladesh.html

[40] Riaz (2016), p. 68; See UCA NEWS (2014), https://www.ucanews.comlnews/bangladeshi-ruling-party-wins-election-by-default/70019

[41] Riaz (2016), p. 68.

4.2 Contravention of the Convention of Seniority in Appointing the Chief Justice...

elected representatives.[42] Justice Haque sought to justify this deviation from the short order on the basis that the Thirteenth amendment permitted a group of unelected individuals to run the affairs of the country during the interim period between the dissolution of the Parliament and a general election, which was not only undemocratic but also inconsistent with one of the basic structures of the Constitution, namely, the concept of democracy.[43] To this end, Justice Haque relied on:

(a) the preamble of the Constitution, which lists "democracy" as one of the fundamental principles of the Constitution; and
(b) Article 56 of the Constitution, which provides that if the necessity arises in the interim period between "a dissolution of Parliament" and the next general election for the appointment of the Prime Minister and other members of the Cabinet, such appointments should be made only from those persons who were members of the Parliament immediately before its dissolution.[44]

Thus, it seems that Justice Haque had written the majority judgment in a manner which was very much in line with the changes brought forth by the BAL regime through the Fifteenth Amendment Act of 2011. It is further evident that the deletion of the system of NPCG, on the basis of Justice Haque's contention that it went against the democratic fibre of the Constitution, has facilitated Bangladesh's lapse into a one-party dictatorship.

Justice Haque in articulating his arguments for invalidating the Thirteenth Amendment, had also purposefully overlooked the fact that elections held under the supervision of political governments had invariably been rigged to favour the incumbent, which had the impact of undermining the concept of democracy as enshrined in the Constitution. It is this troubling electoral history of the nation which had necessitated the insertion of the system of NPCG in the Constitution by merely rendering the provisions of Article 56 inoperative during the interregnum between the dissolution of the Parliament and a general election. Subsequently, the system of NPCG had succeeded in assisting the Election Commission in holding three credible general elections in 1996, 2001, and 2008 respectively. Thus, contrary to Justice Haque's assertions, it can be strongly argued that the system of NPCG had further consolidated the concept of democracy in Bangladesh.

Finally, Justice Haque in his judgment held that the system of NPCG, in addition to being destructive of the concept of democracy as recognised by the Constitution of Bangladesh, had an adverse impact on the independence of the superior judiciary. To this end, he made reference to the fact that the consideration of political

---

[42] See *Abdul Mannan Khan us. Bangladesh*, Civil Appeal No. 139 of 2005 with Civil Petition for Leave to Appeal No. 596 of 2005, at 14, 252, 340–41.

[43] Ibid., p. 383 ("Thus, our preamble contains the clue to the fundamentals of the Constitution and the basic constituent of our Constitution is the administration of the Republic through their elected representatives. These two integral parts of the Constitution form a basic element which must be preserved and cannot be altered.").

[44] Ibid., p. 385.

allegiance, instead of seniority, had been the dominant factor, as discussed in Sects. 4.2.1 and 4.2.2, in appointing the Chief Justice since the introduction of the system of NPCG.[45] Consequently, the learned judge observed that a caretaker government composed of elected representatives was more conducive to prevent the intrusion of extraneous considerations, such as political favouritism, in the selection process of the judges of the superior judiciary.[46] Thus, it is evident that Justice Haque's solution for obviating the possibility of patronage appointments to the bench was to put an end to the constitutional practice of requiring retired Chief Justices to head caretaker governments. However, contrary to the solution put forward by Justice Haque, as would be evident from the forthcoming discussion, patronage appointments to the bench, including supersession of the senior-most judges in appointing the Chief Justice, has not stopped following the deletion of the system of NPCG from the Constitution.

However, before discussing the final instance of supersession in appointing the Chief Justice, it is apposite to mention here that 10 months after the publication of the full judgment in the Thirteenth Amendment case, on 23 July 2013, the BAL regime appointed Justice Haque as the Chairman of the Law Commission for a period of 3 years. Justice Haque received this appointment with the rank, status, salary, allowance, and other benefits equivalent to those of the Chief Justice of the country.[47] This appointment gave the impression to the politically-conscious citizens of the country that Justice Haque was being rewarded for his services in ensuring that the BAL had perpetuated its grip on power.

The current BAL regime violated the convention of seniority in appointing the Chief Justice for the third time on 2 February 2018, when it appointed Justice Syed Mahmud Hossain as the Chief Justice in supersession of the senior-most judge of the AD, Justice MA Wahab Miah.[48] It is, indeed, striking that the regime overlooked Justice Miah for appointment as the Chief Justice notwithstanding the fact that he had been serving as the Acting Chief Justice of the country for 4 months since October 2017. In this context, it should be noted that Justice Miah was appointed as the Acting Chief Justice in pursuance of Article 97 of the Constitution of Bangladesh, which, as pointed out earlier in Sect. 3.2, in an attempt to prevent patronage appointment obliges the President to follow the mechanical rule of seniority in appointing the Acting Chief Justice when a vacancy arises in the office of Chief Justice or when "absence, illness, or any other cause" renders the Chief Justice incapable of discharging the duties of his office.

Thus, it is evident that the BAL regime frustrated Justice Miah's legitimate expectation of being appointed to the highest judicial office of the land notwithstanding his seniority and his performing the functions of such office on an interim

---

[45] Ibid., pp. 14, 252, 313.

[46] Ibid., p. 339.

[47] See The Daily Star (2016), http://www.thedailystar.net/city/ex-cj-khairul-haque-reappointed-law-commission-chair-1248835

[48] Sarkar (2018), https://www.thedailystar.net/frontpage/justice-mahmud-hossain-made-cj-1529263

4.2 Contravention of the Convention of Seniority in Appointing the Chief Justice... 107

basis. Consequently, Justice Miah considered it dignified to resign as a judge of the AD within hours of the appointment of Justice Hossain as the new Chief Justice.[49] Hence, the BAL regime's decision to flout the principle of seniority in appointing the Chief Justice deprived the nation of the services of a senior and experienced judge.

Although the regime did not offer any reasoning for depriving Justice Miah the Chief Justiceship, it seems that he was overlooked for the position as he went against the wishes of the BAL regime by pronouncing a dissenting judgment in the *Thirteenth Amendment Case* upholding the constitutionality of the system of NPCG. The learned judged reached such a conclusion in light of the fact that the system had further consolidated the principle of democracy in Bangladesh.[50] Instead, Justice Hossain was deemed more trustworthy for appointment as the Chief Justice as it was the BAL regime which had: (a) appointed him to serve as the Deputy Attorney General in 1999; (b) appointed him to the HCD as an additional judge in 2001; and (c) ultimately, elevated him to the AD in 2011.[51]

Thus, the BAL has now surpassed the previous record set by the BNP government (2001–2006), as discussed above in Sect. 4.2.1, in violating the principle of seniority to appoint the Chief Justice of the county. It is further evident that contrary to Justice Haque's prescription as articulated in the *Thirteenth Amendment Case*, the deletion of the system of NPCG from the Constitution has not had the desired effect of preventing the violation of the convention of appointing the senior-most judge of the AD as the Chief Justice. It should be stressed here that the violation of the principle of seniority in appointing the Chief Justice not only causes injustice to the superseded judge by frustrating his legitimate expectation of being appointed to the highest judicial official of the nation, but also makes room for further injustices likely to be meted out in the future against litigants, particularly in cases where the government is a party. This also has the disastrous impact of making the highly dignified and prestigious office of the Chief Justice controversial and of, consequently, lowering public confidence in the impartiality of the highest court of the land. It is difficult to calculate the aggregate amount of evil inflicted on the community by such a decision to violate the convention of seniority. Furthermore, if the superseded judges resign in protest or take leave until retirement, as had occurred when Justice Miah resigned from office in February 2018 as a mark of protest upon being superseded by the BAL regime for appointment as the Chief Justice of Bangladesh, the country will be deprived of the services of senior, experienced, and competent judges. It can hardly be expected, especially in third world countries, that the junior judge appointed as the Chief Justice overlooking the claim of his senior colleagues, will refuse to accept such an appointment to save the highest court from political clout and controversy.

---

[49] BDNEWS24.COM (2018), https://bdnews24.com/bangladesh/2018/02/02/justice-wahhab-miah-resigns-after-justice-mahmud-hossain-is-named-chief-justice

[50] *Abdul Mannan Khan v. Bangladesh*, Civil Appeal No. 139 of 2005 with Civil Petition for Leave to Appeal No. 596 of 2005 (Bangl.), at 35.

[51] See above n 48.

4.3 The Violation of the Convention of Seniority in Appointing the Judges of the AD

The convention of following seniority in appointing judges of the AD was consistently followed for about 4 years following the coming into force of the Constitution of Bangladesh, i.e., from 16 December 1972 to 12 August 1976. But since 13 August 1976, this convention has been transgressed at regular intervals by successive governments. These instances of contravention of the principle of seniority can be grouped under two categories, namely, supersession during Martial Law and autocratic regimes, and supersession during civilian regimes. It would be evident from this discussion that political considerations only became a motivating factor for superseding senior judges of the HCD in elevating judges to the AD during the tenure of the second BAL regime (1996–2001) following the restoration of parliamentary democracy in Bangladesh in 1991.

4.3.1 Contravention of the Principle of Seniority in Appointing Judges of the AD during Martial Law and Autocratic Regimes

An attempt will now be made to examine the instances of supersession of the senior most judges of the HCD in appointing judges to the AD of the SC during the Martial Law regimes of 1975 and 1982, and the autocratic regime of 1986.

4.3.1.1 Contravention of the Principle of Seniority in Appointing Judges of the AD by the First Martial Law Regime (August 1975– April 1979)

Martial Law, as pointed out earlier in Sect. 3.5.2, was declared for the first time in the history of Bangladesh on 15 August 1975 following the assassination of the President of the country, Sheikh Mujibur Rahman (Muib). Subsequently, the convention of the principle of seniority in appointing judges to the SC was violated for the first time in the history of Bangladesh when the President and Chief Martial Law Administrator, Justice Sayem, elevated Justice Debesh Chandra Bhattachari to the AD superseding the senior-most judge of the HCD, Justice Ruhul Islam.[52] Although the first martial law regime set in motion the disturbing practice of superseding senior-most judges of the HCD in appointing judges of the AD, no political or other motivation was apparent behind this lone instance of supersession during the life of this regime.

---

[52] Bari (2016), p. 56.

4.3 The Violation of the Convention of Seniority in Appointing the Judges of the AD 109

Bangladesh, as mentioned earlier in Sect. 3.5.2, returned to civilian rule on 6 April 1979, at the initiative of President Ziaur Rahman (Zia), who was the founder of the BNP. During the rule of the BNP from 6 April 1979 to 23 March 1982, there were no violations of the principle of seniority in appointing judges of the AD.

4.3.1.2 Violation of the Principle of Seniority in Elevating Judges to the AD by the Second Martial Law Regime (March 1982–November 1986)

Bangladesh's return to civilian rule, as pointed out earlier in Sect. 3.5.2, was short-lived as Zia was assassinated on 30 May 1981. Within only 9 months and 25 days of Zia's assassination, on 24 March 1982, the Chief of Army Staff, Lt General HM Ershad, executed a bloodless coup disposing the democratically elected government of the BNP. Ershad, subsequently, placed the entire country under Martial Law for the second time in its history and suspended the operation of the Constitution. This declaration of Martial Law belied the assertion of Shah Azizur Rahman, who served as the Prime Minister of the BNP government from April 1979 to March 1982, made in the Parliament on 2 March 1982—merely 22 days before the proclamation of the second Martial Law—that there was no possibility of the imposition of another martial law in Bangladesh as "democracy ha[d] found firm roots in the soil of Bangladesh".[53]

After the declaration of Martial Law, the convention of seniority in appointing judges to the AD amongst the judges of the HCD was violated on two occasions, in April 1982 and December 1985 respectively. On 21 April 1982, Ershad, as the Chief Martial Law Administrator, promoted Justice ATM Masud to the AD, bypassing the senior-most judge of the HCD—Justice Mohsin Ali.[54] Three years and eight months later, on 26 December 1985, Ershad, as the President of Bangladesh, elevated Justices MH Rahman and ATM Afzal to the AD superseding three senior HCD judges, namely, Justices ARM Amirul Islam Chowdhury, Md Habibur Rahman (CSP) and Abdul Matin Khan Chowdhry.[55] Similar to the first Martial Law regime, no extraneous considerations could be found behind the decision of the second Martial Law regime to violate the principle of seniority in appointing the judges of the AD.

---

[53] Thomas (1982).

[54] International Ecological Safety Collaborative Organization (2016), http://www.iesco-iesco.org/content/en-US/p2068_k913.aspx; The Daily Star (2015), http://www.thedailystar.net/justice-masud-passes-away-573

[55] The Observer (2015), https://www.observerbd.com/2015/01/10/65593.php

4.3.1.3 Breach of the Principle of Seniority in Appointing Judges of the AD by the Civilian Regime of HM Ershad (1986–1990)

More than 4 years after the declaration of Martial Law, Ershad sought to become a civilian President by contesting on the ticket of his newly established party, namely, the Jatiya Party. He, subsequently, won a controversial Presidential election on 15 October 1986.[56] Three years later in 1989, Ershad breached the convention of following seniority in appointing Justice Mustafa Kamal, a HCD Judge, as a judge of the AD ignoring the two senior-most judges of the HCD—Justice ARM. Amirul Islam Chowdhury and Justice Sultan Hossain Khan.[57]

4.3.2 *Breach of the Violation of the Principle of Seniority in Appointing the Judges of the AD following the Return to Parliamentary Democracy*

After more than 8 years of iron-fist rule, Ershad was forced out of office on 6 December 1990 after people from all walks of life, including doctors, lawyers, university teachers, journalists, government officials and workers and employees, brought the country to a standstill demanding his resignation.[58] Following Ershad's resignation, Chief Justice Shahabuddin Ahmed was sworn in as the Acting President and his interim government was given the responsibility of assisting the Election Commission to hold a free and fair general election, which was held on 27 February 1991.[59] Following the election, the BNP formed a government after masterminding a simple majority in the Parliament with the support of the principal Islamic party of the country, *Jamaat-e-Islami*. Within 6 months of forming a government, the BNP introduced the Constitution (Twelfth Amendment) Bill, 1991, which was unanimously passed by the Parliament on 6 August 1991. This Twelfth Amendment Act, among other things, reintroduced parliamentary democracy in Bangladesh by vesting the "executive power of the Republic" in the Prime Minister,[60] while making the President the ceremonial head of the state.[61]

An attempt will now be made to discuss the instances of the contravention of the principle of seniority in appointing the judges of the AD following the restoration of

---

[56] See above n 5, p. 181.

[57] See above n 53.

[58] Bari, States of Emergency, 184–185.

[59] Ibid.

[60] Constitution of Bangladesh, 1972 (Bangladesh) art. 55(2) (as amended by s 3 of the Constitution (Twelfth Amendment) Act, 1991.

[61] Constitution of Bangladesh, 1972 (Bangladesh) art. 48(3) (as amended by s 3 of the Constitution (Twelfth Amendment) Act, 1991.

4.3 The Violation of the Convention of Seniority in Appointing the Judges of the AD 111

parliamentary democracy in Bangladesh during the successive regimes of the BNP and BAL.

4.3.2.1 Violation of the Principle of Seniority in Elevating Judges to the AD during the BNP Regime (1991–1996)

During the regime of BNP, President Abdur Rahman Biswas elevated Justices Abdur Rouf and Ismail Uddin Sarkar to the AD on 8 June 1995, bypassing the senior-most judge of the HCD, Justice ARM Amirul Islam Chowdhury.[62] Thus, Justice Chowdhury was ignored on four occasions in elevating junior judges to the AD—twice each by Presidents Ershad and Biswas.

4.3.2.2 Violation of the Convention of Seniority in Appointing Judges to the AD during the Regime of the BAL (1996–2001)

During the second regime of the BAL, the two senior-most judges of the HCD, Justices Md Mozammel Haque and Qazi Shafiuddin, fell victim to supersession on three separate occasions. These two judges were overlooked for appointment to the AD for the first time when President Shahabuddin Ahmed elevated Justice Mahmudul Amin Chowdhury to the highest court of appeal on 28 June 1999. Subsequently, the learned judges were superseded when the President elevated Justices Kazi Ebadul Haque and Mainur Reza Chowdhury to the AD on 19 January and 28 November 2000 respectively.[63]

It seems that both Justices Haque and Shafiuddin were victimized for their bold decisions in certain sensitive cases. In November 2000, Justice Haque held the preventive detention orders of four leaders of the opposition political party, BNP, as illegal and ordered the BAL government to pay BD Taka four lac (four hundred thousand) as compensation to the BNP leaders for unnecessarily keeping them in preventive custody.[64] Furthermore, in *Mainul Hosein v. Sheikh Hasina Wazed*—[65] a case which required the HCD to rule on the merit of three petitions seeking the institution of contempt of court proceedings against Prime Sheikh Hasina for her allegation made in an interview with the British Broadcasting Corporation (BBC) that both the lower and superior judiciary had turned into a sanctuary for criminals as they were released on bail whenever they approached the courts—Justice Haque made the following courageous observations:

---

[62] See above n 53.

[63] Ibid.

[64] Ibid.; The Daily Star (1997), https://www.thedailystar.net/news/detention-of-4-bnp-leaders-declared-illegal

[65] *Mainul Hosein v. Sheikh Hasina Wazed* 53 DLR (2001) 138 (HCD 2000)

112   4   The Intrusion of Extraneous Considerations in the Appointment of the Chief Justice...

> We are disposing of three applications for drawing of proceedings of contempt of Court against the Honourable Prime Minister Sheikh Hasina with a note of desire that the Honourable Prime Minister shall be more careful and respectful in making any statement or comment with regard to the Judiciary or the judges or the courts of Bangladesh in future.[66]

On the other hand, it seems Justice Shafiuddin had to pay a heavy price for his decision in 1995 in *Anwar Hossain Khan v. Speaker of Bangladesh Sangsad Bhaban and Others.*[67] The case involved a challenge to the legality of Members of Parliament (MPs) belonging to the BAL boycotting eight sessions of the Parliament for 101 days from February 1994 to July 1995 during the regime of the BNP Government (1991–1996). Justice Shafiuddin gave an order directing the abstaining opposition members to attend the Parliament in order to perform and discharge their constitutional obligations. He further observed:

> We declare that the salary, emoluments, allowances and other benefits so received by the respondents are illegal and unauthorised. The aforesaid illegal and unauthorised receipts of salaries, emoluments and allowances by the absentee members of the Parliament without leave of the Parliament are recoverable by appropriate authority upon the processes of law.[68]

Although Justice Haque quietly went into retirement on 1 December 2000, Justice Shafiuddin preferred to resign from office on 9 November 2000—almost a year before was supposed to retire on 1 November 2001—as a mark of protest against his supersession on three separate occasions. Two days after retirement, Justice Shafiuddin in an interview with one of the national dailies claimed that he might have been superseded for his above decision given against the BAL MPs in the *Anwar Hossain Case.*[69]

Notwithstanding the controversies surrounding the political overtones in the above instances of supersessions, President Ahmed violated the convention of seniority for the fourth time on 10 January 2001 in elevating: (a) Justice Golam Rabbani in preference to his senior colleague in the HCD, Justice KM Hasan, and (b) Justice Ruhul Amin ahead of his senior colleague, Justice JR Mudassir Husain. Furthermore, these instances of supersession took place despite the Chief Justice's recommendation that all these four senior judges should be elevated to the AD and that seniority should be respected in elevating them.

Since the appointment of these judges—ranked second and fourth respectively in the list of four senior judges of the HCD recommended by the Chief Justice for elevation to the AD—disregarded a time-honoured convention, it sparked unprecedent protests by lawyers of the SC, including 13 senior lawyers. A meeting between the President of the SCBA, senior lawyers, and former presidents and secretaries of the SCBA, was held at the SCBA office on 10 January 2001.[70] In the meeting, these senior lawyers decided to form a new forum, the Supreme Council of Lawyers, with

---

[66] *Mainul Hosein v. Sheikh Hasina Wazed* 53 DLR (2001) 138, 142 (HCD 2000).

[67] *Anwar Hossain Khan v. Speaker of Bangladesh Sangsad Bhaban and Others* 47 DLR (1995) 42.

[68] *Anwar Hossain Khan v. Speaker of Bangladesh Sangsad Bhaban and Others* 42, 53.

[69] Bari (2016), p. 60.

[70] Ibid.

4.3 The Violation of the Convention of Seniority in Appointing the Judges of the AD

Ishtiaque Ahmed—a distinguished lawyer—as its Convener, to "unite all lawyers to protect the judiciary from interference and keep its independence".[71] It was further agreed that the two superseded judges, Justices Hasan and Husain, who were in the "list of senior judges" submitted by the Chief Justice, should be appointed to the AD. The five-member Committee was given the task of pursuing the matter with the relevant authorities. Accordingly, the Committee met with President Ahmed on 13 January 2001, and requested that he take the necessary measures for elevating the two superseded HCD Judges to the AD. The President told the Committee that "the proposal should have been given due consideration but he has constitutional limitations as he acts on the recommendation of the Prime Minister".[72]

Realizing that they were knocking on the wrong door, the members of the Committee sought an appointment to meet with Prime Minister Hasina. But the Prime Minister refused to meet the members of the Committee, which showed how committed she was to her position. Subsequently, on 15 January 2001, the Minister of Law, Justice, and Parliamentary Affairs made a statement before the Parliament stating that the appointment of judges to the AD was not a matter of promotion and, as such, seniority was not the only criterion for making appointments.[73] Rather, the Minister remarked that qualities, such as competence, knowledge of law, and commitment to the rule of law, were also taken into account in appointing judges to the AD.[74]

Notwithstanding the explanation put forward by the Law Minister, a group of lawyers of the SC—considered "pro-opposition" lawyers—urged the Chief Justice not to administer the oath of office to Justices Rabbani and Amin, who were elevated to the AD in supersession of their senior colleagues.[75] But Chief Justice Rahman, nevertheless, proceeded with the scheduled oath taking ceremony, which was attended by all the judges of the SC. The ceremony took place on 10 January 2001, at his Chamber instead of the Judges' Lounge due to a demonstration organized by the lawyers for voicing their displeasure.[76] The judges were confined in Lounge for more than 2 hours by the agitating lawyers.[77] Furthermore, the lawyers forced suspension of the SC's functioning on 11 January 2001. Consequently, a case was filed against 16 "Pro-Opposition" lawyers, including BNP lawmakers Nazmul Huda and Khandaker Mahbub Uddin, under the Public Safety Act of 2000 for their involvement in the demonstration at the SC.[78]

Furthermore, it seems that Justice Ruhul Amin was not elevated to the AD solely based on the criteria, as had been proffered by the Law Minister in the Parliament,

---

[71] Ibid.

[72] Ibid, 61.

[73] See above n 2, p. 61.

[74] Ibid.

[75] Ibid.

[76] Ibid.

[77] See above n 70.

[78] Bari (2016), p. 61.

but rather as a reward for his verdict upholding of the death penalties of 10 of the 15 accused in the *Bangabandhu Sheikh Mujibur Rahman* (the father of the Prime Minister) *Murder Case* as a member of the Death-Reference Bench of the HCD.[79] Conversely, Justice KM Hasan, the senior most judge of the HCD, was victimized for his decision to recuse himself from the proceedings of the Death-Reference Bench due to his familial relationship with one of the accused. A further ulterior motive in not elevating Justice Hasan to the AD was his previous connection with the BNP as had been divulged by the Prime Minister herself in a public address given in *Sitakunda* on 17 January 2001, when she said that the BNP wanted their former party leader to be elevated to the AD for politicizing the court, which had duly been frustrated.[80]

Within a few months, the elevations of Justices Rabbani and Amin as judges of the AD in supersession of two of their senior colleagues in the HCD were challenged by a junior Advocate of the SC and the Secretary General of an NGO, namely, the Bangladesh Human Rights Commission, before the HCD in the case of *SN Goswami, Advocate v. Bangladesh*.[81] This was the first time in the history of Bangladesh that instances of supersession of senior judges in the appointment of judges to the AD was challenged before a court of law. Justice Syed Amirul Islam, who delivered the judgment on 3 June 2001, upheld the legality of the said appointments. As he observed:

> Question of supersession can only arise in a case of promotion to a higher post. In the present case we are not concerned with the promotion of the judges of the High Court Division, to the Appellate Division. It is rather the appointment of two new judges in the Appellate Division which is in dispute. An appointment of a judge to the Appellate Division from amongst the judges of the High Court Division is not a promotion, it is a fresh appointment made by the President under Article 95(1) of the Constitution from amongst the qualified persons as contained in Sub Article (2) of Article 95 of the Constitution … The actions of the President in the matter of appointment of judges of either Division of this Court are not unfettered in that in appointing a person in the judgeship of either Division the precedent condition as laid down in Article 95(2) has to be complied with. Once the requirements as laid down in Article 95(2) are fulfilled and the President acts on the advice of the Prime Minister, this Court cannot cause an inquiry as to the reason of appointing that person as a Judge.[82]

It is noticeable that the learned Justice himself held that the qualification requirements, as laid down in Article 95 of the Constitution, are equally applicable to the appointment of judges of both the Divisions of the SC. Thus, the Constitution itself has not provided for any specific criteria, such as: (a) number of cases disposed of as a HCD judge, thereby demonstrating merit and quality; (b) handling of complex cases particularly involving constitutional issues; and (c) analytical ability and professional standard which are in higher demand for an AD judge than a HCD judge.

---

[79] The Hindu (2009), https://www.thehindu.com/news/international/Mujibrsquos-killers-case-A-chronology-of-events/article16892929.ece

[80] Bari (2016), p. 62.

[81] *SN Goswami, Advocate v. Bangladesh* 55 DLR (2003) 332.

[82] *SN Goswami, Advocate v. Bangladesh* 55 DLR (2003) 332, 342.

4.3 The Violation of the Convention of Seniority in Appointing the Judges of the AD

Furthermore, there is no provision for the advertisement of vacant posts in the AD and selection of candidates by a judicial committee consisting of majority members from the highest court of the land. Therefore, contrary to the learned judge's claim, the appointment of judges to the AD from amongst the HCD judges appears to be in essence a promotion rather than a fresh appointment.

Regarding the recommendation of the Chief Justice that all the relevant four judges of the HCD were equally competent and that seniority should be respected, the learned Justice held:

> Be that as it may, if all the judges were equally competent, the Executive did not commit any illegality in choosing any two from the equal four inasmuch as there is no law or constitutional provision or convention, requiring the seniors to be appointed.[83]

Thus, it is evident that the convention, as pointed out above in Sects. 3.3 and 4.3, of respecting seniority in appointing judges to the AD from amongst the judges of the HCD, was unknown to Justice Islam. However, he offered some guidance as to the matters to be taken into consideration in elevating a judge of the HCD to the AD. As he observed:

> We are aware of the opinion that if a judge of this Division is elevated to the Appellate Division it should not be on the basis of seniority alone, rather it should be on the basis of seniority-cum-merit. The hard reality is that the quality of the judges of this Division, though are of a satisfactory level, all are not equal. Some are more brilliant than others. Thus, if seniority be the sole criterion for elevation then the most brilliant may be left behind and the less competent may be elevated to the Appellate Division simply because he was appointed a judge of this Division at an earlier point of time than the others. This will have the following effect on the highest judiciary; firstly, the most brilliant judges may be left behind though they could make better contribution to the judiciary. Secondly, if seniority-cum-merit becomes the criterion then right after the appointment of a judge in this Division he will do his best to improve the quality of his judgment and his overall performance as a judge and there will be a sense of competitiveness among the judges in performing their judicial duties. This will immensely benefit the nation as a whole and the judiciary in particular and the most meritorious will move ahead the less meritorious. The judges of this Division will then leave no stone unturned to devote themselves whole-heartedly to the job–day in and day out during the tenure of their office.[84]

It is difficult to agree with the above observations. For manifestation of merit and its objective assessment are very difficult to ascertain. If the President is to decide these, then, to use the words of the same judge, "the independence of judiciary will never be attained". As he observed in *State v. Chief Editor, Manabjamin*[85]:

> [C]an the Government, namely, the major litigant, be justified in enjoying absolute authority in nominating and appointing its arbitrators? The answer would be in the negative. The executive cannot be allowed to enjoy the absolute primacy in the matter of appointment of judges as its "royal privilege". If such a process is allowed to continue, the independence of judiciary will never be attained.[86]

---

[83] *SN Goswami, Advocate v. Bangladesh* 55 DLR (2003) 332, 343–344.

[84] *SN Goswami, Advocate v. Bangladesh* 55 DLR (2003) 332, 349.

[85] *State v. Chief Editor, Manabjamin* 31 CLC 3805, 3806 (HCD, 2002).

[86] *State v. Chief Editor, Manabjamin* 31 CLC 3805, [253].

116   4   The Intrusion of Extraneous Considerations in the Appointment of the Chief Justice...

In the same vein, if the Chief Justice alone is given the task of evaluating the merits of the judges of the HCD, there is again the possibility, as articulated by the same judge, of the following apprehension:

> [A]fter all the Chief Justice is a man with all the failings, all the sentiments and all the prejudices which we as common people have and therefore we think that the matter should not be left in the hands of the learned Chief Justice alone and a better result would be derived if the opinion is formed in the matter of appointment of judges in the Full Court Meeting of the Supreme Court.[87]

However, during the pendency of the *SN Goswami Case*, President Ahmed once again contravened the principle of seniority in appointing a judge of the AD. On 15 May 2001, President Ahmed elevated Justice Md Fazlul Karim to the AD in supersession of three senior judges of the HCD, namely, Justices KM Hasan, Syed JR Mudassir Husain and Abu Sayeed Ahmed.[88] In this context, it is pertinent to note that Justice Karim due to a split decision of the two-member Death Reference Bench of the HCD in the *Bangabandhu Murder Case*, had delivered the final judgment as the third judge in a second HCD bench confirming the death sentences of 12 of the accused.

Thus, the convention of seniority in appointing judges of the AD from amongst the HCD judges was violated on five occasions during the government of the BAL, and both Justices Hasan and Husain became the victim of supersession on two occasions.

4.3.2.3   Contravention of the Convention of Seniority in Appointing Judges of the AD during the BNP Regime (2001–2006)

The BNP government, which was in office from October 2001 to October 2006, adhered to the convention of seniority in elevating judges to the AD from amongst the HCD judges for about 2 years. Justice KM Hasan, who, as pointed out above in Sect. 4.3.2.2, had been superseded twice during the BAL regime, was elevated to the AD on 20 January 2002.[89] Nearly 2 months later, on 5 March 2002, Justice Syed JR Mudassir Husain, who had also been superseded twice by the BAL government, and Justice Abu Syed Ahmed, who had been bypassed once, were appointed to the AD. Justices Kazi ATM Monowaruddin, Fazlul Hoque and Md. Hamidul Hoque were also appointed to the AD on 25 June 2002, 17 July 2002 and 29 June 2003, respectively, without any deviation from the principle of seniority.[90]

But the BNP regime departed from the convention of following seniority for the first time on 13 July 2003, when Justice MM Ruhul Amin was appointed to the AD

---

[87] *State v. Chief Editor, Manabjamin* 31 CLC 3805, [248].

[88] Shamsuddin   and   Jahan   (2016),   http://www.thedailystar.net/law-our-rights/long-way-gone-1246612; See above n 79.

[89] The Daily Star (2003), http://archive.thedailystar.net/2003/06/23/d3062301033.htm

[90] See above n 2, p. 65.

4.3 The Violation of the Convention of Seniority in Appointing the Judges of the AD   117

in supersession of Justice Syed Amirul Islam, who, as discussed above, had given the judgment in the *SN Goswami Case*, opposing the principle of seniority in elevating judges to the AD. Justice Islam was superseded for the second time the very next month, when, on 27 August 2003, Justice Md Tofazzal Islam was appointed as a judge of the AD.[91] He was superseded for the third and fourth times in appointing Justices MA Aziz and Amirul Kabir Chowdhury to the AD on 7 January 2004, and 26 February 2004 respectively.[92] When Justice Aziz received appointment as the Chief Election Commissioner on 23 May 2005, Justice Md Joynul Abedin succeeded him to the AD in supersession of three senior judges of the HCD—Justices Syed Amirul Islam, Md Hassan Ameen, and AK Badrul Hoque.[93]

In this context, it is pertinent to reiterate that it was Justice Syed Amirul Islam who in the *SN Goswami Case* had upheld the instances of supersession in elevating judges to the AD supposedly due to the absence of any "constitutional provision or convention" to that effect and had maintained that appointment should be made on the basis of "seniority-cum-merit" for instilling a sense of competitiveness among the judges. Thus, it appears that he had failed to make an impression on his appointing authority during the BNP regime on five occasions, to use his own words, as "the most meritorious" judge for moving "ahead the less meritorious."[94] However, it can be argued that his repeated supersessions might have finally made him realize that in most cases of supersession, political considerations or affiliations instead of merit had been the dominant factors.

4.3.2.4   Contravention of the Convention of Seniority in Appointing Judges of the AD during the Present BAL Regime (January 2009- to Date)

The Supreme Judicial Commission, which, as discussed earlier in Sect. 3.7, was established on 16 March 2008, through a Presidential Ordinance during the regime of the NPCG for selecting and recommending "competent persons for appointment as judges of the Supreme Court," in its first meeting held on 17 October 2008, recommended four senior-most judges of the HCD, namely, Justices Shah Abu Nayeem Mominur Rahman, Md Abdul Quddus, Md Abdul Aziz and Bijan Kumar Das, for appointment against the two vacant posts in the AD. Although the life of the Supreme Judicial Commission, as will be evident from the forthcoming discussion, was calculatedly brought to an abrupt end in February 2009 by the current government of the BAL following its election in January 2009, the President on 4 March

---

[91] Ibid.

[92] Ibid.

[93] Liton (2005), http://archive.thedailystar.net/2005/05/24/d5052401011.htm

[94] *SN Goswami v. Bangladesh*, 55 DLR (HCD) 332, 343–49 (2003).

118   4   The Intrusion of Extraneous Considerations in the Appointment of the Chief Justice...

2009, appointed Justices Shah Abu Nayeem Mominur Rahman and Md Abdul Aziz—both recommended by the defunct Commission, as judges of the AD.[95]

After increasing the number of posts of judges in the AD of SC from seven to 11 on 9 July 2009, President Rahman on 14 July 2009, appointed four senior-most judges of the HCD, Justices Bijan Kumar Das, ABM Khairul Haque, Md Muzzammel Hossain and Surendra Kumar Sinha, as judges of the AD.[96] The principle of seniority was also observed in the elevation of Justices MA Wahab Miah, Nazmun Ara Sultana, Syed Mahmud Hossain and M Imman Ali to the AD on 23 February 2011.[97]

Thus, it seems that the present regime of the BAL, which has the previous track record of violating the convention of seniority in appointing the Chief Justice of Bangladesh and judges of the AD on numerous occasions, had initially complied with the convention of seniority in appointing judges from the HCD to the AD, perhaps keeping in mind the SCBA's persistent and assiduous demand for conforming to the principle of seniority in the "promotion process".[98]

However, the regime returned to its previous tradition of overlooking senior judges of the HCD in making appointments to the AD approximately 8 months prior to the completion of its tenure in office. On 28 March 2013, the President elevated four judges, Justices Mohammad Anwarul Haque, Siddiqur Rahman Miah, Hasan Foez Siddique and AHM Shamsuddin Chowdhury Manik, of the HCD to the AD.[99] Of these four, the principle of seniority was followed only in respect of the appointment of Justice Haque. Justice Miah was promoted in supersession of three of his colleagues in the HCD while Justices Siddique and Manik were elevated in supersession of an astounding 38 senior judges.[100] Both Justices Siddique and Manik had received their initial appointments as additional judges of the HCD in 2001 when the BAL was in power. The SCBA maintained its tradition of protesting the supersession of senior judges of the HCD in appointing the judges of the AD. It arranged for demonstration on the walkway of the first floor of the SC Building where the said judges were administered oath on 31 March 2013.[101]

It should be stressed here that among the above four appointees, the elevation of Justice Manik was the most controversial. First, Justice Manik, during his tenure as a judge of the HCD, not only made political statements but also sided with the ruling party during a TV talk show in April 2010, in contravention of the Code of

---

[95] The Daily Star (2009a), http://www.thedailystar.net/news-detail-78543

[96] The Daily Star (2009b), http://archive.thedailystar.net/newDesign/print_news.php?nid=96998

[97] The Daily Star (2011b), http://www.thedailystar.net/news-detail-175201

[98] Sarkar (2010b), http://www.thedailystar.net/news-detail-167079

[99] The Daily Star (2013a, b), https://www.thedailystar.net/news-detail-96998

[100] The Daily Star (2013b), https://www.thedailystar.net/news/skip-oath-to-4-new-sc-judges; NEWS FROM BANGLADESH.NET (2013), http://newsfrombangladesh.net/new/readers-opinion/11293-controversial-appointment-of-judges-in-the-appalate-division-of-the-supreme-court-bad-precedent-has-been-created

[101] See above n 99.

4.3 The Violation of the Convention of Seniority in Appointing the Judges of the AD 119

Conduct for Judges of the SC of 2000,[102] which was in force at the time prohibiting judges from expressing their views in public on political matters.[103] Second, he used his bench, which also included a junior judge, as an avenue for persecuting academicians, civil society members, journalists, and lawyers on account of their political beliefs which went against the party in power. For instance, Justice Manik ordered the arrest of MU Ahmed, a Pro-BNP lawyer and a former Assistant Attorney General, for allegedly obstructing the law enforcement agencies from performing their duties during a scuffle that broke out between the Pro-BNP and Pro-BAL lawyers before his bench. The scuffle had broken out after the judge had remarked during a hearing on 2 August 2011 that the statement of Begum Khaleda Zia, the BNP Chairperson and former Prime Minister, about the adverse impact of the Constitution (Fifteenth Amendment) Act, 2011, which, as discussed above in Sect. 4.2.3, repealed the system of NPCG, on the Constitution was "tantamount to sedition".[104]

In pursuance of the order, Ahmed was arrested in the early hours of 11 August 2011. He was allegedly tortured in police custody to the extent that within 5 hours of his arrest he suffered a massive heart attack. Although he was admitted to a local hospital for medical treatment, he passed away on 26 August 2011—15 days after his arrest.[105] The arrest and subsequent death of Ahmed outraged the legal fraternity. The SCBA passed a resolution blaming Justice Manik for his death.[106] However, Justice Manik's response to this was not befitting the high office he was holding at the time. For he once again, in contravention of the Code of Conduct of 2000, which not only required judges to maintain a degree of aloofness consistent with the dignity of their office but also prohibited them from making their views public on matters "that… [were] pending or …[were] likely to arise for judicial determination,"[107] participated in a TV talk-show, and claimed that Ahmed had died of his pre-existing physical condition and not due to police persecution.[108]

---

[102] The Constitution in Article 96(4)(a) empowered the Supreme Judicial Council, which was entrusted with the task of investigating allegations of incapacity or misconduct against judges of the SC and of, subsequently, recommending removal, if proved, of such judges, to "prescribe a Code of Conduct to be observed by the Judges". Accordingly, on 7 May 2000, the Council headed by then Chief Justice Latifur Rahman formulated a Code of Conduct for the Judges of the Supreme Court. However, the BAL after returning to power through the controversial election of 2014 used its overwhelming majority in the Parliament to get the Constitution (Sixteenth Amendment) Act 2014 passed, which replaced the provisions concerning the Supreme Judicial Council in Article 96 of the Constitution with provisions which gave the Parliament the *carte blanche* power to recommend the removal of judge of the Supreme Court from office.

[103] Bangladesh Law House (2011b), http://bdlawhouse.blogspot.com/2011/10/code-of-conduct-for-judges.html

[104] Ibid.

[105] Ibid.

[106] Jasim (2015), http://thedailynewnation.com/news/67594/unprecedented-departure-of-justice-shamsuddin.html

[107] See above n 103.

[108] The Daily Star (2012), https://www.thedailystar.net/news-detail-251310; The Daily Star (2011a), http://www.thedailystar.net/news-detail-205906

120   4 The Intrusion of Extraneous Considerations in the Appointment of the Chief Justice…

Seven months later, on 5 March 2012, Justice Manik's bench issued an order directing the authorities of the Bangladesh Open University to file a criminal complaint against a number of academics for allegedly distorting the history of the Liberation War in two of the University's textbooks on Civics and Sociology respectively.[109] These academics included one of the former Vice-Chancellors of the University, M Ershadul Bari, who was a Professor of Law and was not involved in the writing of either of the said books.[110] It seems that he was sought to be implicated in the complaint solely because of his political ideology. In this context, it is noteworthy that mentioning Zia, the founder of the BNP, instead of Mujib as the proclaimer of independence of Bangladesh from then West Pakistan in the said textbooks, *inter alia*, was construed as constituting distortion of history. To this end, these books relied on the two declarations made by General Zia which were broadcast on *Biplobi Betar Kendra* [Revolutionary Radio Station], Chittagong on 27 and 28 March 1971 respectively. In the first declaration, Zia proclaimed Bangladesh's independence from Pakistan in his capacity as the provisional "President and Commander-in-Chief of the Bangladesh liberation army", while in the second declaration he made the same declaration but this time on behalf of Mujib.[111] However, in June 2009, a bench of the HCD composed of Justices ABM Khairul Haque and Mamtazuddin Ahmed, relying on the Proclamation of Independence, 1971, which stated that Mujib had made "a declaration of independence" on 26 March 1971, declared that it is Mujib who had proclaimed the independence of Bangladesh.[112] It seems that Justice Manik had relied on this decision for issuing the above order against the academics. But in doing so he overlooked the facts that: (a) the said textbooks were initially published in 2002 and later reprinted in the years 2005 and 2009 respectively, and (b) Article 35(1) of the Constitution of Bangladesh expressly prohibits the retrospective use of laws to criminalize conduct.[113]

Third, Justice Manik, during his time as a judge of the HCD, did not write the judgments of many cases. He also did not deliver judgments in several cases. These omissions on the part of Justice Manik, which were also at odds with the Code of Conduct of 2000,[114] significantly disadvantaged litigants as they were deprived of the opportunity to institute appeal petitions before the AD. In light of these, it is

---

[109] U.S. Department Of State, Bureau of Democracy (2012) 13, http://www.state.gov/j/drl/rls/hrrpt/2012humanrightsreport/index.htm?dlid=204395&year=2012#wrapper; The Daily Star (2012), http://www.thedailystar.net/news-detail-225298

[110] Ibid.

[111] N.Y. Times (1981), https://www.nytimes.com/1981/05/30/world/bangladesh-reports-death-of-president-ziaur-rahman.html; Manik and Sarkar (2009), https://www.thedailystar.net/news-detail-93650

[112] The Proclamation Of Independence, 1971 (Bangladesh); Manik and Sarkar (2009), https://www.thedailystar.net/news-detail-93650

[113] Constitution of Bangladesh, 1972 (Bangladesh) art. 35(1) ('No person shall be convicted of any offence except for violation of a law in force at the time of the commission of the act charged as an offence, nor be subjected to a penalty greater than, or different from, that which might have been inflicted under the law in force at the time of the commission of the offence').

[114] See above n 103.

4.3 The Violation of the Convention of Seniority in Appointing the Judges of the AD

evident that Justice Manik was elevated to the AD not because of his record as a judge of the HCD but rather on political considerations.

Following the retirement of Justices Mohammad Anwarul Haque, Siddiqur Rahman Miah and Shamsuddin Chowdhury Manik, the President on 7 February 2016, elevated Justices Mirza Hussain Haider, Md Nizamul Huq, and Mohammad Bazlur Rahman of the HCD to the AD.[115] The principle of seniority was not adhered to in respect of the appointment of any of these judges. Justice Haider was elevated in supersession of the senior-most judge of the HCD, Justice Dastagir Husain, while Justices Huq and Rahman were elevated in supersession of 28 senior judges.[116] It should be stressed here that Justice Huq was previously the Chairman of the International Crimes Tribunal, which was established for investigating war crimes committed during the War of Independence from Pakistan. In December 2012, the Economist published the transcript of Skype and email conversations between Justice Huq and a Belgium-based lawyer of Bangladeshi origin.[117] It revealed that the BAL government had been unduly pressurising Justice Huq to deliver guilty verdicts against the leaders of *Jamaat-e-Islami*, who had been accused of committing war crimes during the Liberation War, rather hastily.[118] The transcripts further revealed that in lieu of these verdicts, he was promised a promotion to the AD.[119] Few days after the publication of this sensitive news, Justice Huq, on 11 December 2012, resigned as the Chairman of the Tribunal and returned to the HCD.[120] It seems that the promise made to Justice Huq in 2012 was finally fulfilled by the regime through his elevation to the AD.

As vacancies arose in the AD due to, in the first, the death of Justice Mohammad Bazlur Rahman on 1 January 2017 and subsequently, due to the resignation, as discussed earlier in Sect. 4.2.3, of Justice MA Wahab Miah on 2 February 2018 after being overlooked for appointment to the office of the Chief Justice, the President, on 8 October 2018, elevated Justices Zinat Ara, Abu Bakar Siddiquee and Md Nuruzzaman of the HCD to the AD.[121] However, in elevating these judges, the BAL regime yet again violated the convention of seniority. Justice Ara was promoted in supersession of three of her senior colleagues in the HCD. On the other hand, Justices Siddiquee and Nuruzzaman were elevated to the AD in supersession of an astounding 29 senior HCD judges. Both Justices Siddiquee and Nuruzzaman had one thing in common—they were both appointed by the BAL government as additional judges of the HCD in 2009 and were subsequently confirmed by the regime

---

[115] BDNEWS24.COM (2016), https://bdnews24.com/bangladesh/2016/02/08/chief-justice-swears-in-three-judges-to-the-appellate-division

[116] Ibid.

[117] Ibid.; Economist (2012), https://www.economist.com/news/briefing/21568349-week-chairman-bangladeshs-international-crimes-tribunal-resigned-we-explain; Bari and Dey (2019), p. 607

[118] Ibid.

[119] Ibid.

[120] Ibid.

[121] BDNEWS24.COM(2018),https://bdnews24.com/bangladesh/2018/10/09/new-faces-of-appellate-division-three-judges-sworn-in

as regular judges of the same Division in 2011.[122] The SCBA maintained its previous tradition of protesting the supersession of senior judges of the HCD in elevating these three judges to the AD. Furthermore, it refrained from felicitating the new appointees.[123]

Following Justice Ara's retirement on 12 March 2020, the President elevated two more judges of the HCD, namely, Justices Tariq ul Hakim and Obaidul Hassan, to the AD on 3 September 2020. The principle of seniority was followed by the BAL regime only in respect of the appointment of Justice Hakim—then the senior most judge of the HCD.[124] It is striking that the regime finally elevated Justice Hakim to the AD after previously superseding him in elevating his junior colleagues, such as Justices Ara, Siddiquee and Nuruzzaman. It seems the judge fell victim to supersession on previous occasions as it was the BNP government, which had initially appointed him to the HCD as an additional judge in 2002 and had subsequently confirmed his appointment in 2004. The BAL regime's sudden change of heart with regard to Justice Hakim can be explained by reference to the fact that the judge was supposed to retire on 20 September 2020, i.e., within a matter of mere 17 days of his elevation to the AD. Thus, the regime significantly limited the judge's scope to deliver a fearless judgment in any case where the regime was a party, by ensuring that his tenure in the AD was shortest in the judicial history of the country.

However, the other appointee, Justice Hassan, was elevated in supersession of as many as 21 of his senior colleagues in the HCD.[125] Interestingly, like previous appointees, particularly, Justices Siddique and Nuruzzaman, to the AD, Justice Hassan also received his appointment to the HCD first as a regular judge and subsequently as a permanent judge in 2009 and 2011 respectively, during the regime of the BAL.[126]

With these appointments, the current regime of BAL has so far contravened the principle of seniority on 10 occasions in elevating judges of the HCD to the AD, thereby surpassing the previous record of supersession on five occasions, which had been jointly held by the previous BNP (2001–2006) and BAL (1996–2001) regimes. In doing so, the BAL has been able to pack the higher Division of the SC with judges, who had received their initial appointment to the HCD during its tenure in office. Thus, it is evident that the BAL has proceeded in a calculated manner to contravene the principle of seniority for composing an AD of its choice, thereby undermining the AD's status in eyes of the litigants as an independent and impartial tribunal.

---

[122] Ibid.

[123] The Daily Star (2018), https://www.thedailystar.net/country/bangladesh-supreme-court-3-new-appellate-division-justices-sworn-in-1644655

[124] New Age (2020), https://www.newagebd.net/article/115303/tariq-ul-hakim-obaidul-hassan-sworn-in-as-ad-judges

[125] Ibid.

[126] Ibid.

4.4 The Appointment of the Judges of the HCD

It may be recalled from the discussion in Sect. 3.5 that the Constitution of Bangladesh, 1972 stipulates the appointment of two types of judges to the HCD, namely, additional judges for an initial period of 2 years, and regular judges. Furthermore, the Constitution does not determine how many justices should sit on the HCD. Rather the President is given the absolute discretion to determine the strength of judges of the lower Division of the SC. Consequently, successive governments have taken advantage of this lacuna to appoint additional judges to the HCD for a period of 2 years, and extraneous considerations, such as political affiliation, have been the dominant factor behind these appointments. During the period between 1996 and 2001, the BAL government appointed 40 additional judges to the HCD under Article 98 of the Constitution. The subsequent government of the BNP surpassed the record set by its predecessor by appointing 45 judges to the HCD. In order to obviate the possibility of politically motivated appointments that took place during the tenure of the political governments, the President during the term of the military-backed NPCG, as discussed earlier in Sect. 3.7, issued, on 16 March 2008, the Supreme Judicial Commission Ordinance, which provided for the establishment of a Supreme Judicial Commission (SJC) "to select and recommend competent persons for appointment as judges of the Supreme Court".[127] Subsequently, the President, for the first time in the history of the nation, appointed on 12 November 2008, seven additional judges to the HCD for 2 years on the recommendation of the newly formed SJC.[128]

However, notwithstanding the fact that the SJC Ordinance, as amended on 16 June 2008, enabled the senior-most judges of the SC to have the majority voice in the process of selecting and recommending candidates for appointment as judges to prevent patronage appointments, it is ironic that on 26 July 2008, the Bangladesh Awami Lawyers Association (BALA)—a platform of pro-BAL lawyers—demanded that the SJC Ordinance be repealed.[129]

After the BAL assumed power following a landslide victory in the general election on 29 December 2008, it placed 54 out of 122 Ordinances promulgated by the NPCG before the Parliament for its approval. But, in line with the demands of the BALA, the SJC Ordinance was not placed before the newly elected Parliament for passage into law. Therefore, it met a natural death as the life of an ordinance is always subject to the approval of the Parliament. Since it is the BAL which, on 25 January 1975, for the first time deleted the constitutional requirement of Presidential consultation with the Chief Justice in appointing the judges of the SC, it hardly comes as a surprise that the party was not inclined towards following a detailed and time-consuming procedure under the auspices of the SJC in the appointment of judges to the highest court of the land.

---

[127] The Supreme Judicial Commission Ordinance, 2008 (Bangladesh) preamble.

[128] Sarkar (2008), https://www.thedailystar.net/news-detail-67646?amp

[129] The Daily Star (2008b), https://www.thedailystar.net/news-detail-47643

124   4   The Intrusion of Extraneous Considerations in the Appointment of the Chief Justice...

Since dispensing with the SJC in early 2009, the BAL regime has so far appointed 85 Judges to the HCD. Thus, the regime has managed to surpass the total number of judges appointed to the HCD by its predecessor, the BNP Government, which appointed 45 judges during its five-year tenure from 2001 and 2006. However, instead of merit, the criteria for appointing these judges to the HCD has, in most cases, been allegiance to the regime. For instance, out of the 17 judges who received appointment to the HCD in April 2010 as additional judges, nine acquired a Third Class in their LLB exams, while 13 had Third Class/Division in more than one of the public exams in their lives. Furthermore, several of these judges were actively involved with the BALA and did not have any experience practicing in the AD of the SC.[130]

In addition to the above predicaments, and perhaps more damningly, two of these 17 judges—Ruhul Quddus Babu and M. Khasruzzaman—are accused of committing very serious offences in the past. Mr. Babu, who was educated in the University of Rajshahi, is one of the prime accused in a case concerning the murder of an activist of a student organisation at the University of Rajshahi in 1988.[131] On the other hand, Mr. Khasruzzaman was involved in vandalism that took place on the SC premises on 30 November 2006. In fact, he was photographed by the leading newspapers of the country kicking the door of the Chief Justice's office.[132] Taking into account the seriousness of these charges brought against the two newly appointed judges, the then-Chief Justice Mohammad Fazlul Karim, who was ultimately appointed as the Chief Justice on 8 February 2010 after previously being overlooked for the position on five occasions, in an unprecedented move in the judicial history of the country, decided against administering the oath of office to these two judges citing "unavoidable reasons".[133] Such a bold move on the part of the Chief Justice of Bangladesh to brighten the image of the judiciary deeply embarrassed the BAL government. However, unlike the BNP government (1991–1996)—which, as pointed out earlier in Sect. 3.5.4, due to the eruption of a controversy over the appointment of certain judges of the HCD in 1994 without consultation with the then Chief Justice, cancelled the Gazette Notification concerning the appointment of those judges —the BAL government showed no signs of retreat. The government ultimately managed to secure the administration of oath to these two controversial judges nearly 6 months after their appointment when Justice Karim's tenure as the Chief Justice came to an end, and its preferred candidate, Justice ABM Khairul Haque, who, as pointed out earlier in Sect. 4.2, was ranked third in the list of senior-most judges of the AD, took over the helm of the office of Chief Justice.

Despite the widespread outcry concerning the appointment of the above-mentioned controversial judges, the government has nevertheless continued to appoint judges based on political considerations. For instance, on 20 October 2019,

---

[130] Bari (2014), p. 14.

[131] The Daily Star (2010c), https://www.thedailystar.net/news-detail-148395

[132] The Daily Star (2010a), https://www.thedailystar.net/news-detail-134740

[133] Ibid.; See also Sarkar (2010a), https://www.thedailystar.net/news-detail-161341

4.4 The Appointment of the Judges of the HCD

the President appointed Md Akhtaruzzaman—then a District and Session Judge—as an additional judge of the HCD. This appointment was made only 1 year and 8 months after Judge (as he then was) Akhtaruzzaman had sentenced Begum Khaleda Zia—the BNP Chairperson and former Prime Minister—to 5 years rigorous imprisonment in a graft case, which had been instituted by the military-backed NPCG (2007–2008) as part of its agenda of implementing the notorious "minustwo" formula.[134] Notably, Zia in her statement given before the court under Section 342 of the Code of Criminal Procedure, 1898 strenuously denied that she had abused power during her time in office and instead rhetorically asked the Judge "whether indiscriminate killing [at the instigation of the BAL regime] of people, including students and teachers, for protesting injustice were misuse of power or she had abused power".[135] However, it seems the judge had purposefully misconstrued Zia's rhetorical statement as an admission that she had, in fact, abused power.[136] Consequently, the Judge held that "there.. [was] no bar to punishing her under section 409 of Penal Code and 5(2) [sic] of Corruption Prevention Act-1947".[137] Khaleda's conviction and the consequent imposition of a five-year jail term, had the effect of disqualifying her under Article 66(2)(d) of the Constitution from contesting the general election scheduled for December 2018,[138] thereby serving the political interests of Prime Minister Hasina of removing her arch-rival in the election. Accordingly, the appointment of Md Akhtaruzzaman as a judge of the HCD of the SC has been viewed by politically conscious citizens of the nation as a reward for services rendered in securing Khaleda's conviction so as to bar her from contesting the general election.

The above patronage appointments in blatant disregard of desirable qualities such as independent character, keen intellect, high legal knowledge and acumen, professional ability, equanimity, dignity, and judicial temperament, annoyed even a ruling party MP, Abdul Matin Khasru, who was also the Minister for Law, Justice and Parliamentary Affairs during the 1996–2001 BAL Regime. As he remarked:

> They [newly appointed Judges] have not been seen in the corridor of the Supreme Court. Despite being Law Secretary of the Ruling party, I knew nothing and I have not been even consulted. They do not have [the] skills to become upper division clerk, yet they are made Judges![139]

---

[134] Bari (2018), p. 62.

[135] Moneruzzaman and Rashid (2018), https://www.newagebd.net/article/35223/khaleda-confessed-to-power-abuse-judge

[136] Halder, Adhikary, and Habib (2018), https://www.thedailystar.net/frontpage/sentencing-graft-case-khaleda-may-file-appeal-today-1537300

[137] Ibid.

[138] Constitution of Bangladesh, 1972 (Bangladesh) art. 66(2)(d) ('A person shall be disqualified for election as, or for being, a member of Parliament who…has been, on conviction for a criminal offence involving moral turpitude, sentenced to imprisonment for a term of not less than 2 years, unless a period of 5 years has elapsed since his release').

[139] See above n 130, p. 15.

126   4   The Intrusion of Extraneous Considerations in the Appointment of the Chief Justice...

It is, therefore, evident that the BAL regime deliberately dispensed with the SJC to secure the appointment of those lawyers closely affiliated with the ruling party as judges of the HCD of the SC of Bangladesh. In the 12 years and a half that the regime has been in power, it has routinely violated the convention of seniority in appointing not only the Chief Justice of the country but also the judges of the AD and has also appointed individuals with questionable academic and professional credentials as judges of the HCD, thereby causing irreparable damage not only to the fair administration of justice, but also to the public faith in the highest court of law's competence to dispense justice.

References

Bangladesh Law House. (2011a). *SC sets aside caretaker govt system*. Available at http://bdlawhouse.blogspot.com.aul2011/06/sc-sets-aside-caretaker-govt-system.html

Bangladesh Law House. (2011b). *Code of conduct for the judges*. Available at http://bdlawhouse.blogspot.com/2011/10/code-of-conduct-for-judges.html.

Bari, M. E. (2014). The natural death of the Supreme Judicial Commission of Bangladesh & the consequent patronage appointments to the Bench: Advocating the establishment of an Independent Judicial Commission. *International Review of Law, 1*(1), 14–15.

Bari, M.E. (2016). Supersession of the Senior-Most Judges in Bangladesh in Appointing the Chief Justice and the Other Judges of the Appellate Division of the Supreme Court: A Convenient Means to a Politicized Bench. *San Diego International Law Journal* 18(1), 45, 46, 47, 56, 60, 61, 62, 65.

Bari, M.E. (2017). *States of emergency and the law: The experience of Bangladesh* (p. 181, 186, 187, 188, 191). Routledge.

Bari, M.E. (2018). The Incorporation of the System of Non-Party Caretaker Government in the Constitution of Bangladesh in 1996 as a means of Strengthening Democracy, Its Deletion in 2011 and the Lapse of Bangladesh into Tyranny following the Non-Participatory General Election of 2014: A Critical Appraisal. *Transnational Law and Contemporary Problems*, 28(1), 59, 61–65, 70, 75, 80, 81–82.

Bari, M. E., & Dey, P. (2019). The enactment of digital security laws in Bangladesh: No place for dissent. *George Washington International Law Review, 51*(4), 607.

Barry, E. (2014). *Low turnout in Bangladesh elections amid boycott and violence*. Available at https://www.nytimes.com/2014/01/06/world/asia/boycott-and-violence-mar-elections-in-bangladesh.html

BDNEWS24.COM. (2016). *Chief justice swears in three judges to the appellate division*. Available at https://bdnews24.com/bangladesh/2016/02/08/chief-justice-swears-in-three-judges-to-the-appellate-division

BDNEWS24.COM. (2018). *Justice Wahhab Miah resigns after Justice Mahmud Hossain is named chief justice*. Available at https://bdnews24.com/bangladesh/2018/02/02/justice-wahhab-miah-resigns-after-justice-mahmud-hossain-is-named-chief-justice

Dyzenhaus, D. (2006). *The constitution of law: Legality in a time of emergency* (p. 19). Cambridge University Press.

Hakim, T. (2020). *Obaidul Hassan sworn in as AD judges*. Available at https://www.newagebd.net/article/115303/tariq-ul-hakim-obaidul-hassan-sworn-in-as-ad-judges

International Ecological Safety Collaborative Organization. (2016). *Hussain Muhammed Ershad*. Available at http://www.iesco-iesco.org/content/en-US/p2068_k913.aspx.

References

Jasim, E. H. (2015). *Unprecedented Departure of Justice Shamsuddin: No farewell by AG Office SCBA*. Available at http://thedailynewnation.com/news/ 67594/unprecedented-departure-of-justice-shamsuddin.html.

Liton, S. (2005). *Justice Aziz becomes CEC*. Available at http://archive.thedailystar.net/2005/05/24/d5052401011.htm

Manik, J. A. & Sarkar, A. (2009). *It's Bangabandhu, not Zia: HC rules Sheikh Mujib declared independence*. Available at https://www.thedailystar.net/news-detail-93650

Mondal, A. L. (2010). *Averting controversy in appointment of Chief Justice*. Available at http://www.thedailystar.net/news-detail-157772

N.Y. Times. (1981). *Bangladesh reports death of President Ziaur Rahman*. Available at https://www.nytimes.com/1981/05/30/world/bangladesh-reports-death-of-president-ziaur-rahman.html

NEWS FROM BANGLADESH.NET. (2013). *Controversial appointment of judges in the appellate division of the Supreme Court: Bad precedent has been created*. Available at http://newsfrombangladesh.net/new/readers-opinion/11293-controversial-appointment-of-judges-in-the-appalate-division-of-the-supreme-court-bad-precedent-has-been-created

Riaz, A. (2016). Bangladesh. In N. De Votta (Ed.), *An introduction to South Asian politics* (p. 68). Routledge.

Sarkar, A. (2008). *Appellate Division running with fewer judges for long*. Available at https://www.thedailystar.net/news-detail-67646?amp

Sarkar, A. (2010a). *Oath of 2 angers pro-BNP lawyers*. Available at https://www.thedailystar.net/news-detail-161341

Sarkar, A. (2010b). *SC may get new judges next month*. Available at http://www.thedailystar.net/news-detail-167079

Sarkar, A. (2018). *Justice Mahmud Hossain made CJ*. Available at https://www.thedailystar.net/frontpage/justice-mahmud-hossain-made-cj-1529263

Shamsuddin, A., & Jahan, S. A. (2016). *A long way gone*. Available at http://www.thedailystar.net/law-our-rights/long-way-gone-1246612

The Daily Star. (1997). *Detention of 4 BNP leaders declared illegal*. Available at *https://www.thedailystar.net/news/detention-of-4-bnp-leaders-declared-illegal*

The Daily Star. (2003). *KM Hasan new CJ*. Available at http://archive.thedailystar.net/2003/06/23/d3062301033.htm

The Daily Star. (2006). *KM Hasan was involved in BNP politics in 1979 Moudud tells parliament, says there was no question of his integrity as judge*. Available at http://archive.thedailystar.net/2006/09/21/d6092101022.htm

The Daily Star. (2008a). *Hasina rolls out AL's charter for change*. Available at http://www.thedailystar.net/news-detail-66898

The Daily Star. (2008b). *No UZ elections before JS polls: AL Awami Ainjibi Parishad to form human chains*. Available at https://www.thedailystar.net/news-detail-47643

The Daily Star. (2009a). *SC appellate division gets 2 new judges*. Available at http://www.thedailystar.net/news-detail-78543

The Daily Star. (2009b). *SC appellate division gets 4 more judges*. Available at http://archive.thedailystar.net/newDesign/print_news.php?nid=96998

The Daily Star. (2009c). *Tafazzul new chief justice*. Available at https://www.thedailystar.net/news-detail-117925

The Daily Star. (2010a). *Controversial 2 left out of oath*. Available at https://www.thedailystar.net/news-detail-134740

The Daily Star. (2010b). *Justice Khairul Haque new chief justice*. Available at http:// www.thedailystar.net/news-detail-156149

The Daily Star. (2010c). *Murder case against Ruhul Quddus stayed*. Available at https://www.thedailystar.net/news-detail-148395

The Daily Star. (2011a). *No greetings for SC judges: Bar leaders protest death of pro-BNP leaders*. Available at http://www.thedailystar.net/news-detail-205906

128   4   The Intrusion of Extraneous Considerations in the Appointment of the Chief Justice...

The Daily Star. (2011b). *SC gets 1st woman judge*. Available at http:// www.thedailystar.net/news-detail-175201

The Daily Star. (2012). *DU, BOU teachers to face criminal charge*. Available at http://www.thedailystar.net/news-detail-225298

The Daily Star. (2013a). *Plea to remove Justice Manik*. Available at *https://www.thedailystar.net/news-detail-251310*

The Daily Star. (2013b). *Skip oath to 4 new SC judges: Outgoing Bar President urges CJ*. Available at https://www.thedailystar.net/news/skip-oath-to-4-new-sc-judges

The Daily Star. (2015). *Justice Masud passes away*. Available at http://www.thedailystar.net/justice-masud-passes-away-573

The Daily Star. (2016). *Ex CJ Khairul Haque reappointed as law commission chair*. Available at http://www.thedailystar.net/city/ex-cj-khairul-haque-reappointed-law-commission-chair-1248835

The Daily Star. (2018). *Three Appellate Division judges sworn in*. Available at https://www.thedailystar.net/country/bangladesh-supreme-court-3-new-appellate-division-justices-sworn-in-1644655\

The Economist. (2012). *Trying war crimes in Bangladesh: The trial of the birth of a nation*. Available at https://www.economist.com/news/briefing/21568349-week-chairman-bangladeshs-international-crimes-tribunal-resigned-we-explain

The Hindu. (2009). *Mujib's killers case: A chronology of events*. Available at https://www.thehindu.com/news/international/Mujibrsquos-killers-case-A-chronology-of-events/article16892929.ece

The Observer. (2015). *Justice Habibur Rahman's first death anniversary tomorrow*. Available at https://www.observerbd.com/2015/01/10/65593.php

Thomas, K.K. (1982). President's address to parliament: Martial law ruled out. *Asian Recorder* 27, 16519.

U.S. Department of State. Bureau of Democracy. (2012). *Bangladesh* 13. Available at http://www.state.gov/j/drl/rls/hrrpt/2012humanrightsreport/index.htm?dlid=204395&year=2012#wrapper

UCA NEWS. (2014). *Bangladeshi ruling party wins election by default*. Available at https://www.ucanews.comlnews/bangladeshi-ruling-party-wins-election-by-default/70019

Chapter 5
The Guarantee of Security of Tenure of the Judges of the Supreme Court under the Constitution of Bangladesh, 1972

5.1 Introduction

An attempt will be made in this Chapter to examine the provisions of the Constitution of Bangladesh, 1972, concerning the security of tenure of the judges of the Supreme Court (SC)—a constituent element of judicial independence. To this end, this Chapter will shed light on the two principal components of the security of tenure of judges, namely, their mandatory retirement age and the method of their removal from office, as originally stipulated by the Constitution and the various amendments introduced to these components over the years. The objective of this examination is to demonstrate that the method of removal of judges involving the Supreme Judicial Council, as introduced by the Martial Law regime of General Zia, was more conducive to maintaining the independence of the judiciary.

5.2 The Original Provisions of the Constitution of Bangladesh, 1972, Concerning the Retirement Age and the Method of Removal of the Judges of the Superior Courts

The Constitution of Bangladesh, 1972 originally provided that a judge of the SC could hold office until he attains the age of 62 years.[1] He could only be removed from his office "by an order of the President passed pursuant to a resolution of Parliament supported by a majority of not less than two-thirds of the total number of members of Parliament, on the ground of proved misbehaviour or incapacity".[2]

---

[1] Constitution of Bangladesh, 1972 (Bangladesh) art. 96(1).

[2] Constitution of Bangladesh, 1972 (Bangladesh) art. 96(2).

© The Author(s), under exclusive license to Springer Nature Singapore Pte Ltd. 2022
M. E. Bari, *The Independence of the Judiciary in Bangladesh*,
https://doi.org/10.1007/978-981-16-6222-5_5

129

130   5 The Guarantee of Security of Tenure of the Judges of the Supreme Court...

The Parliament was further empowered to regulate by law the procedure in relation to a resolution for removal, investigation and proof of the misbehavior or incapacity of a judge of the SC. It seems that these constitutional provisions empowering the Parliament to regulate by law the procedure for removal of the judges were closely modeled on Article 124(4) and (5) of the Constitution of India, 1950. For Article 124(4) of the Indian Constitution stipulates that a judge of the Supreme Court cannot be removed from office unless the President passes an order pursuant to a resolution passed by two-thirds of the members of each house of the Parliament praying for such removal on the ground of "proved misbehaviour or incapacity".[3] Furthermore, Article 124(5) empowers the Parliament to regulate by law the procedure "for the investigation and proof of the misbehaviour or incapacity of a Judge".[4] However, unlike the Parliament of India which in pursuance of Article 124(5) of the Constitution enacted the Judges (Inquiry) Act, 1968 laying down the procedure for the removal of a judge on the ground of proved misbehaviour or incapacity, the Parliament of Bangladesh did not pass any such Act in pursuance of the constitutional provisions.

Thus, it is evident that under the original constitutional provisions in Bangladesh, the judges of the SC were to hold office for a long term and could not be removed during their tenure by the President acting alone even for misbehaviour or incapacity. However, since the Constitution of Bangladesh does not provide for strict separation of powers between the executive and legislative branches of the government by mandating that at least "nine tenths of cabinet members shall be appointed from among members of Parliament,"[5] it can be argued that the executive could adversely influence the removal procedure of the judges if it commanded the support of two-thirds of the total number of members of the Parliament.

5.3 The Changes Introduced to the Security of Tenure of the Judges of the SC of Bangladesh by the Constitution (Fourth Amendment) Act, 1975

The most controversial amendment to the Constitution of Bangladesh, i.e. the Constitution (Fourth Amendment) Act, was enacted, as mentioned earlier in Sect. 3.5.1, by the regime of Bangladesh Awami League (BAL) on 25 January 1975.[6] This amendment in an effort to perpetuate the rule of Sheikh Mujibur Rahman (Mujib), fundamentally diminished the liberal spirit of the Constitution.[7] In addition to vesting President Mujib with the unfettered power, as discussed earlier in Sect. 3.5.1, to

---

[3] Constitution of India, 1950 (India) art. 124(4).

[4] Constitution of India, 1950 (India) art. 124(5).

[5] Constitution of Bangladesh, 1972 (Bangladesh) proviso to art. 56(2).

[6] Bari (2017), p. 173.

[7] Ibid., p. 175, 177.

appoint the judges of the SC, the amendment also changed the method of removal of the judges. Although it retained the original provision of the Constitution that a judge of the SC would hold office until he attains the age of 62 years, it inserted a new provision which stated that: "A judge may be removed from his office by the President on the ground of misbehaviour or incapacity."[8] Thus, Mujib was invested with the blanket unilateral power to both appoint and remove the judges of the SC, thereby essentially signalling the end of the independence of the superior judiciary.

5.4 The Changes Introduced to the Security of Tenure of the Judges by the Martial Law Regime of 1975

Since the changes introduced by the Fourth Amendment turned Bangladesh, as discussed earlier in Sects. 3.5.1 and 3.5.2, into a dictatorship obviating the possibility of a democratic change of government, a group of army officers on 15 August 1975, assassinated Mujib and and subsequently placed the nation under Martial Law.

Although the Martial Law regime refrained from taking the drastic step, as discussed earlier in Sect. 3.5.2, of either abrogating or suspending the Constitution of Bangladesh, it nevertheless made the Constitution subservient to the First Proclamation, which was issued on 20 August 1975, and Martial Law Regulations or Orders issued by the regime from time to time.[9] Notwithstanding the fact that the Constitution only empowers the Parliament to amend its provisions and does not authorize the President under any circumstances to either alter or suspend any provision of the Constitution in exercise of his power of making ordinances, the President assumed such powers on 19 September 1975 through the Proclamation of the (First Amendment) Order, 1975 (Proclamation Order no. 1 of 1975). Consequently, he amended various provisions of the Constitution, including the provisions concerning the method of removal of judges of the superior courts by issuing Proclamations (Amendments) Orders during the continuance of the Martial Law (1975–1979).

The Second Proclamation (Seventh Amendment) Order, 1976 increased the retirement age of the judges of the SC by stipulating that "a Judge of the Supreme Court shall hold office until he attains the age of sixty-five years".[10] Furthermore, the Amendment Order reinstated the original constitutional provisions concerning the removal of the judges of the SC, which, as pointed out above in Sect. 5.2, were repealed by the Fourth Amendment. For the Order stipulated that a judge of the SC could not be removed from office except by an "order of the President made pursuant

---

[8] Constitution (Fourth Amendment) Act, 1975 (Bangladesh) s 15.

[9] Banglapedia, https://en.banglapedia.org/index.php?title=Proclamation

[10] Second Proclamation (Seventh Amendment) Order, 1976 (Bangladesh) art. 4. However, the Constitution (Fourteenth Amendment) Act 2004 increased the retirement of the judges of the Supreme Court from 65 to 67 years. Thus, judges of the Supreme Court of Bangladesh are to remain in office until they have attained the age of 67 years.

132   5 The Guarantee of Security of Tenure of the Judges of the Supreme Court ..

to a resolution of Parliament passed by a majority of not less than two-thirds of the total number of members of Parliament on the ground of proved misbehaviour, or incapacity".[11] The Parliament was also given the discretion to regulate the procedure in relation to a resolution of removal and for investigation and proof of misbehaviour or incapacity of a judge of the SC.[12]

However, only a day after assuming the office of the President, on 22 April 1977, General Ziaur Rahman—the Chief Martial Law Administrator (CMLA)—issued the Proclamations (Tenth Amendment) Order, 1977, which changed the above constitutional method of removal of the judges of the SC. The Proclamations (Tenth Amendment) Order provided that a judge of the SC could only be removed from office by the President on the recommendation of the Supreme Judicial Council (SJC), which was to be composed of "the Chief Justice of Bangladesh and the two next senior judges of the Supreme Court,"[13] following an inquiry to determine whether the judge had "ceased to be capable of properly performing the functions of his office by reason of physical or mental incapacity" or had been "guilty of gross misconduct".[14]

Following the revocation of Martial Law on 6 April 1979, the above changes introduced by the Proclamations (Tenth Amendment) Order, 1977 regarding the removal of the judges of the SC involving the SJC were validated by the Constitution (Fifth Amendment) Act, 1979.[15]

This new constitutional method of removal of judges of the SC, as introduced by the Martial Law regime, was more conducive to maintaining the integrity and independence of the judiciary. For by confining the membership of the SJC solely to the most senior judges of the Court, the Constitution did not afford either the executive or the legislature with any opportunity to influence its inquiry into the conduct of a judge, thereby safeguarding the fairness and objectivity of the Council's processes. It should be further stressed here that this procedure for removing judges of the SC was also in conformity with the international norms, as discussed earlier in Sect. 2.4.2, concerning judicial independence.

Accordingly, the AD of the SC shed light on the efficacy of the removal method involving the SJC in two landmark constitutional cases. In *Anwar Hossain Chowdhury v. Bangladesh*,[16] popularly known as the Eight Amendment Case, Justice Badrul Haider Chowdhury observed that:

> Judges cannot be removed except in accordance with provisions of Article 96- that is the Supreme Judicial Council. Sub-article (5) says if after making the inquiry, the Council reports to the President that in its opinion the Judge has ceased to be capable of properly performing the functions of his office or has been guilty of gross misconduct, the President, shall by order remove the Judge from office. This is [sic] unique feature because the Judge

---

[11] Ibid.

[12] Ibid.

[13] Proclamations (Tenth Amendment) Order, 1977 (Bangladesh) art. 2.

[14] Ibid.

[15] Bari (2018), p. 80.

[16] *Anwar Hossain Chowdhury v. Bangladesh* (1989) 18 CLC (AD).

is tried by his own peers- 'thus there is secured a freedom from political control' (1965 A.C.P 190).[17]

Twenty years later, the AD in *Khondker Delwar Hossain v. Bangladesh Italian Marble Works Ltd., and others*[18] (the Fifth Amendment Case) in unequivocal terms observed that

> the procedure for removal of a Judge of the Supreme Court of Bangladesh by the Supreme Judicial Council… [is a] more transparent procedure than that of the earlier ones [namely, Parliamentary and Presidential method of removal] and also [for] safeguarding the independence of the judiciary.[19]

5.5 The Changes Introduced to the Security of Tenure of the Judges by the Martial Law Regime of HM Ershad (1982–1986)

Nine months and 24 days after Zia's assassination, on 24 March 1982, HM Ershad—then the Chief of Army Staff—disposed of the government of Bangladesh Nationalist Party (BNP) and placed the nation under Martial Law for the second time in its short history. The Proclamation of Martial Law was followed by the suspension of the Constitution, which also had the adverse impact of rendering the transparent method of removal of judges involving the SJC inoperative. Eighteen days after the declaration of Martial Law, on 11 April 1982, the Proclamation (First Amendment) Order was issued authorising Ershad, in his capacity as the CMLA, to exercise not only the power to appoint judges of the SC but also to remove them from office "without assigning any reason".[20] Thus, it is evident that Ershad followed in the footsteps of Mujib to assume the unfettered power to appoint and remove judges of the SC at his pleasure.

Within a few months of the issuance of the First Amendment Order, Ershad exercised his unconstrained power to remove three judges of the SC without assigning any reason whatsoever.[21] This Order also fixed the tenure of the office of the Chief Justice at three years.[22] This meant that a Chief Justice had to mandatorily step down from office after three years even if he had not attained the retirement age of 65 years. The stipulation of a fixed tenure for the Chief Justice yielded a rather embarrassing and unfortunate outcome for Justice Kemaluddin Hussain, who was the occupier of the office of the Chief Justice at the time the First Amendment Order

---

[17] Ibid., [292 (21)].

[18] *Khondker Delwar Hossain v. Bangladesh Italian Marble Works Ltd., Dhaka and others*, (2009) Civil Petition for Leave to Appeal Nos 1044 and 1045.

[19] Ibid., p. 77.

[20] The Proclamation (First Amendment) Order, 1982 (Bangladesh) [10(4)].

[21] Nariman (1984), p. 44.

[22] The Proclamation (First Amendment) Order, 1982 (Bangladesh) [10(1)].

134   5   The Guarantee of Security of Tenure of the Judges of the Supreme Court..,

was issued and had already served for more than three years in that role. Since the gazetted copy of the Order was not served on Justice Hussain, he was unaware of the impact of Order on his fate as the Chief Justice. Subsequently, on 12 April 1982, he proceeded to hear a number of cases when an Advocate pleaded *coram non judice* in view of the fact that the former ceased to hold the office as a consequence of the First Amendment Order—the details of which were published in the newspapers that morning. When the Attorney General confirmed the veracity of the claim made by the Advocate, Justice Hussain left the court and bade farewell to his colleagues and the advocates.[23]

The events following the suspension of the operation of the SJC, including the removal of three judges of the SC and the unceremonious manner in which Justice Hussain was forced out of the high office of Chief Justice, had an adverse impact on the independence of the judges of the court to dispense justice, particularly in cases where the regime was a party, in accordance with the terms of their oath of office. For instance, in April 1984, judges in as many as three benches of the High Court Division (HCD) "refused to hear a petition for a writ of *habeas corpus*" due to the apprehension of suffering personally, as is evident from the remarks made by one judge in open court: "my heart trembles".[24]

The judiciary was finally allowed to breathe a sigh of relief when the Constitution was finally restored on 11 November 1986 following the revocation of the Martial Law on the same day. As this restoration also had the impact of reinstating the method of removal of judges of the SC involving the SJC, thereby depriving Ershad of the power to remove judges at his pleasure.

5.6   The Changes Introduced to the Retirement Age of the Judges by the BNP Government (2001–2006)

The BNP government used its overwhelming majority in the Parliament in June 2004 to pass the Constitution (Fourteenth Amendment) Act, 2004, which, among other things, increased the retirement age of the judges of the SC from 65 to 67.[25] The objective underlying this amendment, as discussed earlier in Sect. 4.2.1, was to ensure that the BNP's preferred candidate—Justice KM Hasan—would be constitutionally destined to head the "Non-Party Care-taker Government". Nevertheless, by dint of this amendment, judges of the SC were to remain in office for a long time. They could only be removed from office after the SJC recommended such removal following an inquiry into allegations of misbehaviour or incapacity.

---

[23] See above n 21, p. 45.

[24] Ibid., p. 47.

[25] Constitution of Bangladesh, 1972 (Bangladesh) article 96(1) (as amended by section 4 of the Constitution (Fourteenth Amendment) Act, 2004, stipulates that '[A] Judge [of the Supreme Court] shall hold office until he attains the age of sixty-seven years).

References

Banglapedia. *Proclamation*. Available at https://en.banglapedia.org/index.php?title=Proclamation

Bari, M. E. (2017). *States of emergency and the law: The experience of Bangladesh* (p. 173, 175, 177). Routledge.

Bari, M. E. (2018). The incorporation of the system of non-party caretaker government in the constitution of Bangladesh in 1996 as a means of strengthening democracy, its deletion in 2011 and the lapse of Bangladesh into tyranny following the non-participatory general election of 2014: A Critical Appraisal. *Transnational Law and Contemporary Problems, 28*(1), 80.

Nariman, F. S. (1984). The judiciary under martial law regimes. *Centre for the Independence of Judges and Lawyers Bulletin, 14*, 44–45.

Chapter 6
The Functioning of the Supreme Judicial Council, the Changes Introduced to the Method of Removal of Judges of the Supreme Court of Bangladesh in 2014 and the Subsequent Scathing Attack on the Judiciary

6.1 Introduction

It might be recalled from the discussion in Chap. 5 that in order to further the principle of judicial independence, the Constitution of Bangladesh, 1972, as amended by the Proclamations (Tenth Amendment) Order, 1977 and later validated by the Constitution (Fifth Amendment) Act, 1979, stipulated a transparent procedure for the removal of judges of the Supreme Court (SC)—the highest court of law which is composed of the High Court Division (HCD) and the Appellate Division (AD). The Constitution provided that a judge of the SC could only be removed from office on the recommendation of the Supreme Judicial Council—headed by the Chief Justice of the country and additionally composed of the two senior-most judges of the SC.[1] Thus, the Constitution guaranteed the security of tenure of the judges by ensuring that they could not be removed from office at the whim of the political branches of the government. However, the current regime of Bangladesh Awami League (BAL) used its absolute majority in the Parliament on 17 September 2014 to pass the Constitution (Sixteenth Amendment) Act, 2014, which replaced this transparent method of removal of judges with a controversial parliamentary method of removal.[2]

In order to demonstrate the effectiveness of the method of removal of judges involving the Supreme Judicial Council in safeguarding the independence of the judiciary, this Chapter will, in the first place, critically evaluate the functioning of

---

A significantly edited version of this chapter has been published in a refereed journal. For details, see Bari, M.E. (2021). The Recent Changes Introduced to the Method of Removal of Judges of the Supreme Court of Bangladesh & the Consequent Triumph of an All-Powerful Executive over the Judiciary: Judicial Independence in Peril. *Cardozo International & Comparative Law Review.* 4(2), 653–696.

---

[1] Constitution of Bangladesh, 1972 (Bangladesh) art. 96(5) and (6).

[2] Constitution (Sixteenth Amendment) Act, 2014 (Bangladesh) s. 2.

© The Author(s), under exclusive license to Springer Nature Singapore Pte
Ltd. 2022
M. E. Bari, *The Independence of the Judiciary in Bangladesh*,
https://doi.org/10.1007/978-981-16-6222-5_6

the Council. Subsequently, it will be made manifestly evident that the deletion of the constitutional provisions concerning this transparent procedure of removal of the judges of the SC through the Constitution (Sixteenth Amendment) Act, 2014 and the subsequent measures, e.g. forcing the Chief Justice of the country to not only resign from office but also to leave the country for declaring the Sixteenth Amendment unconstitutional, have been preferred for exerting the supremacy of the current government of the Bangladesh Awami League (BAL) over the judiciary. Furthermore, light will be shed on the fact that these adverse measures have substantially impaired the ability of the judges of the SC to administer justice without the fear of adverse consequences.

6.2 The Functioning of the Supreme Judicial Council

In addition to vesting the Supreme Judicial Council (SJC) with the authority to conduct an investigation into allegation of incapacity or misconduct against a judge of the SC, the Constitution also empowered the Council to "prescribe a Code of Conduct to be observed by the Judges".[3] Consequently, on 7 May 2000, the Council in exercise of its constitutional power prescribed a 14-point Code of Conduct for the Judges detailing the "values of judicial life".[4] The formulation of such a code also had "the positive rule of law value of informing judges about the minimum standards of conduct that … [were] expected of them, and provide[d] fair warning to any who may be tempted to transgress those standards".[5]

Since the formulation of the Code, the Council had the opportunity to investigate the allegations into the capacity or conduct of the judges of the SC on three separate occasions. The Council was presented with the opportunity to conduct such an investigation, for the first time, when the President of the Supreme Court Bar Association (SCBA) in October 2003 brought a grave allegation of gross misconduct against Justice Syed Shahidur Rahman—a judge of the HCD. The SCBA President alleged that Justice Rahman had in violation of the Code of Conduct for Judges[6] accepted a bribe of BDT 50,000 to fix bail for an individual accused under the Women and Children Repression Prevention Act.[7] This allegation of bribery against a judge of the HCD seriously undermined and eroded public confidence in

---

[3] Constitution of Bangladesh, 1972 (Bangladesh) art. 94(4).

[4] Bangladesh Law House (2011), http://bdlawhouse.blogspot.com/2011/10/code-of-conduct-for-judges.html (no longer in force). The life of the Code of 2000 came to an abrupt end when the constitutional provisions concerning the Supreme Judicial Council were repealed through the enactment of the Constitution (Sixteenth Amendment) Act, 2014.

[5] Removal from office (2015), p. 525.

[6] Bangladesh Law House (2011), rs. 8–10, http://bdlawhouse.blogspot.com/2011/10/code-of-conduct-for-judges.html

[7] The Daily Star (2015), https://www.thedailystar.net/backpage/sc-upholds-dismissal-judge-shahidur-144355

6.2 The Functioning of the Supreme Judicial Council

the credibility of the superior judiciary of the country as an effective and efficient arbitrator of disputes. Consequently, the President in pursuance of Article 96(5)(b) of the Constitution of Bangladesh directed the Council to inquire into the allegations brought against Justice Rahman. After conducting the inquiry, the Council reported that "on consideration of the facts and circumstances and the materials on record in their entirety it cannot be said that there is total absence of material in support of the allegations nor can it be said that the allegations are without any basis".[8] Accordingly, the Council recommended to the President that in its opinion "Mr. Justice Syed Shahidur Rahman should not continue as... a Judge of the High Court Division of the Supreme Court of Bangladesh".[9] In pursuance of this recommendation, the President on 20 April 2004 issued an order removing Justice Rahman from office, [10] thereby restoring public confidence in the integrity of the SC.

On 30 October 2004—only six months and 10 days after Justice Rahman was removed from office—another grave allegation of serious misconduct surfaced against a judge of the HCD, namely Justice Faisal Mahmud Faizee. Two national dailies ran a story alleging that Justice Faizee had not only tampered with his academic transcript but also forged the certificate of his Bachelor of Laws (LLB) examinations at the University of Chittagong. The dailies ran this story on the basis of an investigation which the University of Chittagong was carrying out at the time into allegations of certificate tampering against 2400 examinees—one of whom was Justice Faizee.[11] Notwithstanding the seriousness of this allegation, the SJC headed by the then Chief Justice—JR Mudassir Husain—did not consider it prudent to seek the President's direction under Article 96(5) of the Constitution for conducting an investigation. However, due to growing pressure from the lawyers of the SC demanding stern action against Justice Faizee, the Chief Justice took a largely symbolic step in withdrawing the concerned Justice from the bench.[12] Furthermore, the Bangladesh Bar Council, which is the licensing and regulatory body for all legal practitioners of the country, served a show cause notice on Justice Faizee on 4 November 2004 requiring him to explain why his enrolment certification as a legal practitioner should not be cancelled due to, among other things, the dispute regarding his LLB certificate.[13] Since Justice Faizee did not furnish any reply to the show cause notice attempting to disprove the allegations brought against him, the Bar Council in an unprecedented move proceeded to cancelling the judge's enrolment certificate as an advocate of the SC.[14]

---

[8] *Md. Idrisur Rahman v. Syed Shahidur Rahman and Others*, (2005) Civil Appeal No. 145 of 2005 with Civil Petition for Leave to Appeal No. 405 of 2005, 56.

[9] Ibid.

[10] BDNEWS24.COM (2005b), https://bdnews24.com/bangladesh/2005/04/24/sc-stays-hc-order-declaring-illegal-shahidur-s-removal

[11] The Daily Star (2007a), http://archive.thedailystar.net/2007/03/04/d7030401011.htm.

[12] BDNEWS24.COM (2005a), https://bdnews24.com/bangladesh/2005/04/24/justice-faizee-s-advocate-ship-certificate-cancelled-faces-criminal-case.

[13] Ibid.

[14] Ibid.

140 6 The Functioning of the Supreme Judicial Council, the Changes Introduced...

The above issues were compounded by the fact that the authorities of the University of Chittagong on completion of the inquiry into allegation of certificate forgery against Justice Faizee, concluded that there was merit to the allegations and as such, they duly cancelled his LLB Certificate.[15] It should be stressed here that the Constitution of Bangladesh stipulates that in order for an individual to be eligible for appointment as a judge of the SC, he should, among other things, be enrolled as an Advocate of the SC[16]—an enrolment which can be attained after successfully completing, among other things, an LLB. Furthermore, in order to maintain the integrity and dignity of the judiciary, judges of the SC must of necessity be of unimpeachable integrity and of spotless character. Therefore, the cancellation of Justice Faizee's LLB certificate on account of forgery and also of his enrolment as an Advocate not only cast serious doubts over his constitutional eligibility to continue as a judge of the SC but also had the dreadful impact of undermining and eroding the integrity and dignity of the superior judiciary.

Accordingly, Chief Justice Md Ruhul Amin, who succeeded Justice JR Mudassir Husein as the Chief Justice, on 10 March 2007—within 9 days of assuming the office of the Chief Justice—wrote to the President stressing on the necessity to resolve the constitutional crisis concerning Faizee's continuation as a judge of the HCD.[17] Consequently, the President directed the SJC headed by Chief Justice Amin to investigate the allegations of forgery against Justice Faizee. The Council found "strong evidence of forgery" against the concerned judge.[18] Sensing the writing on the wall, Justice Faizee considered it prudent to resign as a judge of the HCD on 12 July 2007,[19] thereby depriving the Council of the opportunity to put forward its recommendation to the President.

The SJC was convened for the third and final instance on 25 February 2013 to conduct an allegation of misconduct against Justice Mizanur Rahman Bhuiyan, who was appointed as a judge of the HCD on 29 July 2002 by the government of the BNP and *Jamaat-e-Islami* Alliance. The allegation involved Justice Bhuiyan distributing photocopies of a contentious news report among his colleagues at the SC.[20] The news report in question termed Ahmed Rajib Haider—one of the high-profile activists who demanded death sentence for all those accused of committing of war crimes in 1971, including prominent leaders of the *Jamaat-e-Islami*[21]—an apostate

---

[15] The Daily Star (2007b), http://archive.thedailystar.net/2007/03/04/d7030401011.htm

[16] Constitution of Bangladesh, 1972 (Bangladesh) art 95(2)(a).

[17] BDNEWS24.COM (2007b), https://bdnews24.com/bangladesh/2007/03/28/supreme-judicial-council-holds-first-meeting-on-faizee.

[18] BDNEWS24.COM (2007a), https://bdnews24.com/bangladesh/2007/07/13/hc-judge-faizee-bows-out

[19] Ibid.

[20] Ibid.

[21] Khokon(2017),https://www.indiatoday.in/world/story/ahmed-rajib-blogger-murder-ganajagaran-mancha-killer-dhaka-961678-2017-02-20

6.2 The Functioning of the Supreme Judicial Council

for allegedly defaming the religion of Islam and Prophet Muhammad through his blog posts.[22]

The members of the ruling BAL, which at the time commanded the support of the three-fourths of the elected members of the Parliament,[23] were incensed when news broke about the alleged distribution of the controversial news reports by Justice Bhuiyan. For instance, Sheikh Selim—an influential MP of the ruling BAL—took the parliamentary floor to remark that Justice Bhuiyan by distributing the above report had not only violated the Constitution but had also sided with war criminals in an attempt to thwart the mass movement, which was being carried out at the time demanding the imposition of capital punishment on all war criminals.[24] Selim went further when he demanded that Justice Bhuiyan should be questioned in order to find his possible link with the killing of Rajib.[25] Other ruling party MPs, including the Chief Whip of the Parliament, also echoed Selim's sentiments. Consequently, in light of these demands, the Minister for Law, Justice and Parliamentary Affairs assured his party colleagues in the Parliament that he would discuss the idea of forming a SJC with the Chief Justice for "taking action" against Justice Bhuiyan as his "behaviour … [could] be termed as misconduct".[26] Therefore, it is manifestly evident that the ruling party MPs reached a conclusion regarding Justice Bhuiyan's alleged misconduct even before the Council had the opportunity to impartially investigation the allegation, thereby attempting to exert undue pressure on the Council to recommend the removal of the concerned judge from office.

It should be stressed here that the ruling party MPs, including the Minister for Law, Justice and Parliamentary Affairs, did not shed light on how Justice Bhuiyan, according to them, had violated the Constitution by allegedly distributing the news report. Furthermore, since the Constitution of Bangladesh does not define what would construe as misconduct on the part of a judge of the SC, the SJC, as pointed out above, had prescribed a Code of Conduct for putting flesh on the bare bones of the Constitutional text. The Code, among other things, in rule 5 prescribed that a judge should maintain "a degree of aloofness consistent with the dignity of his high office"[27] and Justice Bhuiyan's alleged distribution of the news report concerning the deceased blogger could only have been construed as a violation of this rule regarding the maintenance of aloofness.

The Council conducted its investigation into the allegation of misconduct against Justice Bhuiyan for more than five months from 25 February to 5 August 2013.

---

[22] The Daily Star (2013a), https://www.thedailystar.net/news/justice-mizanur-replies-to-judicial-council-2; Islam (2018), p. 29.

[23] European Parliament (2008), http://www.epgencms.europarl.europa.eu/cmsdata/uploa d/36287860-18fe-4c47-92b1-5aa527c34129/Election_report_Bangladesh_29_December_ 2008.pdf

[24] The Daily Star (2013b), https://www.thedailystar.net/news-detail-269768

[25] Ibid.

[26] Ibid.

[27] Bangladesh Law House (2011), r. 5, http://bdlawhouse.blogspot.com/2011/10/code-of-conduct-for-judges.html

During this time, Justice Bhuiyan was also given the opportunity to submit a written response to the Council explaining the allegation that had been brought against him.[28] Finally, on 5 August 2013, the Council reported to the President that it had found no merits into the allegation of misconduct against Justice Bhuiyan,[29] thereby clearing him of any wrongdoing and thwarting in the process the BAL's plan to secure his removal.

It is, therefore, evident from the above discussion that the SJC—headed by the Chief Justice and composed of the senior-most judges of the AD as members—since its formation had performed its function in an objective manner by recommending removal of judges guilty of moral turpitude from office, thereby maintaining public confidence in the integrity and dignity of the judiciary. Furthermore, the Council did not succumb to any political pressure while carrying out its investigation into the allegation of misconduct against Justice Bhuiyan, thereby frustrating the design of the ruling BAL to secure the removal of a judge who was appointed by its opposing BNP-Jamaat alliance while it was in power, and maintaining the independence of the judiciary.

6.3 The Omission of the Constitutional Provisions Concerning the SJC by the Constitution (Sixteenth Amendment) Act, 2014

Notwithstanding the effectiveness of the constitutional provisions concerning the SJC in safeguarding the independence of the judiciary, the government of BAL used its brute majority in the Parliament on 17 September 2014 to pass the Constitution (Sixteenth Amendment) Act, 2014 repealing the provisions concerning the SJC from the Constitution. It is necessary to point out here that the Sixteenth Amendment was passed 13 months and three days after the BAL regime's attempt to secure the removal of Justice Bhuiyan of the HCD, as pointed out earlier in Sect. 6.2, from office was duly frustrated by the SJC. The adverse impact of the deletion of the provisions concerning the SJC from the Constitution can be further gathered from the fact that the BAL proceeded to get this amendment passed only seven months after it had cemented its grip on power, as discussed earlier in Sect. 4.2.3, by conducting and subsequently winning a sham general election in January 2014. Since prior to the 2014 election, the BAL in a calculated manner used its three-fourth majority in the Parliament to enact the Constitution (Fifteenth Amendment) Act, 2011 for abolishing the system of NPCG from the Constitution—a system which is credited with supervising three free and fair general elections in 1996, 2001 and 2008 respectively—all the opposition political parties, including the BNP, refused to participate in the election. Consequently, the Parliament resultant of the 2014

---

[28] Sarkar (2013), https://www.thedailystar.net/news/justice-mizanur-cleared

[29] Ibid.

general election was devoid of any opposition. Thus, it is manifestly evident that the BAL regime had purposefully incapacitated the Parliament to act as a check on its powers, thereby reducing it to a mere a rubber stamp.

Having ensured the subservience of the Parliament, the ruling BAL passed, as mentioned above, the Sixteenth Amendment on 17 September 2014 for curtailing the independence of the judiciary. For the Sixteenth Amendment in dispensing with the constitutional provisions concerning the SJC, entrusted the Parliament with the power to remove the judges of the SC.[30] The BAL, however, claimed that it had merely restored the original provisions of the 1972 Constitution of Bangladesh by entrusting the Parliament with the power to remove the judges.[31] It should be stressed here that the BAL's pretension to restoring the sanctity of the 1972 Constitution is unfounded. For it is the BAL government which for the first time, as pointed out earlier in Sect. 5.3, had undermined the sanctity of the Constitution by, among other things, repealing the original provisions concerning the removal of judges through the enactment of the Constitution (Fourth Amendment) Act, 1975. Instead of the Parliament, the Fourth Amendment authorized Sheikh Mujibur Rahman (Mujib)—the father of the current Prime Minister, Sheikh Hasina—to remove the judges of the SC at his pleasure, thereby undermining the independence of the judiciary.

Furthermore, it should be stressed here that the Constitution should be seen as a "living force"[32]—one that is capable of changing to reflect "changing social condition and changing needs".[33]Accordingly, the framers incorporated flexible amendment provisions in the Constitution of Bangladesh.[34] However, in freezing the Constitution according to its original provisions concerning the removal of judges by the Parliament, the BAL overlooked the fact that the method of removal of judges involving the SJC did not leave the fate of the judges at the mercy of the pollical branches of government and, as such, was more in line with the contemporary norms concerning the independence of the judiciary (See Sect. 2.4.2).

It can be strongly argued that like the Fourth Amendment, the Sixteenth Amendment was also preferred for curbing the independence of the judiciary by making it extremely convenient for an "all-powerful executive" [35] to remove any judge of the SC who drew its ire for delivering justice in a fearless and impartial manner in a dispute where it was a party. For in the absence of an actual opposition, the Parliament emerging out of the 2014 election, was reduced, as pointed out above, to a toothless body—subject to the absolute control of the BAL government.

---

[30] Constitution (Sixteenth Amendment) Act, 2014 (Bangladesh) s. 2(2).

[31] Mahbub (2014), https://bdnews24.com/bangladesh/2014/09/17/16th-amendment-passed-to-restore-parliaments-power-to-sack-judges

[32] *Theophanous v. Herald and Weekly Times Ltd* (1994) 182 CLR 104, 174.

[33] Strauss (2010), https://www.law.uchicago.edu/news/living-constitution

[34] Constitution of Bangladesh, 1972 (Bangladesh) art. 142(1)(a) (stipulating that any proposed bill for amendment to the Constitution can be passed by the votes of 'two-thirds of the total number of members of the Parliament'.)

[35] Bari (2018), pp. 80–81.

The argument that the Sixteenth Amendment undermined the independence of the judiciary by granting the executive the unconstrained authority to sack the judges of the SC through the subservient Parliament, gains further momentum by reference to the anti-defection provision contained in Article 70 of the Constitution. Article 70 requires Members of Parliament (MPs) to blindly defer to the directives of their nominating political parties in order to keep their membership in the Parliament.[36] Thus, Article 70 would operate to preclude the competence of MPs to defy arbitrary directives of the BAL government while exercising the potential power of removing a judge of the SC.

6.4 The SC's Invalidation of the Sixteenth Amendment and the Consequent Attack on the Chief Justice

The constitutionality of the Sixteenth Amendment was challenged before the HCD within a few months of its enactment in the case of *Advocate Asaduzzaman Siddiqui v. Bangladesh* (the Sixteenth Amendment Case).[37] A HCD majority of 2:1, on 5 May 2016, invalidated the amendment as being "colourable, void and ultra vires" the Constitution of Bangladesh.[38] Justice Moyeenul Islam, who delivered the majority judgment, articulated three grounds in favour of this finding. First, Justice Islam took notice of the fact that the majority of the Commonwealth nations do not invest the legislative branch of the government with the power to remove judges of the superior courts.[39] Rather these nations, as had been previously discussed in Sect. 2.4.2, invest either *ad hoc* tribunals or permanent disciplinary councils, which are akin to the SJC as had been provided for by the Constitution of Bangladesh prior to the enactment of the Sixteenth Amendment, with the power to remove judges of the superior courts.[40] The learned judge observed that these Commonwealth jurisdictions prefer such a removal mechanism "for upholding the separation of powers among the 3(three) organs of the State and for [ensuring] complete independence of the Judiciary from the other two organs of the State".[41] Accordingly, Justice Islam observed that the constitutional provisions "relating to the Supreme Judicial Council are more transparent in safeguarding the independence of the judiciary".[42]

---

[36] Constitution of Bangladesh, 1972 (Bangladesh) art. 70 (stipulating that "A person elected as a member of Parliament at an election at which he was nominated as a candidate by a political party shall vacate his seat if he … votes in Parliament against that party.").

[37] *Advocate Asaduzzaman Siddiqui v. Bangladesh* (2014) Writ Petition No. 9989/2014 (HCD).

[38] Ibid., p. 165.

[39] Ibid., p. 76.

[40] Ibid.

[41] Ibid.

[42] Ibid., p. 142.

6.4 The SC's Invalidation of the Sixteenth Amendment and the Consequent Attack... 145

Second, Justice Islam shed light on the adverse impact of Article 70 on the independence of MPs to perform their functions in the Parliament. As he observed:

> I must say that this Article has fettered the Members of Parliament unreasonably and shockingly. It has imposed a tight rein on them. Members of Parliament can not [sic] go against their partyline or position on any issue in the Parliament. They have no freedom to question their party's stance in the Parliament, even if it is incorrect and flawed. They can not vote against their party's decision. They are, indeed, hostages in the hands of their party high command.[43]

Consequently, the learned judge held that due to Article 70, MPs would be required to "toe the partyline in case of removal of any Judge of the Supreme Court,"[44] thereby leaving the judge "at the mercy of the party high command,"[45] and impairing in the process the independence of the judiciary.

Finally, Justice Islam took cognizance of the past decisions of the Appellate Division (AD) of the SC, which have identified "Independence of the Judiciary" as one of the basic structures of the Constitution.[46] Since security of tenure is one of the fundamental elements of judicial independence, the learned judge observed that the Sixteenth Amendment by investing the subservient Parliament with the power to remove the judges of the SC had diminished one of the basic structures of the Constitution in violation of the terms of Article 7B of the Constitution. For Article 7B explicitly provides that the constitutional provisions relating to the basic structures are not amenable to the amendatory process.[47] Consequently, Justice Islam held that the "Court... has power to undo any amendment if it transgresses its limits and alters any basic structure of the Constitution".[48]

When the BAL government instituted an appeal against the HCD's declaration of unconstitutionality of the Sixteenth Amendment, the AD—the highest court of appeal in the country—unanimously upheld the decision of the HCD.[49] Chief Justice SK Sinha—the first judge of Hindu faith to ascend to the Muslim majority nation's highest judicial office—delivered the judgment of the Court on 1 August 2017. In affirming the decision of the HCD, Chief Justice Sinha rightly observed that since the Parliament resultant of the sham 2014 general election remained completely under the thumb of the executive branch of government, the "judiciary should not be made answerable to the Parliament."[50] The learned judge also echoed the observations of Justice Islam of the HCD regarding the undue restrictions imposed by

---

[43] Ibid., p. 123.

[44] Ibid., p. 124.

[45] Ibid.

[46] Ibid., pp. 92–100.

[47] Constitution of Bangladesh, 1972 (Bangladesh) art. 7B (providing that "Notwithstanding anything contained in article 142 of the Constitution ... the provisions of articles relating to the basic structures of the Constitution including article 150 of Part XI shall not be amenable by way of insertion, modification, substitution, repeal or by any other means.)

[48] *Advocate Asaduzzaman Siddiqui v. Bangladesh* (2014) Writ Petition No. 9989/2014 (HCD), at 99.

[49] *Bangladesh v. Advocate Asaduzzaman Siddiqui* (2017) Civil Appeal No. 06 of 2017 (AD).

[50] Ibid., p. 205.

146   6   The Functioning of the Supreme Judicial Council, the Changes Introduced...

Article 70 of the Constitution on MPs, which further curtailed the competence of MPs to be independent of partisan political directives, including at the time of exercising the potential power of impeaching a judge of the SC. As he observed:

> [I]t is difficult for a member of Parliament [by reason of Article 70] to form an opinion independently ignoring the directions given by the party high command of the political party in power[51]... [This] leads to the... conclusion that... [the] new mechanism [for removing judges] cannot be expected to function independently and neutrally if a Judge attracts displeasure from the political party in power, he may be subjected to removal by the Parliament. There can be little argument that the function of judicial review by Judges involve dealing with views in respect of which political parties in the government and opposition could have opposing views with which the Judges may not reflect or agree in their judgment. Without a political tradition in which members of Parliament could clearly demonstrate that they can act neutrally and impartially if they are given the power of removal and will not be affected by the party's views under article 70, the purported process of impeachment introduced by Sixteenth Amendment would clearly undermine the independence of judiciary and will definitely alter the basic structure of the constitution.[52]

Finally, Chief Justice Sinha after articulating the reasons for upholding the HCD's decision to invalidate the Sixteenth Amendment, attributed the BAL government's attempt to curb the independence of the Judiciary to its "greed for power". As he observed:

> The greed for power is like a plague, once set in motion it will try to devour everything. Needless to say, this WAS NOT at all the aims and vision of our liberation struggle. Our Forefathers fought to establish a democratic State, not to produce any power-monster. The human rights are at stake, corruption is rampant, Parliament is dysfunctional, crores of people are deprived of basic health care, mismanagement in the administration is acute, with the pace of the developed technology, the crimes dimension is changing rapidly, the life and security of the citizens are becoming utterly unsecured, the law enforcing agencies are unable to tackle the situation and the combined result of all this is a crippled society, a society where good man does not dream of good things at all; but the bad man is all the more restless to grab a few more of bounty. In such a situation, the Executive becomes arrogant and uncontrolled ... Even in this endless challenge, the judiciary is the only relatively independent organ of the State which is striving to keep its nose above the water though sinking. But judiciary too, cannot survive long in this situation ... [However] [i]nstead of strengthening the judiciary, the Executive is now trying to cripple it and if it happens, there could be disastrous consequences.[53]

The decision of the AD to uphold the Sixteenth Amendment's unconstitutionality had the impact of restoring the constitutional provisions concerning the removal of judges of the SC involving the SJC. However, Chief Justice Sinha's judgment, in particular his blunt observations about the BAL's hunger for power, incensed the BAL hierarchy, including its chief—Prime Minister Hasina. As soon as the written judgment was published, Prime Minister Hasina, her cabinet and parliamentary colleagues began using unparliamentary language questioning Chief Justice Sinha's character, integrity and propriety in declaring the Sixteenth Amendment *ultra vires*

---

[51] Ibid., p. 284.

[52] Ibid., pp. 292–293.

[53] Ibid., pp. 228–229.

6.4 The SC's Invalidation of the Sixteenth Amendment and the Consequent Attack... 147

the Constitution. The Prime Minister and her colleagues not only called for Chief Justice Sinha to step down but also advised him to "either leave the country or get treatment in Hemayetpur [a mental facility situated in Pabna, Bangladesh]".[54] These unkind remarks about the head of the judiciary vindicated the concerns raised by both Divisions of the SC in the Sixteenth Amendment Case regarding the prospect of entrusting the Parliament with the power to impeach judges.

However, when the Chief Justice did not step down on his own volition, the BAL regime took matters into its own hands. On 2 October 2017, the Minister for Law, Justice and Parliamentary Affairs, who like his colleagues had also criticized Chief Justice Sinha for his verdict in the Sixteenth Amendment Case,[55] told the media that the Chief Justice would "go on a month's leave... on health grounds".[56] This announcement was followed by the publication of a gazette notifying that Justice MA Wahhab Miah—the senior most judge of the AD—would act as the Chief Justice in the absence of Chief Justice Sinha.[57] The appointment of the Acting Chief Justice was made in pursuance of Article 97 of the Constitution, which, as pointed earlier in Sect. 3.2, in an attempt to prevent patronage appointment obliges the President to follow the rule of seniority in appointing the Acting Chief Justice when a vacancy arises in the office of Chief Justice or when "absence, illness, or any other cause" renders the Chief Justice incapable of discharging the duties of his office.

On 13 October 2017—11 days after the announcement of the Law Minister— Justice Sinha left the country for Australia. However, before leaving, Chief Justice Sinha contradicted the government's claim by telling the journalists gathered at his official residence that:

> *I'm not sick.*[58] I'm not fleeing. I'll come back. I'm a little embarrassed. I'm the guardian of the judiciary. I'm leaving for a brief period in the interest of the judiciary, and so that the judiciary is not polluted.[59]

His one-page long written statement, which was distributed to the journalists, further shed light on the political pressures exerted on him: "[T]he way a political quarter, lawyers, and especially some honourable ministers of the government and the honourable prime minister are criticising me recently over a verdict made me embarrassed."[60]

Within a few hours of Justice Sinha leaving for Australia, the BAL regime took the unprecedented move of instituting 11 charges, including "money laundering,

---

[54] Times News (2017), http://bangladesh.timesofnews.com/denigrating-cj-who-said-what.html; BDNEWS24.COM (2017), https://bdnews24.com/politics/2017/08/27/leave-bangladesh-or-get-treated-for-mental-problem-minister-matia-to-chief-justice.

[55] Ibid.

[56] The Daily Star (2017b), https://www.thedailystar.net/frontpage/cj-goes-months-leave-1470712

[57] Daily Sun (2017), https://www.daily-sun.com/post/258788

[58] The Daily Star (2017c), https://www.thedailystar.net/frontpage/cj-set-leave-australia-1476169.

[59] Ibid.

[60] Ibid.

financial irregularities, corruption, moral turpitude," against him,[61] It is pertinent to mention here that at the time a furore had erupted over the judgment in the *Sixteenth Amendment case*, Justice Sinha had served as the Chief Justice for approximately two years and 9 months.[62] During this period, no allegations of corruption had ever been brought against the learned judge. Rather it is only after the pronouncement of the judgment in the Sixteenth Amendment Case that the BAL regime had suddenly discovered that Chief Justice Sinha was guilty of conduct unbecoming of the holder of highest judicial office in Bangladesh. It is, therefore, manifestly evident that the BAL regime had went to great lengths to persecute Justice Sinha for thwarting its attempt to subjugate the judiciary. Owing to such persecution, Justice Sinha prematurely resigned from his office on 11 November 2017[63]—two months and twenty days before he was supposed to retire. Since retirement, Justice Sinha has been living in exile—first in the US and now in Canada where he has sought asylum.[64]

6.5 The Impact of Justice Sinha's Resignation on the Independence of the Judiciary

Although Justice Sinha resigned as the Chief Justice on 11 November 2017, the BAL Government did not proceed, as pointed earlier in Sect. 4.2.3, to appoint Acting Chief Justice MA Wahhab Miah as the regular Chief Justice in pursuance of Article 95(1) of the Constitution. Rather two months and 20 days after Justice Sinha's resignation, the regime appointed Justice Syed Mahmud Hossain—the second senior-most judge of the AD—as the regular Chief Justice on 2 February 2018.[65] Since Justice Miah did not defer to the wishes of the BAL regime when he, as pointed out earlier in Sect. 4.2.3, pronounced a dissenting judgment upholding the constitutionality of the system of NPCG in the Thirteenth Amendment Case,[66] it seems the regime did not consider him trustworthy to implement its agenda of securing the reversal of the AD's unanimous decision in the *Sixteenth Amendment Case* on the basis of the review petition that it had filed on 24 December 2017 under

---

[61] The Daily Star (2017a), http://www.thedailystar.net/frontpage/11-charges-against-cj-1476448.

[62] The Economic Times (2015), https://economictimes.indiatimes.com/news/international/world-news/bangladesh-appoints-surendra-kumar-sinha-as-new-chief-justice/articleshow/45852712.cms?from=mdr

[63] The Daily Star (2017d), https://www.thedailystar.net/politics/chief-justice-cj-surendra-kumar-sinha-resigns-1489639.

[64] The Daily Star (2019), https://www.thedailystar.net/country/news/sk-sinha-seeks-asylum-canada-1777318

[65] The New Nation (2017), http://m.thedailynewnation.com/news/163639/justice-mahmud-hossain-made-new-cj

[66] *Abdul Mannan Khan v. Bangladesh*, Civil Appeal No. 139 of 2005 with Civil Petition for Leave to Appeal No. 596 of 2005 (Bangl.), at 35.

6.5 The Impact of Justice Sinha's Resignation on the Independence of the Judiciary 149

Article 105 of the Constitution.[67] Rather it seems that Justice Hossain, who was initially appointed in 1999 as the Deputy Attorney General and was subsequently appointed to the HCD as an additional judge in 2001 during the rule of the BAL, was considered more dependable to give effect to this grand design.

It should be stressed here that although the judgment of the AD in the Sixteenth Amendment Case, as pointed out earlier in Sect. 6.4, had the effect of restoring the constitutional provisions concerning the SJC, the then Attorney General, Mahbubey Alam—a pro BAL lawyer[68] who even sought nomination from the BAL for contesting the 2018 general election[69]—casted doubt on such restoration due to the pendency of the review petition before the AD. However, it is difficult to agree with this interpretation offered by the then principal law officer of the country. For, according to a unanimous decision of the full bench of the AD, which also consisted of the current Chief Justice—Justice Hossain—a review petition should not be "equated with an appeal".[70] Accordingly, it can be strongly argued that unlike the pendency of the BAL regime's appeal against the decision of the HCD in the Sixteenth Amendment Case, which prevented the restoration of the constitutional provisions concerning the SJC, the pendency of a review petition instituted against the determination of the final court of appeal, namely, the AD, in the Sixteenth Amendment Case cannot be said to have the same effect.

Furthermore, a review of a decision of the AD is only permissible when there is a manifest error of law or fact on the face of the decision which either "undermines its soundness or results in miscarriage of justice".[71] In light of the detailed examination of the AD's decision in the Sixteenth Amendment Case in Sect. 6.4, it is evident that the decision does not exhibit any "apparent and patent"[72] error which casts doubt on its reasonableness. Rather the AD had prevented the executive's attempt to encroach on the independence of the judiciary—a basic structure of the Constitution—by unanimously nullifying the Sixteenth Amendment. In this context, the observations of Justice Hossain—the current Chief Justice—in the Sixteenth Amendment case are noteworthy:

> The Sixteenth Amendment impairs the independence of the judiciary by making the judiciary vulnerable to a process of impeachment by the legislature which would be influenced by political influence and pressure.[73]

---

[67] Constitution of Bangladesh, 1972 (Bangladesh) art. 105 (stipulating that the "Appellate Division shall have power, subject to the provisions of any Act of Parliament and of any rules made by that division to review any judgment pronounced or order made by it").

[68] Asian Human Rights Commission (2009), http://www.humanrights.asia/news/ahrc-news/AHRC-STM-016-2009/

[69] Jishnu, Brahmaputra (2018), https://www.dhakatribune.com/bangladesh/politics/2018/04/29/attorney-general-mahbub-hopes-awami-league-nomination-next-election

[70] *Abdul Quader Mollah v. The Chief Prosecutor*, International Crimes Tribunal, Dhaka, Criminal Review Petition Nos. 17–18 of 2013, at 21.

[71] Ibid.

[72] Ibid., p. 22.

[73] *Bangladesh v. Advocate Asaduzzaman Siddiqui*, (2017) Civil Appeal No. 06 of 2017 (AD), 549

Justice Hossain in his judgment also termed the method of removal of judges on the recommendation of the SJC a more "transparent procedure"[74] when compared to the procedure concerning removal of judges by the Parliament. However, notwithstanding such observations, it is striking that Justice Hossain after being sworn in as the Chief Justice in supersession of Justice Miah, has not proceeded to promptly dispose of the review petition seeking the reversal of the decision of the AD in the Sixteenth Amendment Case. Rather it seems that out of "a sense of gratitude"[75] to the BAL regime, Justice Miah has now radically transformed his views regarding the efficacy of the provisions concerning the SJC for safeguarding the independence of the judiciary. Such transformation became evident when it came to the fore that Chief Justice Hossain had unilaterally carried out a primary investigation against three judges of the HCD—accused of misconduct or incapacity.[76] Subsequently, Justice Hossain upon consultation with the head of the state—President Md Abdul Hamid, who has been elected to the office on a BAL ticket[77]—ordered the concerned judges to refrain from their judicial duties.[78]

This method adopted by the Chief Justice for taking disciplinary action against the judges of the SC in consultation with the executive branch of government, is not only devoid of any constitutional foundation but also lacks the objectivity and transparency of the process involving the SJC. For unlike the functioning of the SJC, it does not represent the plurality of opinion of the senior-most judges of the nation for precluding the likelihood of arbitrariness or bias, even subconsciously, against the judge accused of wrongdoing and permits the executive branch to adversely influence such a method. Furthermore, unlike the SJC, there is no evidence to suggest that the method adopted by the Chief Justice provides the accused judge any opportunity to defend the charges brought against him.

The unceremonious ouster of Justice Sinha from the office of the Chief Justice coupled with the adoption of an unconstitutional and arbitrary method by Justice Hossain for taking disciplinary action against judges accused of misconduct, have had the impact of unduly curtailing the competence of the judiciary to impartially adjudicate cases where the executive is a party, and to act as the final bulwark against executive encroachment on the liberty of individuals. In this context, reference can be first made to a recent deferential decision of the HCD in dismissing a writ petition challenging the constitutionality of the anti-defection provision contained in Article 70 of the Constitution for contravening, among other things, the tenets of the principle of democracy as enshrined in various provisions of the Constitution.[79] It is

---

[74] Ibid., p. 545.

[75] Campbell and Lee (2001), p. 95.

[76] BDNEWS24.COM (2019), https://bdnews24.com/bangladesh/2019/08/22/three-high-court-judges-facing-probe-ordered-to-refrain-from-judicial-activities.

[77] The Daily Star (2018b), https://www.thedailystar.net/politics/abdul-hamid-elected-president-of-bangladesh-second-term-1531225

[78] See above n 76.

[79] Constitution of Bangladesh, 1972 (Bangladesh) arts. 7, 19, 26, 27, 31, 44 and 119; The Daily Star (2018a), https://www.thedailystar.net/backpage/article-70-constitution-its-safeguard-democracy-1581670

6.5 The Impact of Justice Sinha's Resignation on the Independence of the Judiciary

striking that in dismissing the petition, Justice Abu Taher adopted an erroneous interpretation of the observations of both the AD and HCD in the *Sixteenth Amendment Case*, as discussed earlier in Sect. 6.4, regarding the adverse impact of Article 70 on the independence of MPs to act as an effective check on the powers of the executive branch of government. For he observed that the observations of both the Divisions of the SC regarding Article 70 in the *Sixteenth Amendment Case* were not of precedential value as these were incidental or collateral to the delivery of their judicial opinion in the case.[80] Justice Taher reached such a conclusion notwithstanding the fact that the detrimental impact of Article 70 on the independence of MPs was, as pointed out earlier in Sect. 6.4, one of the grounds on the basis of which both the HCD and AD had declared the Sixteenth Amendment *ultra vires* the Constitution. Justice Moyeenul Islam Chowdhury in delivering the majority judgment of the HCD to strike down the amendment shed light on the undesirable impact of Article 70, which has become a principal tool for the government of the day to ensure the subservience of the MPs. As he observed:

> Because of Article 70 of the Constitution, a Member of Parliament effectively loses his character as an agent of the people and becomes the nominee of his party. What is dictated by the cabinet of the ruling party or the shadow cabinet of the opposition, Members of Parliament must follow them meekly ignoring the will and desire of the electorate of their constituencies. There starts a process of distance and apathy between the Members of Parliament and their electors. Such Members are dummies in Parliament. Having a solid grip over the majority of the Members of Parliament, the party-in-power moves to influence the executive, judiciary and other instrumentalities. It eventually results in what we say, 'daleokaran'- the political terminology to indicate a 'group oriented society'.[81]

Consequently, Justice Chowdhury held that the terms of Article 70 coupled with the parliamentary method of removal of judges as contemplated by the Sixteenth Amendment would firmly put the fate of judges in the hands of the party in power, thereby undermining the independence of the judiciary.

On appeal, Chief Justice Sinha in delivering the judgment of the AD, as discussed earlier in Sect. 6.4, had endorsed the observations of the HCD by maintaining that due to the unwarranted restrictions imposed by Article 70 on the independence of MPs to carry out their functions in the Parliament, the method of removal of judges as envisaged by the Sixteenth Amendment "would clearly undermine the independence of the judiciary".[82]

It is evident from the above analysis that the both the HCD and AD in the Sixteenth Amendment Case drew a clear connection between the parliamentary method of impeachment of judges of the SC sought to be introduced by the Sixteenth Amendment, and the undesired consequences of the simultaneous operation of Article 70. Therefore, these observations of the two Divisions of the SC cannot be downplayed as obiter. It seems that the judge of the highest court of the nation

---

[80] Constitution of Bangladesh, 1972 (Bangladesh) art. 70.

[81] *Advocate Asaduzzaman Siddiqui v. Bangladesh* (2014) Writ Petition No. 9989/2014 (HCD), at 123–124.

[82] *Bangladesh v. Advocate Asaduzzaman Siddiqui* (2017) Civil Appeal No. 06 of 2017 (AD), at 293.

engaged in a deliberate attempt to downplay the precedential value of a landmark constitutional case in order to shield himself from the wrath of the ruling of BAL.

Second, the HCD has also proved reluctant in recent times to stand between the individual and the encroachment on his liberty by the executive. In this context reference can be made to the arrest of Shahidul Alam—an internationally celebrated photographer—on 5 August 2018 and the subsequent refusal of the HCD to grant him bail on several occasions.

Alam was arrested by plain-clothes policemen for: a) documenting the BAL regime's violent suppression of peaceful protests organized by high school students from 29 July 2018 to 2 August 2018 demanding safer roads and stringent road safety regulations, through photos and live recorded videos posted on Facebook, and b) giving an interview to *Al Jazeera* on 5 August 2018, in which he remarked that the student protests reflected deeper popular anger at the "looting of the banks and the gagging of the media," and the "extrajudicial killings, disappearings, bribery and corruption" executed by an "unelected government ... clinging on by brute force".[83] Subsequently, the regime charged Alam under the draconian Section 57 of the Information and Communication Technology Act, 2006, which had criminalized the publication of "fake, obscene or defaming information in electronic form".[84] If convicted, Alam could face a maximum jail term of fourteen years and a maximum fine of USD 11,920,400.[85]

It is manifestly evident that the regime of BAL was victimizing Alam for merely exercising his constitutionally protected right to freedom of speech and expression to criticise the regime's controversial policies or decisions. Furthermore, when the police produced Alam before the Chief Metropolitan Magistrate's Court, there was clear visible physical evidence that the law enforcement agencies had tortured him as "he was unable to walk by himself".[86] In fact, he described to the court the manner in which he was tortured, thus: "I was hit [in custody]. [They] washed my blood-stained Punjabi [a traditional Bangladeshi attire] and then made me wear it again."[87] Notwithstanding the infringement of Alam's fundamental rights, including the right not to be "subjected to torture or to cruel, inhuman, or degrading punishment or

---

[83] Barth (2018), https://www.fairobserver.com/region/central_south_asia/bangladesh-shahidul-alam-arrest-free-press-latest-asian-news-this-week-32380/; The Guardian (2018), https://www.theguardian.com/world/2018/nov/20/bangladeshi-activist-shahidul-alam-released-from-prison

[84] Information & Communication Technology Act, 2006 (Bangladesh), s. 57 (amended by Information & Communication Technology (Amendment) Act, 2013 (Bangladesh).

Section 57 became a tool for the BAL regime to put down its critics in contravention of the fundamental rights guaranteed by the Constitution. This controversial provision was ultimately repealed through the enactment of the Digital Security Act, 2018 (Bangladesh). See Digital Security Act, 2018 (Bangladesh) s. 61.

[85] Information & Communication Technology Act, 2006 (Bangladesh) s. 57, amended by Information & Communication Technology (Amendment) Act, 2013 (Bangladesh).

[86] Perrigo (2018), http://time.com/5359850/bangladesh-photographer-arrest-shahidul-alam-protests

[87] NEWAGE (2018), http://www.newagebd.net/article/47782/shahidul-on-seven-day-remand

6.5 The Impact of Justice Sinha's Resignation on the Independence of the Judiciary 153

treatment",[88] the lower court not only refused to grant him bail but also placed him on a seven-day remand.[89]

However, the HCD also refused to thwart the BAL regime's arbitrary encroachment on the fundamental human rights of Alam in dereliction of its constitutional mandate.[90] Furthermore, the HCD in following in the footsteps of the lower court refused to grant Alam bail on 4 separate occasions,[91] which resulted in him spending 107 days in prison.[92] It should be stressed here that such refusal to grant bail stands in stark contrast to HCD's previous tradition of offering efficacious remedy to petitioners to further "the cause of justice".[93] For instance, during the last declared state of emergency in January 2007 in Bangladesh, when the military-backed NPCG ousted the jurisdiction of the courts to release individuals arbitrarily detained by it under the Emergency Power Rules,[94] the HCD notwithstanding such ouster proceeded to order the release of many detainees in exercise of its inherent power to grant bail under Section 498 of the Code of Criminal Procedure (CrPc), 1898.[95] The HCD observed that its inherent jurisdiction to grant bail to secure the release of individuals under Section 498 of the CrPc could not be taken away even during a state of emergency by any subordinate law.[96]

It is, indeed, striking that the HCD in departing from the practices followed by courts elsewhere of adopting a highly deferential approach when called on to examine actions taken by the government during states of emergency,[97] did not shy away from holding the executive to account. Yet during ordinary times, the superior judiciary due to the BAL regime's hostility towards it has proved to be extremely deferential.

In light of the above discussion, it is evident that the measures adopted in the aftermath of the decision of Justice Sinha in the Sixteenth Amendment Case, have enabled the BAL regime to ensure the subservience of the judiciary, thereby realising its aspiration of becoming "the unlimited master of the state".[98]

---

[88] Constitution of Bangladesh, 1972 (Bangladesh) art. 35(5).

[89] Dhaka Tribune (2018), https://www.dhakatribune.com/bangladesh/court/2018/11/13/100-days-on-from-shaidul-alam-s-arrest.

[90] Constitution of Bangladesh, 1972 (Bangladesh) art. 102(1) (stipulating that "The High Court Division on the application of any person aggrieved, may give such directions or orders to any person or authority, including any person performing any function in connection with the affairs of the Republic, as may be appropriate for the enforcement of any the fundamental rights conferred by Part III of this Constitution.").

[91] Agence France Presse (2018), https://www.yahoo.com/news/bangladesh-photographer-freed-months-detention-161543306.html?soc_src=community&soc_trk=tw.

[92] Ibid.

[93] *AKM Reazul Islam v. State* [2008] 13 BLC (HCD) 111, 119.

[94] Bari (2017), pp. 208–209.

[95] Ibid., pp. 209–210.

[96] *Moyezuddin Sikder v. State* [2007] 59 DLR (HCD) 287, 297.

[97] Bari (2017), pp. 110, 136–141.

[98] Laski (2015), p. 542.

References

(2015) Chapter 3: Removal from office. *Commonwealth Law Bulletin*, 41(4), 525.

Agence France Presse. (2018). *Shahidul alam, Bangladesh photographer freed after months in detention*. Available at https://www.yahoo.com/news/bangladesh-photographer-freed-months-detention-161543306.html?soc_src=community&soc_trk=tw

Asian Human Rights Commission. (2009). *Bangladesh: End the politically chosen "disposable" attorney and prosecutorial*. Available at http://www.humanrights.asia/news/ahrc-news/AHRC-STM-016-2009/

Bangladesh Law House. (2011). *Code of conduct for the judges*. Available at http://bdlawhouse.blogspot.com/2011/10/code-of-conduct-for-judges.html

Bari, M. E. (2017). *States of emergency and the law: The experience of Bangladesh* (pp. 209–210). Routledge.

Bari, M. E. (2018). The incorporation of the system of non-party caretaker government in the constitution of Bangladesh in 1996 as a means of strengthening democracy, its deletion in 2011 and the lapse of Bangladesh into tyranny following the non-participatory general election of 2014: A critical appraisal. *Transnational Law and Contemporary Problems, 28*(1), 81–82.

Barth, P. (2018). *Bangladesh prevents freedom of opinion*. Available at https://www.fairobserver.com/region/central_south_asia/bangladesh-shahidul-alam-arrest-free-press-latest-asian-news-this-week-32380/

BDNEWS24.COM. (2005a). *Justice Faizee's advocate ship certificate cancelled, faces criminal case*. Available at https://bdnews24.com/bangladesh/2005/04/24/justice-faizee-s-advocate-ship-certificate-cancelled-faces-criminal-case

BDNEWS24.COM. (2005b). *SC stays HC order declaring illegal Shahidur's removal*. Available at https://bdnews24.com/bangladesh/2005/04/24/sc-stays-hc-order-declaring-illegal-shahidur-s-removal

BDNEWS24.COM. (2007a). *HC Judge Faizee bows out*. Available at https://bdnews24.com/bangladesh/2007/07/13/hc-judge-faizee-bows-out

BDNEWS24.COM. (2007b). *Supreme Judicial Council holds first meeting on Faizee*. Available at https://bdnews24.com/bangladesh/2007/03/28/supreme-judicial-council-holds-first-meeting-on-faizee

BDNEWS24.COM. (2017). *Leave Bangladesh or get treated for mental problem*. Available at https://bdnews24.com/politics/2017/08/27/leave-bangladesh-or-get-treated-for-mental-problem-minister-matia-to-chief-justice

BDNEWS24.COM. (2019). *Three high court judges facing probe, ordered to refrain from judicial activities.*. Available at https://bdnews24.com/bangladesh/2019/08/22/three-high-court-judges-facing-probe-ordered-to-refrain-from-judicial-activities

Brahmaputra, J. (2018). *Attorney General Mahbubey hopes for Awami League nomination in next election*. Available at https://www.dhakatribune.com/bangladesh/politics/2018/04/29/attorney-general-mahbub-hopes-awami-league-nomination-next-election

Campbell, E., & Lee, H. P. (2001). *Australian Judiciary* (p. 95). Cambridge University Press.

Daily Sun. (2017). *Wahhab Miah made acting Chief Justice*. Available at https://www.daily-sun.com/post/258788

Dhaka Tribune. (2018). *100 Days on from Shahidul Alam's arrest.*. Available at https://www.dhakatribune.com/bangladesh/court/2018/11/13/100-days-on-from-shaidul-alam-s-arrest

European Parliament. (2008). *Legislative elections in Bangladesh. Election Observation Delegation, 2*. Available at http://www.epgencms.europarl.europa.eu/cmsdata/upload/36287860-18fe-4c47-92b1-5aa527c34129/Election_report_Bangladesh_29_December_2008.pdf

The Economic Times. (2015). *Bangladesh appoints Surendra Kumar Sinha as new chief justice*. Available at https://economictimes.indiatimes.com/news/international/world-news/bangladesh-appoints-surendra-kumar-sinha-as-new-chief-justice/articleshow/45852712.cms?from=mdr

References

Islam, M. (2018). Secularism in Bangladesh: An unfinished revolution. *South Asia: Journal of South Asian Studies, 38*(1), 29.

Khokon, S.H. (2017). *Ganajagaran Mancha blogger Ahmed Rajib's killer held in Dhaka.* Available at https://www.indiatoday.in/world/story/ahmed-rajib-blogger-murder-ganajagaran-mancha-killer-dhaka-961678-2017-02-20

Laski, H. J. (2015). *A grammar of politics* (p. 542). Routledge.

Mahbub, S. (2014). *16th Amendment passed to restore Parliament's power to sack judges.* Available at https://bdnews24.com/bangladesh/2014/09/17/16th-amendment-passed-to-restore-parliaments-power-to-sack-judges

NEWAGE. (2018). *Shahidul on seven-day remand.* Available at http://www.newagebd.net/article/47782/shahidul-on-seven-day-remand

Perrigo, B. (2018). *What the arrest of photographer Shahidul Alam means for press freedom in Bangladesh.* Available at http://time.com/5359850/bangladesh-photographer-arrest-shahidul-alam-protests.

Sarkar, A. (2013). *Justice Mizanur cleared.* Available at https://www.thedailystar.net/news/justice-mizanur-cleared

Strauss, D.A. (2010). *The living constitution.* Available at https://www.law.uchicago.edu/news/living-constitution

The Daily Star. (2007a). *CU cancels certificate of Judge Faizee, 2,350 others.* Available at http://archive.thedailystar.net/2007/03/04/d7030401011.htm.

The Daily Star. (2007b). *Mark sheet tampering: CU cancels certificates of Judge Faizee, 2350 others.* Available at http://archive.thedailystar.net/2007/03/04/d7030401011.htm

The Daily Star. (2013a). *Alleged misconduct: Justice Mizanur replies to judicial council.* Available at https://www.thedailystar.net/news/justice-mizanur-replies-to-judicial-council-2

The Daily Star. (2013b). *Justice faces JS music.* Available at https://www.thedailystar.net/news-detail-269768

The Daily Star. (2015). *Bangladesh top court upholds dismissal of judge Shahidur.* Available at https://www.thedailystar.net/backpage/sc-upholds-dismissal-judge-shahidur-144355

The Daily Star. (2017a). *11 'Charges' against CJ.* Available at http://www.thedailystar.net/frontpage/11-charges-against-cj-1476448\

The Daily Star. (2017b). *Chief justice goes on a month's leave.* Available at https://www.thedailystar.net/frontpage/cj-goes-months-leave-1470712

The Daily Star. (2017c). *I'm not sick.* Available at https://www.thedailystar.net/frontpage/cj-set-leave-australia-1476169

The Daily Star. (2017d). *SK Sinha resigns from chief justice post, says president's press secretary.* Available at https://www.thedailystar.net/politics/chief-justice-cj-surendra-kumar-sinha-resigns-1489639

The Daily Star. (2018a). *Article 70 of constitution: It's a safeguard for democracy..* Available at https://www.thedailystar.net/backpage/article-70-constitution-its-safeguard-democracy-1581670

The Daily Star. (2018b). *Hamid elected president for a second term.* Available at https://www.thedailystar.net/politics/abdul-hamid-elected-president-of-bangladesh-second-term-1531225

The Daily Star. (2019). *SK Sinha seeks asylum in Canada.* Available at https://www.thedailystar.net/country/news/sk-sinha-seeks-asylum-canada-1777318

The Guardian. (2018). *Bangladeshi photographer Shahidul Alam released from prison.* Available at https://www.theguardian.com/world/2018/nov/20/bangladeshi-activist-shahidul-alam-released-from-prison

The New Nation. (2017). *Justice Mahmud Hossain made new CJ.* Available at http://m.thedailynewnation.com/news/163639/justice-mahmud-hossain-made-new-cj\

Times News. (2017). *Denigrating CJ: Who said what.* Available at http://bangladesh.timesofnews.com/denigrating-cj-who-said-what.html

Chapter 7
Conclusion

7.1 Introduction

This Chapter will endeavour to summarise the key arguments articulated in the preceding six Chapters of this book with a view to highlighting the weaknesses of the provisions of the Constitution of Bangladesh, 1972 concerning the appointment of the judges of the Supreme Court of Bangladesh and to shed light on the adverse measures taken by the current government of the Bangladesh Awami League (BAL) to adversely affect the security of tenure of the judges. Subsequently, based on these findings, an attempt will be made in this Chapter to put forward concrete recommendations for incorporating changes in the Constitution of Bangladesh to rule out the possibility of patronage appointments to the highest court of the land and to enable the judges to enjoy security of tenure, thereby safeguarding the independence of the judiciary.

7.2 The Constituent Elements of Judicial Independence

The Constitution of a nation, which embodies in it the power of the people, entrusts the judiciary with the vigilant task of keeping the political branches of government, namely, the executive and legislature, within the bounds of constitutionality by nullifying the unconstitutional acts of these two organs. By preventing the executive and the legislature from overstepping the constitutional limits of their authority, the judiciary, in fulfilment of the pious trust reposed on it by the people, acts as the guardian not only of the Constitution but also of democracy values, such as the rule of law and human rights of individuals. In order for the judiciary to carry out these pivotal tasks, its independence from the two other organs of the government should be adequately secured. For doing so would enable the judges to interpret and apply

© The Author(s), under exclusive license to Springer Nature Singapore Pte Ltd. 2022

M. E. Bari, *The Independence of the Judiciary in Bangladesh*, https://doi.org/10.1007/978-981-16-6222-5_7

the law free from any political pressure or interference. This is referred to as the traditional meaning of judicial independence.

Over the years, several international and regional organisations have developed standards, which are based on the conception that the independence of the judiciary carries four meanings:

1. **Substantive Independence**— which refers to the independence of an individual judge to "dispense justice according to law without regard" to the dictates of the government of the day;[1]
2. **Personal Independence**— which relates to the independence of an individual judge from the executive with regard to his security of tenure;
3. **Collective Independence**— which is based on the idea of safeguarding the institutional, administrative and financial independence of the judiciary from the executive and the legislature; and
4. **Internal Independence**—which refers to the independence of the judges from their judicial colleagues and superiors.

The notions of substantive and personal independence comprise the independence of an individual judge while the notions of internal and collective independence constitute the independence of the judiciary as a whole. However, as discussed in Sects. 1.2, 2.3 and 2.4, it is more common for constitutions around the world to guarantee the individual independence, i.e., substantive and personal independence, of judges. Inextricably linked with the individual independence of judges is the procedures governing their appointment and security of tenure. It is, therefore, imperative to stipulate a transparent method of appointment of judges and to guarantee their security of tenure. As doing so has the beneficial impact of enabling judges to decide cases according to law and fact, without being unduly influenced by the political branches of government and without the fear of suffering adverse consequences for objective decision-making.

7.2.1 The Importance of a Transparent Method of Appointment

In light of the international norms concerning judicial independence, which recommend the appointment of judges of the superior courts involving a judicial appointments commission, modern constitutions invest a judicial appointments commission with the responsibility to select and subsequently nominate candidates to the head of the state for appointment to the bench. In this context, reference can be made to the constitutional process of appointment of judges introduced in recent times in the UK and Pakistan (See Sect. 2.4.1).

---

[1] Stephen (1985), p. 531.

In the UK, the Constitutional Reform Act, 2005 (CRA) provides for the establishment of two types of selection commissions. First, in pursuance of the terms of the CRA, most of the judicial appointments in the UK are made on the recommendation of the Judicial Appointments Commission, which is headed by a lay person and is further composed of 14 members chosen through open competition among members of the public, the judiciary, the legal profession and non-legally qualified judicial office holders. Second, the CRA provides for the establishment of special selection commissions for nominating candidates for appointment to the superior courts, including the highest court of appeal in the UK, namely, the Supreme Court. The CRA, as amended in 2013 by the Crime and Courts Act, also provides for the membership of such ad-hoc commissions. In all cases, the appointments to the bench should be on "merit".[2] In this context, it is noteworthy that in an effort to further the cause of ensuring the appointment of the meritorious candidates, the CRA contains a number of safeguards. The CRA, in the first instance, does not provide either of the political branches of the government representation in the JAC and the ad-hoc commissions. Furthermore, it significantly curtails the authority of the executive to reject the candidates recommended by the commissions or to request the reconsideration of the nominations. As any such action of the executive must be accompanied by appropriate reasons. After the commissions have put forward the recommendation on three separate occasions, the appointing authority will be constrained to appoint the candidate. The objective underlying the incorporation of these safeguards is to reduce the role of the executive in the process of appointing the judges to "almost a purely formal one" (See Sect. 2.4.1).[3]

In the same vein, the Constitution of Pakistan, 1973, as amended in 2010, stipulates a new method for selecting and recommending candidates for appointment to the superior courts. It entrusts a Judicial Commission with the responsibility to select and recommend candidates for appointment to the bench. Although the Constitution envisages a role for each of the three branches of the government in the new process of appointing judges, past and present members of the judiciary have been given the dominant voice in the Commission in order to limit the possibility of appointment of judges on extraneous considerations (See Sect. 2.4.1).

On the other hand, in view of the issues surrounding the appointment of the judges of the superior courts in India involving the "collegium" system, which, as discussed earlier in Sect. 2.4.1, is an invention of the Supreme Court of India to deprive the executive of the final say in appointing judges of superior courts, the Constitution of India, 1950, was amended by the Constitution (Ninety-Ninth Amendment) Act on 14 August 2014, to provide for the establishment of a National Judicial Appointments Commission (NJAC). The NJAC was invested with the responsibility to select and recommend candidates to the executive for appointment to the bench. However, unlike the Constitution of Pakistan, the Constitution of India, as amended in August 2014, did not allow senior members of the judiciary to

---

[2] Constitutional Reform Act, 2005 (UK) s. 63(2).

[3] Bogdanor (2010), p. 67; Bevir (2010), p. 163.

constitute a majority in the NJAC. Furthermore, the Constitution not only allowed the Law Minister representation in the Commission but also provided for the inclusion of two "eminent persons". Finally, any two members of NJAC had the discretion to veto nomination, which could have been potentially exercised by the Law Minister in conjunction with either of the "eminent persons" to prevent the nomination of any candidate considered unfriendly to the government of the day. This grant of wide discretion had the effect of defeating the objective of securing the appointment of most deserving candidates to the bench. Consequently, the Supreme Court invalidated the Ninety-Ninth Amendment for undermining the independence of the judiciary (See Sect. 2.4.1).

It is, therefore, evident that the idea of entrusting a judicial appointments commission to carry out the pivotal task of selecting and recommending suitable candidates for appointment to the bench, has found favour in modern democracies in recent times. However, in order for such a commission to realise its purpose, this book stresses that a constitution should contain the following safeguards:

(a) The judicial appointments commission should be chaired by the head of the judiciary and should additionally be composed, among others, of the senior-most judges of the superior courts— together these senior members of the judiciary should constitute, as is the case in Pakistan, the majority in the commission. This arrangement would impede the ability of the political branches of the government to unduly influence the process of selecting judges to ensure the appointment of their preferred candidates;

(b) the commission should only be competent to select and recommend candidates on merit, which has been construed to include criteria, such as legal knowledge and experience, intellectual and analytical ability, sound judgment, decisiveness, integrity, independence, fairness, impartiality, maturity and sound temperament (See Sect. 2.4.1); and

(c) the recommendations of the commission should have binding effect unless the executive possesses information which cast reasonable doubt on the competence of the nominee to serve as a judge of the superior courts. In such a scenario, the executive should reserve the right to ask the commission to reconsider its recommendation by sharing with the latter the relevant information regarding the unsuitability of the candidate.

It can be strongly argued that a judicial appointments commission possessing the above characteristics will be inclined towards recommending those candidates for judgeship who possess unimpeachable integrity, spotless character, judicial temperament, firmness, keen intellect, and the ability to analyse facts. In this context, the observations of Gerald L Gall are noteworthy:

> The dictates of tradition require the greatest restraint, the greatest propriety and the greatest decorum from the members of our judiciary. We expect our judges to be almost superhuman

7.2 The Constituent Elements of Judicial Independence

in wisdom, in propriety, in decorum and in humanity. There must be no other group in society which must fulfil this standard of public expectation.[4]

7.2.2 The Importance of Security of Tenure

One of the most important elements for safeguarding the independence of the judges to decide cases without fear or favour is security of tenure. As the guarantee security of tenure "reinforces the independence of mind and action" of judges "essential to the proper discharge of their functions"[5] and consequently, enables them to hold the executive to account. Therefore, once appointed judges should either remain in office "for life"[6] or should enjoy "guaranteed tenure until a mandatory retirement age".[7] They should only be removed from office on account of incapacity or misbehaviour "that renders them unfit to discharge" the functions of their office.[8] However, such removal must be made a difficult process, depriving the political branches of government, particularly the executive, to remove judges at whim. Otherwise, judges would be inclined to decide cases in accordance with the wishes of the government of the day to keep their job.

Accordingly, the international norms concerning judicial independence, as discussed earlier in Sect. 2.4.2, recommend that any process for removing a judge from office should involve an independent and impartial body of judicial character. Such a body should be entrusted with the responsibility to investigate the allegations brought against a judge and to, consequently, recommend the removal of such a judge if the allegations are proven. In light of these norms, a majority of the Commonwealth nations invest either ad hoc or permanent disciplinary tribunals with the responsibility to investigate allegations brought against a judge before putting forward their recommendations.

However, this book has demonstrated in Sect. 2.4.2 that it is common for national constitutions to not specify the composition of ad hoc tribunals, which in turn provides the executive with the discretion to pack the tribunals with loyalists for unduly influencing the investigation against a judge. In this context, the constitutional arrangement in Malaysia, as discussed in Sect. 2.4.2, is instructive. For the weaknesses of the Malaysian Constitution's provisions concerning the institution of an ad hoc tribunal was exploited by the government of Mahathir Mohamad in 1988 to orchestrate the removal of the then head of the judiciary, Lord Tun Salleh Abas, for his proclivity to hold the government to account for depriving the courts of the judicial power of the Federation (See Sect. 2.4.2).

---

[4] Quoted in *Re Therrien* [2001] 2 SCR 3, 76.

[5] *Fingleton v The Queen* (2005) 216 ALR 474, 507 (J. Kirby).

[6] International Bar Association (1982), Art. 22.

[7] United Nations (1985), Art. 12.

[8] The Commonwealth Latimer House Principles (1998), pp. 28–29.

162   7   Conclusion

On the other hand, when a constitution provides for the institution a permanent disciplinary tribunal and confines the membership of such a body to senior members of the judiciary, it preserves the objectivity and fairness of the investigation initiated against a judge of the superior court. This argument is bolstered by reference to the provisions concerning the Supreme Judicial Council as contained in the Constitution of Pakistan, 1973, for investigating the allegations brought against a judge of the superior judiciary and for recommending, if proved, his removal from office. The Constitution of Pakistan confines the membership of the Council to senior members of the superior judiciary, thereby depriving the executive of the opportunity to interfere with the removal proceedings initiated against the concerned judge. Thus, it is manifestly evident that entrusting a permanent disciplinary tribunal body— the membership of which is confined to the senior members of the judiciary— with the pivotal task of conducting disciplinary proceedings against an accused judge, is more conducive to maintaining the independence of the judiciary (See Sect. 2.4.2).

When a constitution invests bodies of judicial character with the responsibility to select and recommend judges and to conduct disciplinary proceedings against judges, it insulates judges from political pressure, thereby enabling them to impartially decide cases on their merits. In this context, the observations of Justice Murray Gleeson, who served as the Chief Justice of the High Court of Australia from 1998 to 2008, are noteworthy:

> It is the right of citizens that there be available for the resolution of civil disputes between citizen and citizen or between citizen and government, and for the administration of criminal justice, an independent judiciary whose members can be assured with confidence to exercise authority without fear or favour.[9]

Furthermore, appointing and removing judges on the recommendation of bodies of a judicial character have the salutary effect of safeguarding the independence of the judiciary as a whole. For these bodies while performing their tasks tend to "view the collective needs of the institution or branch rather than look to individual interests".[10]

The utility of a transparent method of appointment of judges and of adequate security of tenure to safeguard the independence of the judiciary, can be gathered from the manner in which the Pakistani superior judiciary, as discussed earlier in Sect. 2.5, has held the executive accountable in recent times. Arguably, this has been possible due to the safeguards contained in the Constitution of Pakistan, 1973, for shielding the judges from political pressure (See Sects. 2.4.1, 2.4.2 and 2.5).

---

[9] *Fingleton v The Queen* (2005) 216 ALR 474, 486.

[10] Dakolias and Thachuk (2000), p. 379.

7.3 The Constitution of Bangladesh and the Principle of Judicial Independence

The framers of the Constitution of Bangladesh, 1972, as discussed earlier in Sects. 1.3 and 2.6, sought to establish a democratic society in which an independent judiciary would operate to uphold the rule of law and the human rights of individuals. To this end, the Constitution not only speaks of the necessity to separate the judiciary from the executive but also to safeguard the personal independence of the judges by stipulating that "[s]ubject to the provisions of this Constitution, the Chief Justice and the other Judges shall be independent in the exercise of their judicial functions".[11] Consequently, judges are required to swear to "faithfully discharge the duties of …[their] office according to law" and to hold the scale of justice even between the humblest citizen and an all-powerful executive, regardless of the consequences to themselves.

Furthermore, the Constitution guarantees every accused the fundamental right to have a "speedy and public trial" by not only an independent but also by an impartial judiciary.[12] Thus, the principle of the independence of judiciary is recognised as a cornerstone in the scheme of the Constitution of Bangladesh. In fact, the principle is one of the basic pillars upon which the nation's constitutional edifice is built. However, notwithstanding such recognition, there exists a significant gap between the enunciation of the principle of judicial independence in the Constitution and the manner in which the Constitution seeks to give effect to such a principle.

7.4 Does the Constitution of Bangladesh Guarantee a Transparent Method of Appointment of Judges of the Superior Judiciary?

The Constitution of Bangladesh, as discussed earlier in Sect. 3.1, provides for the appointment of three kinds of judges to the superior judiciary, namely, the Chief Justice of Bangladesh, the judges of the Appellate Division (AD)— the higher Division of the Supreme Court (SC)— and the judges of the High Court Division (HCD)— the lower Division of the SC. However, since the Constitution vests the executive with the power to appoint these judges, it paves the way for the intrusion of extraneous considerations into the appointment process.

---

[11] Constitution of Bangladesh, 1972 (Bangladesh) article 94(4).

[12] Constitution of Bangladesh, 1972 (Bangladesh) article 35(3).

164   7 Conclusion

7.4.1 The Appointment of the Chief Justice

The Constitution of Bangladesh, 1972, as discussed earlier in Sect. 3.2, empowers the President— the Head of the State—to appoint the Chief Justice of Bangladesh. It is striking that the Constitution does not obligate the President to consult any constitutional entity or a selection committee before appointing the head of the judiciary. This issue is further compounded by the fact that the Constitution does not specify any qualifications for the appointment of the Chief Justice. Thus, the President, who can hardly be expected to know about the judicial qualities of a candidate or his performance as a puisne judge of the SC, is given the unfettered discretion to appoint the Chief Justice.

Article 95 of the Constitution stipulates for the appointment of the regular Chief Justice, while Article 97 speaks of the appointment of an Acting Chief Justice as a stop-gap arrangement for a shorter period. Although Article 97 obligates the President to appoint the senior-most judge of the AD as the Acting Chief Justice when a vacancy arises in the office of the Chief Justice or when the Chief Justice is unable to perform the functions of his office due to "absence, illness or any other cause" to obviate the possibility of a patronage appointment, the Constitution in Article 95 does not impose any such obligation on the President to follow the rule of seniority in appointing the regular Chief Justice from amongst the judges of the AD. Consequently, a convention of appointing the senior-most judge of the AD as the regular Chief Justice, had been developed to prevent the appointment of the head of the judiciary on irrelevant considerations. The convention of seniority was an effective safeguard for preserving public confidence in the integrity of the highest judicial office of the nation.

However, this convention has been transgressed at regular intervals since June 2003— twice during the tenure of the government of the Bangladesh Nationalist Party (BNP) (2001-2006), once in May 2008 when the military-backed "Non-Party Care-taker" government (NPCG) was in office, and thrice since the government of the Bangladesh Awami League (BAL) took office in January 2009 (See Sects. 4.2.1, 4.2.2, and 4.2.3). It is, therefore, evident the BAL regime has gone further than its predecessors in superseding the senior-most judges of the AD to appoint the Chief Justice. Furthermore, these supersessions have been perpetrated by the BAL regime to secure the appointment of those judges of the AD as Chief Justice who would, for instance, implement its various parochial agendas, such as securing:

(a) the declaration of the system of NPCG, which was incorporated in the Constitution by the Constitution (Thirteenth Amendment) Act, 1996, unconstitutional so as to enable it to rig the outcome of general elections in its favour (See Sect. 4.2.3); and

(b) the reversal of the decision of the AD nullifying the Constitution (Sixteenth Amendment) Act, 2014 to bring the superior judiciary under its control. (See Sect. 6.5).

It is noteworthy that Justice Khairul Haque in his decision in the *Thirteenth Amendment Case* drew a connection between the incorporation of the system of

7.4 Does the Constitution of Bangladesh Guarantee a Transparent Method... 165

NPCG in the Constitution and the supersession of the senior-most judges of the AD in appointing the Chief Justice on account of political allegiance, thereby inferring that the system was counterproductive to judicial independence (See Sect. 4.2.3). However, contrary to this prescription of the learned judge, the deletion of the system of NPCG from the Constitution in July 2011 has not, as is evident from the discussion in Sects. 4.2.3 and 6.5, put an end to the violation of the convention of seniority in appointing the Chief Justice.

7.4.2 *The Appointment of the Judges of the AD*

Since the Constitution of Bangladesh also does not provide any guideline as to the qualifications or judicial qualities necessary for appointment as judges of the AD, a convention was developed to elevate the senior-most judges of the HCD to the AD to prevent appointment on extraneous considerations. However, since 13 August 1976, the convention of appointing the judges of the AD from amongst the judges of the HCD based on seniority after consultation with the Chief Justice has been violated both by the civilian and martial law regimes on numerous occasions (See Sect. 4.3.2). In fact, the current government of BAL has gone further than its predecessors by violating the convention of seniority on 10 occasions (See Sect. 4.3.2.4).

In this context, the example set by Justice Syed Mahboob Morshed, the then Chief Justice of the East Pakistan (Dacca) High Court, is noteworthy. Justice Morshed in 1967 had recommended Mr Tayyabuddin Talukder for appointment as the judge of the High Court. The Chief Justice of Pakistan, Justice AR Cornelius, for unknown reasons did not support his recommendation and, because of this, the President did not make the appointment. In protest of the flouting of his recommendation, Justice Morshed resigned from the office of the Chief Justice of the High Court of East Pakistan on 15 November 1967,[13] thereby setting a shining example in the judicial history of former East Pakistan (now Bangladesh) for upholding the dignity and authority of the office of the Chief Justice and for demonstrating his conviction in effective and meaningful consultation with the said office. However, no Chief Justice of Bangladesh has ever stepped into the shoes of Justice Morshed in similar circumstances. Furthermore, it has not been kept in mind that the violation of the established convention of appointing the senior most judge of the HCD as the judge of the AD is obviously a breach of his legitimate expectation. The tendency of the Supreme Court Bar Association to protest violation of the convention of seniority on political considerations has made the appointees controversial, which in turn has had the disastrous impact of eroding public faith, confidence, and trust in the highest court of appeal.

---

[13] Quoted in *Al-Jehad Trust v. Pakistan*, 1996 PLD (SC) 324, 384

7.4.3 The Appointment of the Judges of the HCD

The Constitution of Bangladesh provides for appointment of two types of judges to the HCD— regular and additional. While the President is required to consult the Chief Justice in appointing the regular puisne judges in pursuance of Article 95(1) of the Constitution, no such requirement is prescribed for the appointment of additional judges for an initial period of two years in accordance with the provisions of Article 98. Consequently, Article 98 has become a gateway which every judge is required to pass to prove their case to the executive for appointment as a permanent judge. To this end, reference can be made to the 85 additional judges appointed by the BAL regime in the past 12 years and a half. Many of these appointments, as pointed out earlier in Sect. 4.4., has been made on purely political considerations in blatant disregard of academic qualifications or judicial qualities.

7.4.4 The Fate of the Supreme Judicial Council, 2008

The President of Bangladesh during the tenure of the military-backed NPCG in March 2008 promulgated the Supreme Judicial Commission Ordinance providing for the establishment of a Supreme Judicial Commission (SJC). The SJC was composed of nine ex-officio members, six of whom were from the judiciary—the Chief Justice of Bangladesh, the three senior-most judges of the AD, and two senior-most judges of the HCD of the SC—who constituted the majority in the Commission (See Sect. 3.7.1). This domination of the Commission by the judicial members was more conducive to selecting and recommending candidates objectively, keeping in mind the needs of the office. However, the BAL regime in order to implement its agenda of packing the bench with loyalists, deliberately refrained from placing the SJC Ordinance before the Parliament, which was elected as a result of the 2008 general election, for approval. Thus, the life of the SJC came to an abrupt end (See Sect. 4.4).

In light of the above, it is evident that the Constitution neither stipulates a transparent method of appointment of judges, which is one of the primary mechanisms for safeguarding the independence of the judges to decide cases on their merit without being unduly influenced by the policy of the government of the day, nor mandates that appointments to the bench should be made on merit.

7.5 Does the Constitution Adequately Safeguard the Security of Tenure of the Judges of the SC?

The Constitution of Bangladesh, as discussed earlier in Sect. 5.2, originally stipulated that the judges of the SC were to remain in office for a long term and could not be removed by the President at its whim. However, President Sheikh Mujibur Rahman arrogated to himself through the enactment of the Constitution (Fourth Amendment), 1975, the unfettered discretion to fire judges, which had a dreadful impact on the independence of the judges to perform their functions without fear or favour (See Sect. 5.3).

Since security of tenure of the judges is a key ingredient for maintaining judicial independence, the Martial Law regime of General Zia in April 1977 took the salutary step of incorporating a transparent procedure in the Constitution for removal of the judges of the SC (See Sect. 5.4). This procedure invested the Supreme Judicial Council (SJC)— chaired by the Chief Justice and additionally composed of the two senior-most judges of the SC as members— with the responsibility to maintain the independence of the judiciary by protecting the judges of the SC from arbitrarily being dismissed at the whim of either the executive or the legislature.

However, the current BAL regime after rendering the Parliament toothless following the sham general election of 2014, has embarked on the journey to institute a tyrannical regime. Since an independent judiciary can act as a bulwark against tyranny, the regime sought to exert its supremacy over the Judiciary by dispensing with the above transparent constitutional method of removal of judges through the enactment of the Constitution (Sixteenth Amendment) Act in September 2014. This amendment, instead, entrusted the Parliament with the power to remove judges of the SC. Although the SC restored the constitution provisions concerning the SJC by invalidating the Sixteenth Amendment for altering one of the basic structures of the Constitution, namely, the independence of judiciary, the BAL regime has shown no signs of retreating from its effort to undermine the independence of the judiciary (See Sects. 6.3, 6.4, and 6.5).

First, in retaliation for Chief Justice Sinha's fearless judgment in the *Sixteenth Amendment Case* derailing the BAL government's plan to rob the judiciary of its independence, the regime not only forced him out of the highest judicial office but also the country. Owing to well-founded fear of persecution in Bangladesh, Justice Sinha has been living in exile in Canada. Second, following Justice Sinha's resignation, the regime appointed its preferred candidate— Justice Hossain— as the Chief Justice in supersession of the senior most judge of the AD— Justice Miah. This appointment was made with the expectation that Justice Hossain would reverse the decision in the *Sixteenth Amendment Case* in pursuance of a review petition filed by the government in December 2017 notwithstanding the fact that he was part of the AD which unanimously declared the amendment *ultra vires* the Constitution. Although Justice Hossain has not yet formally reversed the decision in the *Sixteenth Amendment Case*, he has indirectly executed this plan of the government. As he has validated the regime's ploy of casting doubts on the automatic restoration of the constitutional provisions concerning the SJC by adopting, in consultation with the executive, an arbitrary and unconstitutional method of initiating disciplinary action against judges accused of misconduct (See Sect. 6.5). Through these maneuverers, the regime has instilled fear of adverse consequences in the minds of the judges of the SC, thereby substantially impeding their ability to impartially discharge their duties, as is evident from the recent decisions of the HCD (See Sect. 6.5).

7.6 Recommendations: Incorporation of Effective Safeguards in the Constitution of Bangladesh, 1972 for Guaranteeing the Independence of the Judiciary

It is manifestly evident from the discussion in the preceding Chapters of this book and summarised above that successive governments in Bangladesh, particularly the current government of the BAL, have exploited the weaknesses constitutional provisions concerning the appointment of the judges of the SC to pack the bench with loyalists. Furthermore, the current BAL regime has taken one measure after another to adversely impact the security of tenure of the judges of the highest court of law. These events have not only unduly impaired the independence of the judges to decide cases free from the pressure of the executive but have also undermined the public confidence in the independence and impartiality of the judiciary. Accordingly, it is imperative that the following reforms are incorporated within the Constitution of Bangladesh, 1972, by means of an amendment:

(a) Appointment of the Chief Justice of Bangladesh on the basis of Seniority

It is striking that in the case of an unexpected vacancy, the Constitution of Bangladesh provides that the President will appoint an Acting Chief Justice solely on the basis of seniority, which negates the possibility of a patronage appointment. It can be strongly argued that a similar approach should be adopted for appointing the regular Chief Justice of Bangladesh, as well. Thus, Article 95(1) of the Constitution should stipulate that the President shall appoint only the senior-most judge of the AD of the SC as the Chief Justice of Bangladesh, as has been done in the case of the Constitution of Pakistan, 1973, by the Constitution (Eighteenth Amendment Act), 2010 (See Sects. 2.4.1 and 3.2).

Although it is quite possible that in a given case the inflexible rule of seniority can lower judicial performance as the senior-most judge might not be the most suitable choice or might not be able to live up to the highest standard expected of him, the rule of seniority must be adhered to in appointing the Chief Justice for the following reasons:

(i) there is a greater safety in appointing the senior-most judge as the Chief Justice, the *sentinel qui vive* of the independence of the judiciary. For, doing so would deprive the President from picking and choosing among the judges on the basis of extraneous considerations, e.g., political or personal favouritism.

7.6 Recommendations: Incorporation of Effective Safeguards in the Constitution... 169

(ii) the supersession of the senior-most judge in appointing the Chief Justice of Bangladesh will hurt his dignity and self-respect as the cause list is printed in accordance with the seniority of the judges and the judges sit in that order. He might also feel belittled in the eyes of others as an incompetent and inefficient judge. Consequently, he may take retirement (as had been done by Justice MA Wahab Miah in February 2018 after he was overlooked for appointment as the Chief Justice notwithstanding his seniority and his performing the functions of the office of the Acting Chief Justice for four months) or take leave until retirement, thereby creating a vacuum in the AD of experienced and competent judges.

(iii) The appointment of the Chief Justice by seniority will prevent a scramble among judges of the SC for the highest office. This scramble would be nothing but a competition to show who has better imbibed the gospel of the ruling party so as to capture the eye and ear of the appointing authority whenever a vacancy arises. Even the junior-most judge may think that by giving a decision in favour of the executive in a case and by cultivating good relationship with it, he would stand a good chance of becoming the Chief Justice of Bangladesh. This in turn has the disturbing impact of shattering public confidence in the highest judicial office of the nation.

(b) Abolition of the System of Appointment of Additional Judges to the HCD of the SC

The system of appointing additional judges to the HCD of the SC in pursuance of Article 98 of the Constitution of Bangladesh, which has become the principal tool for the executive to determine the fitness of candidates for appointment as permanent judges, should be abolished on the following grounds:

First, since the additional judges are initially appointed for a period of two years, they can hardly be expected to hold the scale of justice as independently and courageously as regular judges in cases, particularly in which the executive is involved.

Second, if they pronounce a fair and fearless judgment against the executive, which is the largest litigant before the HCD, it may cost them either appointment as regular judges or "for a further period."

Third, a litigant's confidence in the independence and impartiality of additional judges, whose continuance in office after the specified period is subject to the pleasure of the executive, is bound to suffer from the thought that these judges are likely to be biased towards the government of the day.

Finally, international norms concerning the independence of judiciary disapprove the system of appointing temporary judges like additional judges. For instance, the Montreal Declaration on the Independence of Justice, 1983, provides that the appointment of temporary judges is inconsistent with the principle of judicial independence and, as such, it calls for gradually discontinuing such appointments where they exist.[14]

(c) **Establishment of a Supreme Judicial Commission for Selecting and Recommending Candidates for Appointment to the SC**

The present method for the appointment of the judges of both the Divisions of the SC in Bangladesh, which grants the executive significant leeway to make appointments to the bench through political or personal patronage, should be replaced with a transparent method. In order to strengthen the independence and impartiality of the judiciary, Article 95(1) of the Constitution should invest an independent, effective and meaningful Supreme Judicial Commission, representing various interests with pre-eminent position in favour of the senior-most members of judiciary, with the power to select and recommend best candidates to the President for judicial appointment. For, the principles on the independence of the judiciary, formulated and adopted by various international and regional organisations, particularly in the 1980s and thereafter, favour the appointment of judges of superior courts by, on the recommendation, proposal/advice of, or after consultation with an appropriately constituted and representative judicial body. Furthermore, the Constitutions of some of the modern democracies provide for the establishment of a judicial appointments commission which enjoy high degree of independence from the political branches of the government (See Sect. 2.4.1).

The proposed Supreme Judicial Commission should be headed by the Chief Justice of Bangladesh. It should additionally be composed of the 4 senior-most judges of the SC, the last retired Chief Justice and a Professor of Law chosen on the basis of seniority from public universities by rotation, as ex-officio members. Given the political branches of the government have time and again sought to undermine the independence of the judiciary of Bangladesh, allowing the senior members of the judiciary to constitute a majority in the proposed Commission will insulate the process of selecting and recommending the judges from political pressure, thereby maintaining the integrity and fairness of the process.

Furthermore, the Commission should be empowered to select and recommend candidates for appointment as judges of the SC on merit, i.e., "legal excellence and experience coupled with good character and suitable temperament".[15] As Sir Harry Gibbs aptly pointed out:

> Judicial Commissions, advisory Committees and procedures for consultation [with the Chief Justice] will all be useless unless there exists … the will to appoint only the best.[16]

The recommendation of the Commission should be binding on the executive unless the latter claims to possess information which casts reasonable doubt on a candidate's fitness to serve as a judge of the SC of Bangladesh. In that case, the executive

---

[14] Montreal Declaration (1983), article 2.20.

[15] Gibbs (1987), p. 11.

[16] Ibid.

7.6 Recommendations: Incorporation of Effective Safeguards in the Constitution...

should have the discretion to ask the Commission to reconsider its recommendation in light of the information in the former's possession.

(d) **Strength of Judges**

Since the Constitution of Bangladesh provides the executive with the discretion to increase the number of judges of both the Divisions of the SC on political considerations, such as creating berths on the bench to reward those favourites who have delivered as law officers, as party men and judges, rather than on judicial considerations (e.g. to deal with increased number of cases), such a power should only be exercised by the President on the recommendation of the proposed Supreme Judicial Commission, as is provided for by Article 5 of the Constitution of Puerto Rico, 1952.

Since the BAL regime, as pointed out earlier in Sects. 6.3, 6.4 and 6.5 and summarised above, has adversely impacted the security of tenure of the judges by taking a number of measures, including dispensation with the process of removal of judges involving the SJC and forcing the Chief Justice SK Sinha out of office, it is necessary to adopt, in addition to the above reforms, a few other concrete measures for upholding the independence of the judiciary.

First, it is striking that despite the passing of almost four years, the AD has not disposed of the review petition filed by the regime seeking the reversal of the decision in the *Sixteenth Amendment Case*, which restored the provisions concerning the SJC by invalidating the Sixteenth Amendment. Since the decision in the *Sixteenth Amendment Case*, as pointed out earlier in Sect.6.4, does not manifest any "apparent and patent"[17] error which can jeopardize its reasonableness, it is imperative that the AD dismisses the review petition without any further delay. For doing so would remove the impediment, as conveniently claimed by the BAL, to the restoration of the constitutional provisions concerning removal of the judges of the SC on the recommendation of the SJC.

Second, the BAL should realise that impairing the independence of the judiciary in order to ensure the survival of its absolutist project is fundamentally contradictory to the democratic principles on which the nation was founded, as is evident from the third preamble paragraph of the Constitution: "[I]t shall be a fundamental aim of the State to realise through the democratic process a ... society ... free from exploitation— a society in which the rule of law, fundamental human rights and freedom ... will be secured for all citizens."[18]

The adoption of the above reforms would enable those appointed as judges of the SC of Bangladesh to decide cases on their legal and factual merits free from political control, thereby ensuring the observance of the rule of law and restoring in the process the SC's credibility in the eyes of the litigants. As Sir Gerard Brennan, the former Chief Justice of Australia, aptly observed:

---

[17] *Abdul Quader Mollah v. The Chief Prosecutor*, International Crimes Tribunal, Dhaka, Criminal Review Petition Nos. 17–18 of 2013, at 22.

[18] Constitution of Bangladesh, 1972 (Bangladesh), Preamble.

172   7 Conclusion

The reason why judicial independence is of such public importance is that a free society exists only so long as it is governed by the rule of law— the rule which binds the governors and the governed, administered impartially and treating equally all those who seek its remedies or against whom its remedies are sought. However vaguely it may be perceived, however unarticulated may be the thought, there is an aspiration in the hearts of all men and women for the rule of law.

That aspiration depends for its fulfilment on the competent and impartial application of the law by judges. In order to discharge that responsibility, it is essential that judges be, and be seen to be, independent.[19]

References

Bogdanor, V. (2010). *The new British constitution* (p. 67). Hart Publishing; See also, Bevir, M. (2010). *Democratic governance* (p. 163). Princeton University Press.

Brennan, G. (1996). *Judicial independence*. Available at https://www.hcourt.gov.au/assets/publications/speeches/former-justices/brennanj/brennanj_ajc.htm

Dakoliasm, M., & Thachuk, K. (2000). Attacking corruption in the judiciary: A critical profess in judicial reform. *Wisconsin International Law Journal, 18*(2), 379.

Gibbs, H. (1987). The appointment of judges. *Australian Law Journal, 61*, 11.

The Commonwealth Latimer House Guidelines. (1998). *Independence of judiciary* 28–29.

United Nations. (1985). *Basic principles on the independence of the judiciary*. GA/RES/40/32 & GA/RES/40/146 (29 November & 13 December 1985). Available at https://www.ohchr.org/EN/ProfessionalInterest/Pages/IndependenceJudiciary.aspx

---

[19] Brenna (1996), https://www.hcourt.gov.au/assets/publications/speeches/former-justices/brennanj/brennanj_ajc.htm

Table of Cases

Domestic Court Judgements

Abdul Mannan Khan v. Bangladesh, Civil Appeal No. 139 of 2005 with Civil Petition for Leave to Appeal No. 596 of 2005. (Bangladesh).

Abdul Quader Mollah v. The Chief Prosecutor, International Crimes Tribunal, Dhaka, Criminal Review Petition Nos. 17–18 of 2013, 22. (Bangladesh).

Additional District Magistrate, Jabalpur v. Shivkant Shukla [1976] AIR (SC) 1207.

Advocate Asaduzzaman Siddiqui v. Bangladesh (2014) Writ Petition No. 9989/2014 (HCD), at 99. (Bangladesh).

AKM Reazul Islam v. State [2008] 13 BLC (HCD) 111, 119. (Bangladesh).

Al-Jehad Trust v. Pakistan, 1996 PLD (SC) 324, 384. (Pakistan).

Anwar Hossain Chowdhury and Others v Bangladesh (1989) 18 CLC (AD). (Bangladesh).

Anwar Hossain Khan v. Speaker of Bangladesh Sangsad Bhaban and Others 47 DLR (1995) 42. (Bangladesh).

Bangladesh and Justice Syed Md Dastagir Hossain and others v. Md Idrisur Rahman 38 CLC (AD) 2009. (Bangladesh).

Bangladesh v. Advocate Asaduzzaman Siddiqui (2017) Civil Appeal No. 06 of 2017 (AD). (Bangladesh).

Commissioner of Taxes v. Justice S. Ahmed 42 DLR (AD) (1990) 162. (Bangladesh).

Fingleton v The Queen (2005) 216 ALR 474, 507. (Australia).

Hind and others v The Queen (1976) 1 All ER 353. (Judicial Committee of the Privy Council, United Kingdom).

Idrisur Rahman v. Bangladesh 37 CLC (HCD) (2008). (Bangladesh).

In re special reference 1 of 1998 AIR 1999 SC 1. (Bangladesh).

Khondker Delwar Hossain v. Bangladesh Italian Marble Works Ltd., Dhaka and others, (2009) Civil Petition for Leave to Appeal Nos 1044 and 1045. (Bangladesh).

© The Author(s), under exclusive license to Springer Nature Singapore Pte Ltd. 2022
M. E. Bari, *The Independence of the Judiciary in Bangladesh*,
https://doi.org/10.1007/978-981-16-6222-5

174   Table of Cases

Kudrat-E-Elahi v. Bangladesh (1992) 44 DLR (AD) 319. (Bangladesh).

Liversidge v Anderson [1942] AC 206, 244. (United Kingdom).

M Saleem Ullah v Bangladesh (2005) 57 DLR (HCD) 171. (Bangladesh).

Mainul Hosein & others v Sheikh Hasina, 53 DLR (2001) 138. (Bangladesh).

Malik Asad Ali v. Federation of Pakistan, (1998) 50 PLD (SC) 161. (Pakistan).

Marbury v. Madison, 5 U.S. (1 Cranch) 137, 165–66 (1803). (United States).

Md Idrisur Rahman, Advocate and others v Secretary, Ministry of Law, Justice and Parliamentary Affairs, Government of the People's Republic of Bangladesh 37 CLC (HCD) 2008. (Bangladesh).

Md. Idrisur Rahman v. Syed Shahidur Rahman and Others, (2005) Civil Appeal No. 145 of 2005 with Civil Petition for Leave to Appeal No. 405 of 2005, 56. (Bangladesh).

Moazzem Hossain v. State 42 DLR (AD) (1990) 162. (Bangladesh).

Moyezuddin Sikder v. State [2007] 59 DLR (HCD) 287, 297. (Bangladesh).

Mujibur Rahman v Bangladesh (1992) 44 DLR (AD). (Bangladesh).

Re Therrien [2001] 2 SCR 3, 76. (Canada).

S.P. Gupta v Union of India, 1981 Supp SC 87 at 347 (as per Justice Gupta). (India).

Sharaf Faridi v the Federation of Islamic Republic of Pakistan PLD 1989 Karachi 404. (Pakistan).

SN Goswami Advocate v Bangladesh 55 DLR (2003) 392. (Bangladesh).

State v Chief Editor, Manabjamin 31 CLC (HCD) (2002). (Bangladesh).

Supreme Court Advocates-on-Record Association v. Union of India (1993) 4 SCC 441. (India).

Supreme Court Advocates-on-Record Association v. Union of India (2016) 4 SCC 357. (India).

Theophanous v. Herald and Weekly Times Ltd (1994) 182 CLR 104, 174. (Australia).

Walter Valente v Her Majesty the Queen (1985) 2 RCS 673. (Canada).

Watan Party and Pakistan Steel People's Workers Union et al v. Federation of Pakistan [2006] PLD (SC) 697.

Bibliography

List of National Constitutions and Constitutional Amendments

A MAGYAR KÖZTÁRSASÁG ALKOTMÁNYA, 2011 (Constitution of the Republic of Hungary) (effective date 25 April 2011).

Basic Law for the Federal Republic of Germany (effective date 8 May 1949).

Basic Law of Saudi Arabia, 1992 (Saudi Arabia) (effective date 31 January 1992).

BUNREACHT NA HÉIREANN, 1937 (Irish Constitution) (effective date 29 December 1937)

Commonwealth of Australia Constitution Act, 1900 (Australia) (effective date 9 July 2000).

Constitución Española, 1978 (Spain) (effective date 27 August 1978).

Constitution (Fifteenth Amendment) Act, 2011 (Bangladesh).

Constitution (Fourteenth Amendment) Act, 2004 (Bangladesh).

Constitution (Fourth Amendment) Act, 1975 (Bangladesh).

Constitution (Ninety-Ninth Amendment) Act, 2014 (India).

Constitution (Sixteenth Amendment) Act, 2014 (Bangladesh).

Constitution (Twelfth Amendment) Act, 1991.

Constitution of Albania, 1998 (Albania) (effective date 21 October 1998).

Constitution of Algeria, 1989 (Algeria).

Constitution of Bangladesh, 1972 (Bangladesh) (effective date 16 December 1972).

Constitution of Ethiopia, 1995 (Ethiopia) (effective date 21 August 1995).

Constitution of India, 1950 (India) (effective date 26 November 1949).

Constitution of Japan, 1946 (Japan) (3 May 1947).

Constitution of Kenya, 2010 (Kenya) (effective date 27 August 2010).

Constitution of Malta, 1964 (Malta) (effective date 21 September 1964).

Constitution of Montenegro, 2006 (Montenegro) (21 May 2006).

Constitution of Nigeria, 1999 (Nigeria) (effective date 29 May 1999).

Constitution of Pakistan, 1973 (Pakistan) (effective day 14 August 1973).

Constitution of the Co-Operative Republic of Guyana, 1980 (Guyana) (effective date 20 February 1980).

Constitution of the Democratic Socialist Republic of Sri Lanka, 1978 (Sri Lanka) (effective date 7 September 1978).

Constitution of the Independent State of Western Samoa, 1960 (West Samoa) (effective date 28 October 1960).

Constitution of the Islamic Federal Republic of the Comoros, 1978.

Constitution of The Republic of Armenia 1995 (Armenia) (effective date 7 May 1995a).

© The Author(s), under exclusive license to Springer Nature Singapore Pte Ltd. 2022
M. E. Bari, *The Independence of the Judiciary in Bangladesh*,
https://doi.org/10.1007/978-981-16-6222-5

176 Bibliography

Constitution of the Republic of Armenia, 1995 (Armenia) (effective date 7 May 1995b).
Constitution of the Republic of Fiji, 2013 (Fiji) (effective date 7 September 2013).
Constitution of the Republic of Korea, 1948 (effective date 7 July 1948).
Constitution of the Republic of Namibia, 1990 (Namibia) (effective date 21 March 1990a).
Constitution of the Republic of Namibia, 1990 (Namibia) (effective date 21 March 1990b).
Constitution of the Republic of Poland, 1997 (Poland) (effective date 7 April 1997).
Constitution of the Republic of Rwanda, 2003 (Rwanda) (effective date 26 May 2003).
Constitution of the Republic of Sudan, 1998 (Sudan) (effective date 1 July 1998).
Constitution of the Republic of Trinidad and Tobago, 1976 (Trinidad and Tobago).
Constitutional Reform Act, 2005a (United Kingdom) (effective date 24 March 2005).
Druk-Gi Cha-Thrims-Chen-Mo, 2008 (Constitution of Bhutan).
Grundloven, 1953 (Constitution of Denmark) (effective date 5 June 1953).
Konstitutsiia Rossiiskoi Federatsii [Konst. Rf], 1993 (Constitution of Russia) (effective date 25 December 1993).
KONSTYTUCJA RZECZYPOSPOLITEJ POLSKIEJ Z DNIA 2 KWIETNIA, 1997 [Constitution of the Republic of Poland], 1997 (Poland) (effective 7 April 1997)
Laws of Malaysia Federal Constitution, 1957 (Malaysia) (effective date 31 August 1957).
Nēpālakō Sanvidhāna, 2015 (Nepal) (effective date 20 September 2015).
Proclamation (First Amendment) Order, 1982a (Bangladesh) (effective date 11 April 1982).
Proclamation of Emergency, 2007 (Pakistan) (effective date 3 Nov 2007).
Proclamation of Independence, 1971 (Bangladesh) (effective date 17 April 1971).
Proclamations (Tenth Amendment) Order, 1977 (Bangladesh).
Provisional Constitution Bangladesh Order, 1972 (Bangladesh) (effective date 11 January 1972).
Puerto Rico Constitution, 1952 (Puerto Rico) (effective date 25 July 1952).
SAKARTVELOS K'ONSTITUTSIA, 1995 (Constitution of Georgia) (effective date 24 August 1995).
Second Proclamation (Seventh Amendment) Order, (Bangladesh) (effective date 28 May 1976).
SYNTAGMA [SYN.], 1975 (Constitution of Greece).
The Supreme Judicial Commission Ordinance, 2008a (Bangladesh) preamble.
Ustav Republike Hrvatske, 1990 (Constitution 0f The Republic of Croatia) (effective date 22 December 1990).
USTAV REPUBLIKE SRBIJE, 2006 (Constitution of Serbia) (effective date 8 November 2006).
КОНСТИТУЦІЯ УКРАЇНИ, 2004 (Constitution of Ukraine) (effective date 8 December 2004)

Statutes/Rules/Treaties/Conventions/General Comments/Principles

UN Basic Principles on the Independence of the Judiciary, Seventh United Nations Congress on the Prevention of Crime and the Treatment of Offenders, GA/RES/40/32 & GA/RES/40/146 (Endorsed on 29 November & 13 December 1985). Available at https://www.ohchr.org/EN/ProfessionalInterest/Pages/IndependenceJudiciary.aspx
Indian Independence Act, 1947 (United Kingdom) (effective date 18 July 1947).
Information & Communication Technology (Amendment) Act, 2013 (Bangladesh) (effective date 9 October, 2013.
Information & Communication Technology Act, 2006 (Bangladesh).
Minimum Standards of Judicial Independence, International Bar Association (Adopted on 1982). Available at https://www.ibanet.org/MediaHandler?id=bb019013-52b1-427c-ad25-a6409b49fe29

Bibliography 177

The Beijing Statement of the Principles of the Independence of the Judiciary in the LAWASIA Region, Law Association for Asia and the Pacific (LAWASIA) (Adopted on 1995). Available at https://www.icj.org/wp-content/uploads/2014/10/Beijing-Statement.pdf

Universal Declaration on the Independence of Justice, Montreal Declaration (Adopted on 1983). Available at https://www.icj.org/wp-content/uploads/2016/02/Montreal-Declaration.pdf

Bangladesh Legal Practitioners and Bar Council Order, 1972 (Bangladesh).

Second Proclamation Order No. I of 1977 (Bangladesh).

Bangladesh Civil Service Recruitment (1995 Amendment) Rules, 1981 Ordinance No. 087 (Bangladesh) pt. XXII.

The Supreme Judicial Commission Ordinance, 2008b (Bangladesh).

Indian High Courts Act, 1911 (United Kingdom).

Government of India Act, 1935 (United Kingdom).

Government of India Act, 1915 (United Kingdom).

Proclamation (First Amendment) Order I of 1982b (Bangladesh).

The Proclamation of Martial Law, 1982 (Bangladesh) (effective date 24 March 1982).

The Proclamation Order No. III of 1983, (Bangladesh) (effective date 11 December 1983).

Courts Administration Act, 1993.

Constitutional Reform Act, 2005b (United Kingdom).

Supreme Court (Judicial Appointments) Regulations 2013 (United Kingdom).

Judicial Appointments Regulations 2013 (United Kingdom).

African Charter on Human and Peoples' Rights. (1981). OAU Doc CAB/LEG/67/3 21 (27 June 1981).

International Covenant on Civil and Political Rights. (1966). UNTS 999 UNTS 171 (16 December 1971).

Convention for the Protection of Human Rights and Fundamental Freedoms. (1950). 213 UNTS 221.

American Convention on Human Rights. (1969). 1144 UNTS 123 (22 November 1969).

Digital Security Act, 2018 (Bangladesh) (effective date 8 October 2018).

Websites/Internet Materials

Agence France Presse. *Shafiqul Alam, Bangladesh Photographer Freed After Months in Detention.* https://www.yahoo.com/news/bangladesh-photographer-freed-months-detention-161543306.html?soc_src=community&soc_trk=tw

Aljazeera. *US gov't shutdown: How long? Who is affected? Why did it begin?.* https://www.aljazeera.com/news/2019/1/25/us-govt-shutdown-how-long-who-is-affected-why-did-it-begin

Amnesty International. *Denying the Undeniable: Enforced Disappearances in Pakistan'.* https://www.amnesty.org/download/Documents/ASA330182008ENGLISH.pdf

Appleton, K., & Stracqualursi, V. *Here's What Happened the Last Time the Government Shut Down.* https://abcnews.go.com/Politics/heres-happened-time-government-shut/story?id=26997023

Asian Human Rights Commission. *Bangladesh, Government Contests the Reappointment of Judges in Supreme Court.* http://www.humanrights.asia/news/ahrc-news/AHRC-STM-201-2008/?searchterm

Asian Human Rights Commission. *Bangladesh: End the politically chosen "disposable" attorney and prosecutorial.* http://www.humanrights.asia/news/ahrc-news/AHRC-STM-016-2009/

Bangladesh Law House. *Code of Conduct for the Judges.* http://bdlawhouse.blogspot.com/2011/10/code-of-conduct-for-judges.html

Bangladesh Law House. SC Sets Aside Caretaker Govt System. http://bdlawhouse.blogspot.com.aul2011/06/sc-sets-aside-caretaker-govt-system.html

178   Bibliography

Bangladesh Law House. *Supreme Court Lawyer Died in Police Custody: Severe Torture Alleged, Judicial Probe Demanded.* http://bdlawhouse.blog spot.com.au/2011/ 08/supreme-court-lawyer-died-in-police.html

Banglapedia. *Proclamation.* https://en.banglapedia.org/index.php?title=Proclamation

BANGLAPEDIA. *Warrant of Precedence.* http://en.banglapedia.org/index.php?title=Warrant_of_Precedence

Barry, E. *Low Turnout in Bangladesh Elections Amid Boycott and Violence.* https://www.nytimes.com/2014/01/06/world/asia/boycott-and-violence-mar-elections-in-bangladesh.html

Barth, P. *Bangladesh Prevents Freedom of Opinion.* https://www.fairobserver.com/region/central_south_asia/bangladesh-shahidul-alam-arrest-free-press-latest-asian-news-this-week-32380/

BDNEWS24.COM. *Chief Justice Swears in Three Judges to the Appellate Division.* https://bdnews24.com/bangladesh/2016/02/08/chief-justice-swears-in-three-judges-to-the-appellate-division

BDNEWS24.COM. *HC Judge Faizee bows out.* https://bdnews24.com/bangladesh/2007/07/13/hc-judge-faizee-bows-out

BDNEWS24.COM. *Justice Faizee's advocate ship certificate cancelled, faces criminal case.* https://bdnews24.com/bangladesh/2005/04/24/justice-faizee-s-advocate-ship-certificate-cancelled-faces-criminal-case

BDNEWS24.COM. *Justice Wahhab Miah resigns after Justice Mahmud Hossain is named chief justice.* https://bdnews24.com/bangladesh/2018/02/02/justice-wahhab-miah-resigns-after-justice-mahmud-hossain-is-named-chief-justice

BDNEWS24.COM. *Leave Bangladesh or Get Treated for Mental Problem.* https://bdnews24.com/politics/2017/08/27/leave-bangladesh-or-get-treated-for-mental-problem-minister-matia-to-chief-justice

BDNEWS24.COM. *SC stays HC order declaring illegal Shahidur's removal.* https://bdnews24.com/bangladesh/2005/04/24/sc-stays-hc-order-declaring-illegal-shahidur-s-removal

BDNEWS24.COM. *Supreme Judicial Council holds first meeting on Faizee.* https://bdnews24.com/bangladesh/2007/03/28/supreme-judicial-council-holds-first-meeting-on-faizee

BDNEWS24.COM. *Three High Court judges facing probe, ordered to refrain from judicial activities.* https://bdnews24.com/bangladesh/2019/08/22/three-high-court-judges-facing-probe-ordered-to-refrain-from-judicial-activities

Boissoneault, L. *The Genocide the U.S. Can't Remember, But Bangladesh Can't Forget.* https://www.smithsonianmag.com/history/genocide-us-cant-remember-bangladesh-cant-forget-180961490/

Boone, J. *Pakistan's prime minister Yosuf Raza Gilani disqualified by Supreme Court.* https://www.theguardian.com/world/2012/jun/19/pakistan-prime-minister-yousuf-gilani-disqualified

Brahmaputra, J. *Attorney General Mahbubey hopes for Awami League nomination in next election.* https://www.dhakatribune.com/bangladesh/politics/2018/04/29/attorney-general-mahbub-hopes-awami-league-nomination-next-election

Brennan, G. *Judicial Independence.* https://www.hcourt.gov.au/assets/publications/speeches/former-justices/brennanj/brennanj_ajc.htm

Burger, W. *Address to the American Bar Association, San Francisco.* Reported in Vital Speeches cited in Kirby, J. (2005). *Independence of the Legal Profession: Global and Regional Challenges.* Presidents of Law Association in Asia Conference, . http://www.hcourt.gov.au/speeches/kirbyj/kirbyj_20mar05.html

Courts and Tribunal Judiciary. *History of the Judiciary.* https://www.judiciary.uk/about-the-judiciary/history-of-the-judiciary/

Daily Sun. *Wahhab Miah made acting Chief Justice.* https://www.daily-sun.com/post/258788

Dhaka Tribune. *100 Days on from Shahidul Alam's Arrest.* https://www.dhakatribune.com/bangladesh/court/2018/11/13/100-days-on-from-shaidul-alam-s-arrest

European Parliament. *Legislative Elections In Bangladesh, Election Observation Delegation 2.* http://www.epgencms.europarl.europa.eu/cmsdata/upload/36287860-18fe-4c47-92b1-5aa527c34129/Election_report_Bangladesh_29_December_2008.pdf

Gul, A. *Pakistan Supreme Court disqualifies Sharif; He steps down.* https://www.voanews.com/east-asia-pacific/pakistan-supreme-court-disqualifies-sharif-he-steps-down

Bibliography

Hakim, T. *Obaidul Hassan sworn in as AD judges*. https://www.newagebd.net/article/115303/tariq-ul-hakim-obaidul-hassan-sworn-in-as-ad-judges

International Commission of Jurists. *African Conference on the Rule of Law*. https://www.icj.org/wp-content/uploads/1961/06/Africa-African-Conference-Rule-of-Law-conference-report-1961-eng.pdf

International Congress of Jurists. *Report of Committee IV, The Judiciary and the Legal Profession under the Rule of Law, Clause I, II*. https://www.icj.org/wp-content/uploads/1959/01/Rule-of-law-in-a-free-society-conference-report-1959-eng.pdf

International Ecological Safety Collaborative Organization. *Hussain Muhammed Ershad*. Available at http://www.iesco-iesco.org/content/en-US/p2068_k913.aspx

Jasim, E. H. *Unprecedented Departure of Justice Shamsuddin: No Farewell by AG Office SCBA*. http://thedailynewnation.com/news/67594/unprecedented-departure-of-justice-shamsuddin.html

Khokon, S. H. *Ganajagaran Mancha blogger Ahmed Rajib's killer held in Dhaka*. https://www.indiatoday.in/world/story/ahmed-rajib-blogger-murder-ganajagaran-mancha-killer-dhaka-961678-2017-02-20

Koshy, S., Ng, C.L.Y., Habib, S., Fung, C., Hock, T.E. and Teh, J. *Events that led to judicial crisis of 88*. https://www.thestar.com.my/news/nation/2008/04/18/events-that-led-to-judicial-crisis-of-88

Law Commission of India. *Report on the Method of Appointment of Judges*. http://lawcommissionofindia.nic.in/51-100/report80.pdf

Liton, S. *Justice Aziz Becomes CEC*. http://archive.thedailystar.net/2005/05/24/d5052401011.htm

Mahbub, S. *16th Amendment passed to restore Parliament's power to sack judges*. https://bdnews24.com/bangladesh/2014/09/17/16th-amendment-passed-to-restore-parliaments-power-to-sack-judges

Manik, J.A. & Sarkar, A. *It's Bangabandhu, not Zia: HC Rules Sheikh Mujib Declared Independence*. https://www.thedailystar.net/news-detail-93650

Mondal, A. L. *Averting controversy in appointment of Chief Justice*. http://www.thedailystar.net/news-detail-157772

N.Y. Times. *Bangladesh Reports Death of President Ziaur Rahman*. https://www.nytimes.com/1981/05/30/world/bangladesh-reports-death-of-president-ziaur-rahman.html

National Commission to Review the Working of the Indian Constitution. *A Consultation Paper on Superior Judiciary*. https://legalaffairs.gov.in/sites/default/files/(XII)Superior%20Judiciary.pdf

NEWAGE. *Shahidul on seven-day remand*. http://www.newagebd.net/article/47782/shahidul-on-seven-day-remand

NEWS FROM BANGLADESH.NET. *Controversial Appointment of Judges in the Appellate Division of the Supreme Court: Bad Precedent has been Created*. http://newsfrombangladesh.net/new/readers-opinion/11293-controversial-appointment-of-judges-in-the-appalate-division-of-the-supreme-court-bad-precedent-has-been-created

Perrigo, B. *What the Arrest of Photographer Shahidul Alam Means for Press Freedom in Bangladesh*. http://time.com/5359850/bangladesh-photographer-arrest-shahidul-alam-protests

Rajagopalan, S. *The elephant in the courtroom*. https://www.livemint.com/Opinion/tWZ7d-VM2608hVfdOyvjP0J/The-elephant-in-the-courtroom.html

Ramkrishnaiah, D. *Rend the Veil of Secrecy*. https://indianexpress.com/article/opinion/columns/rend-the-veil-of-secrecy/

Roosevelt, F. *Fireside Chat*. http://www.presidency.ucsb.edu/ws/?pid.15381

Sarkar, A. *Appellate Division running with fewer judges for long*. https://www.thedailystar.net/news-detail-67646?amp

Sarkar, A. *Justice Mahmud Hossain made CJ*. https://www.thedailystar.net/frontpage/justice-mahmud-hossain-made-cj-1529263

Sarkar, A. *Justice Mizanur Cleared*. https://www.thedailystar.net/news/justice-mizanur-cleared

Sarkar, A. *Oath of 2 angers pro-BNP lawyers*. https://www.thedailystar.net/news-detail-161341

Sarkar, A. *SC May get New Judges Next Month*. http://www.thedailystar.net/news-detail-167079

Shamsuddin, A. & Jahan, S.A. *A Long Way Gone*. http://www.thedailystar.net/law-our-rights/long-way-gone-1246612

180   Bibliography

Singh, Aditi. *Justice Jasti Chelameswar's lasting legacy striking a note of dissent.* https://www.livemint.com/Politics/DsUXbu4j6FWeYzZMnD7SAM/Justice-Jasti-Chelameswars-lasting-legacy-striking-a-note.html

Strauss, D.A. *The Living Constitution.* https://www.law.uchicago.edu/news/living-constitution

The Daily Star. *10 New HC judges to be* Appointed. https://www.thedailystar.net/news-detail-61184

The Daily Star. *11 'Charges' Against CJ.* http://www.thedailystar.net/frontpage/11-charges-against-cj-1476448\

The Daily Star. *Agitating lawyers decide to suspend action.*

The Daily Star. *Alleged Misconduct: Justice Mizanur replies to judicial council.* https://www.thedailystar.net/news/justice-mizanur-replies-to-judicial-council-2

The Daily Star. *Article 70 of Constitution: It's a safeguard for democracy.* https://www.thedailystar.net/backpage/article-70-constitution-its-safeguard-democracy-1581670

The Daily Star. *Bangladesh top court upholds dismissal of judge Shahidur.* https://www.thedailystar.net/backpage/sc-upholds-dismissal-judge-shahidur-144355

The Daily Star. *Chief justice goes on a month's leave.* https://www.thedailystar.net/frontpage/cj-goes-months-leave-1470712

The Daily Star. *Controversial 2 left out of oath.* https://www.thedailystar.net/news-detail-134740

The Daily Star. *CU cancels certificate of Judge Faizee, 2,350 others.* http://archive.thedailystar.net/2007/03/04/d7030401011.htm.

The Daily Star. *Detention of 4 BNP leaders declared illegal. https://www.thedailystar.net/news/detention-of-4-bnp-leaders-declared-illegal*

The Daily Star. *DU, BOU teachers to face criminal charge.* http://www.thedailystar.net/news-detail-225298

The Daily Star. *Ex CJ Khairul Haque Reappointed as Law Commission Chair.* http://www.thedailystar.net/city/ex-cj-khairul-haque-reappointed-law-commission-chair-1248835

The Daily Star. *Hamid elected president for a second term.* https://www.thedailystar.net/politics/abdul-hamid-elected-president-of-bangladesh-second-term-1531225

The Daily Star. *Hasina Rolls Out AL's Charter for Change.* http://www.thedailystar.net/news-detail-66898

The Daily Star. *I'm Not Sick.* https://www.thedailystar.net/frontpage/cj-set-leave-australia-1476169

The Daily Star. *Justice faces JS music.* https://www.thedailystar.net/news-detail-269768

The Daily Star. *Justice Khairul Haque new chief justice.* http:// www.thedailystar.net/news-detail-156149

The Daily Star. *Justice Masud passes away.* http://www.thedailystar.net/justice-masud-passes-away-573

The Daily Star. *KM Hasan new CJ.* http://archive.thedailystar.net/2003/06/23/d3062301033.htm

The Daily Star. *KM Hasan was involved in BNP politics in 1979 Moudud tells parliament, says there was no question of his integrity as judge.* http://archive.thedailystar.net/2006/09/21/d6092101022.htm

The Daily Star. *Mark Sheet Tampering: CU cancels certificates of Judge Faizee, 2350 others.* http://archive.thedailystar.net/2007/03/04/d7030401011.htm

The Daily Star. *Murder case against Ruhul Quddus stayed.* https://www.thedailystar.net/news-detail-148395

The Daily Star. *No greetings for SC judges: Bar leaders protest death of pro-BNP leaders.* http://www.thedailystar.net/news-detail-205906

The Daily Star. *No UZ Elections Before JS Polls: AL Awami Ainjibi Parishad to Form Human Chains.* https://www.thedailystar.net/news-detail-47643

The Daily Star. *Plea to remove Justice Manik. https://www.thedailystar.net/news-detail-251310*

The Daily Star. *Promotion of two HC judges takes lawyers by surprise.*

The Daily Star. *SC Appellate Division gets 2 New Judges.* http://www.thedailystar.net/news-detail-78543

The Daily Star. *SC Appellate Division gets 4 More Judges.* http://archive.thedailystar.net/newDesign/print_news.php?nid=96998

Bibliography

The Daily Star. *SC Appellate Division gets 5 more judges*. http://www.thedailystar.net/newDesign/news-details.php?nid=96998

The Daily Star. *SC gets 1st Woman Judge*. http://www.thedailystar.net/news-detail-175201

The Daily Star. *SK Sinha Resigns from Chief Justice Post, Says President's Press Secretary*. https://www.thedailystar.net/politics/chief-justice-cj-surendra-kumar-sinha-resigns-1489639

The Daily Star. *SK Sinha seeks asylum in Canada*. https://www.thedailystar.net/country/news/sk-sinha-seeks-asylum-canada-1777318

The Daily Star. *Skip Oath to 4 New SC Judges: Outgoing Bar President Urges CJ*. https://www.thedailystar.net/news/skip-oath-to-4-new-sc-judges

The Daily Star. *Tafazzul New Chief Justice*. https://www.thedailystar.net/news-detail-117925

The Daily Star. *Three Appellate Division judges sworn in*. https://www.thedailystar.net/country/bangladesh-supreme-court-3-new-appellate-division-justices-sworn-in-1644655\

The Dainik Manab Zamin. *An interview with Justice Kazi Shafiuddin*.

The Dainik Sangbad. *List of Superseded Judges*.

The Economic Times. *Bangladesh appoints Surendra Kumar Sinha as new Chief Justice*. https://economictimes.indiatimes.com/news/international/world-news/bangladesh-appoints-surendra-kumar-sinha-as-new-chief-justice/articleshow/45852712.cms?from=mdr

The Economist. *Trying War Crimes in Bangladesh: The Trial of the Birth of a Nation*. Available at https://www.economist.com/news/briefing/21568349-week-chairman-bangladeshs-international-crimes-tribunal-resigned-we-explain

The Guardian. *Bangladeshi Photographer Shahidul Alam Released from Prison*. Available at

The Hindu. *Mujib's Killers Case: A Chronology of Events*. https://www.thehindu.com/news/international/Mujibrsquos-killers-case-A-chronology-of-events/article16892929.ece

THE ITTEFAQ. *BNP appointed an individual who had kicked on the door of the Chief Justice as a Judge: Prime Minister in a Public Rally in Sitakunda*.

The New Nation. *Justice Mahmud Hossain Made New CJ*. http://m.thedailynewnation.com/news/163639/justice-mahmud-hossain-made-new-cj\

The Observer. *Justice Habibur Rahman's first death anniversary tomorrow*. https://www.observerbd.com/2015/01/10/65593.php

Times News. *Denigrating CJ: Who Said What*. http://bangladesh.timesofnews.com/denigrating-cj-who-said-what.html

U.S. Department of State. Bureau of Democracy. *Bangladesh*. http://www.state.gov/j/drl/rls/hrrpt/2012humanrightsreport/index.htm?dlid=204395&year=2012#wrapper

UCA NEWS. *Bangladeshi Ruling Party Wins Election by Default*. https://www.ucanews.comlnews/bangladeshi-ruling-party-wins-election-by-default/70019

UN Special Rapporteur on the Independence of Judges and Lawyers. *Civil and Political Rights, including the questions of independence of the judiciary, administration of justice, impunity* [28]. E/CN.4/2004/60 (31 December 2003). https://documents-dds-ny.un.org/doc/UNDOC/GEN/G04/100/26/PDF/G0410026.pdf?OpenElement

UN Transparency International Joint Initiative. *Bangalore Principles of Judicial Conduct*. https://www.unodc.org/pdf/crime/corruption/judicial_group/Bangalore_principles.pdf

United Nations. *Basic Principles on the Independence of the Judiciary Article 1*. GA/RES/40/32 & GA/RES/40/146 (29 November & 13 December 1985). https://www.ohchr.org/EN/ProfessionalInterest/Pages/IndependenceJudiciary.aspx

Universal Declaration of Human Rights. GA Res 217A (III), UN Doc A/810 at 71(10 December 1948). http://hrlibrary.umn.edu/instree/b1udhr.htm

Venkatesan, V. *Judiciary: A Flawed Mechanism*. https://frontline.thehindu.com/the-nation/article30217285.ece

Printed in the United States
by Baker & Taylor Publisher Services